JBoss 3.0

Deployment and Administration Handbook

Meeraj Moidoo Kunnumpurath

Wrox Press Ltd. ®

JBoss 3.0 Deployment and Administration Handbook

© 2002 Wrox Press

First published December 2002

Published by Wrox Press Ltd,
Arden House, 1102 Warwick Road, Acocks Green,
Birmingham, B27 6BH
United Kingdom
Printed in the United States
ISBN 1-86100-812-0

Trademark Acknowledgments

Wrox has endeavored to provide trademark information about all the companies and products mentioned in this book by the appropriate use of capitals. However, Wrox cannot guarantee the accuracy of this information.

Credits

Author
Meeraj M Kunnumpurath

Commissioning Editor
Craig A. Berry

Technical Reviewers
Rahim Adatia
Will Houck
Sing Li
Eric Schley
Robert Stevenson

Technical Editor
Niranjan Jahagirdar

Indexers
Michael Brinkman
Andrew Criddle
Vinod Shenoy

Managing Editors
Matthew Cumberlidge
Kalpana Garde

Project Manager
Helen Cuthill
Cilmara Lion
Abbas Rangwala

Production Coordinators
Abbie Forletta
Sarah Hall
Manjiri Karande

Proof Reader
Dev Lunsford

Cover Design
Natalie O'Donnell

About the Author

Meeraj Kunnumpurath
Meeraj works as a Senior Information Specialist with Electronic Data Systems. He has been using enterprise Java for more than four years. This is the ninth book which he has written with Wrox. He is a Sun Certified Java Programmer and Web Component Developer. He also writes for popular web sites and journals.

He loves football (as it is called outside the US). He is a big fan of Chelsea Football Club, and hopes they win the premiership this season.

You can reach Meeraj at meeraj@lycos.com

I thank Allah for making this possible.

I would like to thank the JBoss group and all the JBoss developers for bringing out such a wonderful product and making the source open. Without their source, I wouldn't have been able to write this book.

I would also like to thank Craig for helping me do this book as well as all the other projects I have been involved at Wrox with Craig.

I also thank Abdul Rahim for the friend and brother he has been.

I would like to dedicate the work I have done for this book to my brothers and sisters, who have been refugees in their own land, for fifty years of endless suffering and misery. Allah says, "Verily hardship follows ease".

JBoss 3.0

Administration and Deployment

Handbook

Table of Contents

Table of Contents

JBoss 3.0

Administration and Deployment

Handbook

Introduction

Introduction

Over the past five years J2EE has evolved as one of the most popular technologies for building enterprise-class applications. J2EE provides a platform for building robust, performing, scalable, manageable, maintainable, and portable enterprise-class applications. One of the key factors, that has contributed significantly towards the success of J2EE as an enterprise platform is portability.

J2EE is an open standard and is not tied to any proprietary vendor-specific implementation. It takes the "Write Once, Run Anywhere" spirit of Java to new heights. J2EE provides portability of applications across J2EE vendors by externalising the run-time behavior of the components such as transactions, security, persistence, lifecycle management, etc. from the compiled binaries of the components into XML-based deployment descriptors.

One of the important features of J2EE is that it leaves to the container providers how they decide to implement the aforementioned run-time services that are provided to the components. In most cases the component developers will be concentrating on the business logic behind the components, whereas application assemblers and component deployers will be taking these components and configuring their run-time behavior based on the target platform on which they will be deployed. Application assemblers and deployers normally do this by amending the standard deployment descriptors that come with the components and adding container-specific deployment descriptors to the components.

Hence to develop powerful J2EE applications that fully utilize the run-time services provided by the platforms in which they run, one should be well versed with the configuration and deployment of J2EE components on specific application servers. Also, to ensure the proper running of the applications once they are deployed, the administrators should be able to monitor and manage the components within the application server environments.

This book is one in a series of books addressing deployment, configuration, management, and maintenance of J2EE components on specific application servers as well as the administration of the application servers that are covered. This book will be concentrating on one of the most popular open source application servers, JBoss Server, with more than 50,000 downloads a month, from the JBoss Group, LLC. We will be covering version 3.0 of JBoss which supports most of the J2EE 1.3 features. In this book we will cover how to configure various J2EE components to fully utilize the run-time services provided by the JBoss server and look at how to configure, manage, and administrate the JBoss server itself.

Throughout this book, we will be using the Petstore application version 1.3.1 from Sun Microsystems to illustrate the various deployment aspects of J2EE components on the JBoss server. The Petstore application comes preconfigured with the deployment information required for the J2EE RI from Sun Microsystems. We will look at how to configure these components to fully utilize the run-time services provided by the JBoss server. In the process, we will also identify the key issues involved in porting J2EE applications from one application server to another. You can get the Petstore application from http://java.sun.com/j2ee/download.html.

What is Covered in this Book?

Now we will have a brief overview of the topics covered in this book. The topics covered in this book are broadly classified into the following categories.

- ❑ Running the server
- ❑ Configuring the server
- ❑ Deploying components

Running the Server

In this section we will cover:

- ❑ Server installation in Chapter 2
- ❑ Server architecture in Chapter 2
- ❑ Operating the server in Chapter 3

Configuring the Server

In this section we will cover:

- ❑ The JBoss JMX management and administration architecture in Chapter 4
- ❑ Configuring run-time properties in Chapter 5
- ❑ Configuring naming services in Chapter 6
- ❑ Configuring security in Chapter 7

❑ Configuring JDBC datasources in Chapter 8

❑ Configuring JMS administered objects in Chapter 9

❑ Configuring mail sessions in Chapter 10

❑ Configuring the Tomcat and Jetty web containers and web servers in Chapters 11 and 12

❑ Configuring cluster environments in Chapter 13

❑ Configuring logging properties in Chapter 14

Deploying Components

In this section we will cover:

❑ The JBoss deployment architecture in Chapter 15

❑ Deploying web components and the JBoss web deployment descriptor in Chapter 16

❑ Deploying EJB components and the JBoss EJB deployment descriptors in Chapters 17, 18, and 19

❑ Deploying EAR applications and the JBoss EAR deployment descriptor in Chapter 20

❑ Deploying custom JBoss components in Chapter 21

Reading XML Structures

Throughout this book, we will be using diagrams generated using XMLSpy from Altova (http://www.altova.com) for illustrating the structure of various XML documents used to configure JBoss and the various components deployed within JBoss. In this section we will provide a brief overview of the notations and icons used by XMLSpy for representing the various aspects of an XML content model. Please note that this section is not a tutorial on XML, XML Schema, or DTD.

XMLSpy uses the notation highlighted in the diagram shown below for representing "Sequence" in an XML schema:

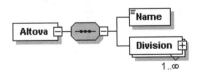

In the diagram above, this therefore means that the Altova element will contain a Name and Division subelement as so:

```
<Altova>
  <Name/>
  <Division/>
</Altova>
```

The notation highlighted in the diagram shown below represents "Choice" in an XML schema:

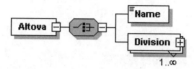

In the diagram above, this therefore means that the Altova element will contain *either* a Name or a Division subelement.

An element that can appear exactly once in its parent's content model is represented by a solid border:

An element that can optionally appear in its parent's content model is represented by a dashed border:

The notation shown below represents an element that can appear zero to many times in its parent's content model:

The notation shown below represents an element that can appear zero to a fixed number of times in its parent's content model. In the diagram below the element may appear zero to ten times.

The notation shown below represents an element that can appear one to many times in its parent's content model:

The notation shown below represents an element that can appear one to a fixed number of times in its parent's content model. In the diagram below the element may appear one to ten times.

Customer Support

We always value hearing from our readers, and we want to know what you think about this book and series: what you liked, what you didn't like, and what you think we can do better next time. You can send us your comments, either by returning the reply card in the back of the book, or by e-mailing us at feedback@wrox.com. Please be sure to mention the book title in your message.

How to Download the Sample Code for the Book

When you log on to the Wrox site, http://www.wrox.com/, simply locate the title through our Search facility or by using one of the title lists. Click on Download Code on the book's detail page.

The files that are available for download from our site have been archived using WinZip. When you have saved the attachments to a folder on your hard-drive, you will need to extract the files using WinZip, or a compatible tool. Inside the Zip file will be a folder structure and an HTML file that explains the structure and gives you further information, including links to e-mail support and suggested further reading.

Errata

We've made every effort to ensure that there are no errors in the text or in the code. However, no one is perfect and mistakes can occur. If you find an error in this book, like a spelling mistake or a faulty piece of code, we would be very grateful for feedback. By sending in errata, you may save another reader hours of frustration, and of course, you will be helping us to provide even higher quality information. Simply e-mail the information to support@wrox.com, your information will be checked and if correct, posted to the Errata page for that title.

To find errata, locate this book on the Wrox web site (http://www.wrox.com/books/1861008120.htm), and click on the View Errata link on the right-hand side of the page:

E-Mail Support

If you wish to query a problem in the book with an expert who knows the book in detail then e-mail support@wrox.com, with the title of the book, and the last four numbers of the ISBN in the subject field of the e-mail. A typical e-mail should include the following:

❑ The name, last four digits of the ISBN (in this case 8120), and page number of the problem, in the Subject field

❑ Your name, contact information, and the problem, in the body of the message

We won't send you junk mail. We need the details to save your time and ours. When you send an e-mail message, it will go through the following chain of support:

❑ **Customer Support**
Your message is delivered to our customer support staff. They have files on most frequently asked questions and will answer anything general about the book or the web site immediately.

❑ **Editorial**
More in-depth queries are forwarded to the technical editor responsible for that book. They have experience with the programming language or particular product, and are able to answer detailed technical questions on the subject. Once an issue has been resolved, the editor can post the errata to the web site.

❑ **The Author**
Finally, in the unlikely event that the editor cannot answer your problem, they will forward the request to the author. We do try to protect the author from any distractions to their writing (or programming) but we are quite happy to forward specific requests to them. All Wrox authors help with the support on their books. They will e-mail the customer and the editor with their response, and again all readers should benefit.

The Wrox support process can only offer support for issues that are directly pertinent to the content of our published title. Support for questions that fall outside the scope of normal book support is provided via our P2P community lists – http://p2p.wrox.com/forum.

p2p.wrox.com

For author and peer discussion, join the P2P mailing lists. Our unique system provides Programmer to Programmer™ contact on mailing lists, forums, and newsgroups, all in addition to our one-to-one e-mail support system. Be confident that the many Wrox authors and other industry experts who are present on our mailing lists are examining any queries posted. At http://p2p.wrox.com/, you will find a number of different lists that will help you, not only while you read this book, but also as you develop your own applications.

To subscribe to a mailing list follow these steps:

- ❑   Go to http://p2p.wrox.com/
- ❑   Choose the appropriate category from the left menu bar
- ❑   Click on the mailing list you wish to join
- ❑   Follow the instructions to subscribe and fill in your e-mail address and password
- ❑   Reply to the confirmation e-mail you receive
- ❑   Use the subscription manager to join more lists and set your mail preferences

JBoss 3.0

Administration and Deployment

Handbook

1

JBoss Server 3.0 Features

JBoss is an open source and free J2EE application server from the JBoss Group, LLC, implemented purely in Java. The JBoss Group, headed by Marc Fleury, is composed of more than a hundred developers all over the world. The current major version of JBoss, 3.0, supports most of the J2EE (Java 2, Enterprise Edition) 1.3 features.

1.1 JBoss Components

The JBoss server uses an extremely modular architecture built around **JMX (Java Management Extensions)**. Out of the box, JBoss provides a JMX implementation, an EJB container, and the basic JBoss server. JBoss also comes with a variety of pluggable components that implement the various J2EE standards such as JMS, JNDI, JAAS, and JTA/JTS, etc.

JBoss allows you to write your own components and plug them into the core JMX implementation, as long as the components you write comply with the JMX specification. This means, for example, if you are not happy with the transaction manager that comes with JBoss, you can write your own transaction manager component and plug it into the JMX bus. You can also add compliant third-party components to JBoss. We'll look at the JBoss JMX implementation in more detail in *Section 4.2: JMX in JBoss*.

The core components that come with JBoss, out of the box, are depicted in this diagram:

These components are:

- **JMX Implementation**

  JBoss provides a JMX implementation for registering and managing components. This is the heart of the JBoss server. JBoss also provides remote management facility for the JMX server and the components running within it.

- **EJB Container**

  This provides the container implementation for the EJB (Enterprise JavaBeans) 1.1 and 2.0 specifications.

- **JBossMQ**

  This component provides the JMS (Java Messaging Service) implementation for messaging support.

- **JBossTX**

  This component provides transaction services using JTA (Java Transaction API) and JTS (Java Transaction Service).

- **JBossCMP**

  This component provides container-managed persistence for entity EJB components. JBoss supports both CMP 2.0 and CMP 1.1.

- **JBossSX**

  This is the JBoss component that provides JAAS-based security.

- **JBossCX**

  This component provided JCA (Java Connector Architecture) connectivity services.

- **Web Container**

  This component provides a pluggable level for integrating J2EE web containers. Currently two web containers that integrate with JBoss are Apache Tomcat and Jetty.

1.2 JBoss Versions

At the time of writing, the current major version of JBoss version was 3.0, and the minor version was 3.0.4. JBoss 3.0 supports most of the J2EE 1.3 features, including EJB 2.0, and comes with an integrated web container, Jetty, which supports the Servlet 2.3 and JSP 1.2 specifications. JBoss 3.0 is available with both Tomcat 4.0.x and Tomcat 4.1.x.

> **Minor versions are primarily bug fixes and the occasional minor feature addition. This book is focused on the major 3.0 release of JBoss, so the minor version you have is relatively unimportant to the material covered in this book.**

1.3 J2EE Support

The latest version of JBoss, along with bundled web container (Jetty or Tomcat), supports the following J2EE APIs:

- **EJB 2.0**
  JBoss CMP supports most of the EJB 2.0 features. It is also backward compatible and supports EJB 1.1 components. This is covered in detail in *Chapters 17, 18*, and *19*.

- **Servlet 2.3**
  Both Jetty and Tomcat supports the Servlet 2.3 specification. This is covered in detail in *Chapters 11, 12*, and *16*.

- **JSP 1.2**
  Both Jetty and Tomcat supports the JSP 1.2 specification. This is covered in detail in *Chapters 11, 12*, and *16*.

- **JMS 1.0.2**
  JBoss comes with a JMS provider that supports both point-to-point and publish/subscribe messaging, compliant with the JMS 1.0.2 specification. This is covered in detail in *Chapter 9*.

- **JTA 1.0.1/JTS 1.0**
  JBoss provides a JTA/JTS-compliant transaction manager that supports distributed transactions.

- **JCA**
  JBossCX provides a JCA implementation and uses JCA for connecting to all external resources including databases. This is covered in detail in *Chapter 8*.

- **JAAS 1.0**
  Jboss provides a highly flexible security service built on top of JAAS. This is covered in detail in *Chapter 7*.

❏ **JavaMail 1.2**

JBoss provides a MBean service for configuring JavaMail sessions. This is covered in detail in *Chapter 10*.

❏ **JNDI**

JBoss provides a highly configurable naming provider that is capable of using multiple protocols including RMI and HTTP. This is covered in detail in *Chapter 6*.

❏ **RMI-IIOP**

JBoss supports RMI invocation over IIOP.

JBoss is not a J2EE 1.3-certified application server. However, the controversies related to JBoss and J2EE certification are mainly political and not technical, and have been well documented.

1.4 Custom Features

In addition to the aforementioned J2EE specific features, JBoss supports:

❏ Fault tolerance and load balancing using clusters.

❏ Web services with an integrated Axis engine.

❏ Logging configuration based on Log4J.

❏ EJB invocation over SSL.

❏ The JBoss server is built around a JMX bus. JBoss uses JMX MBeans for all its configuration and supports deployment of user JMX MBeans within the JBoss environment.

❏ JSR-077 for J2EE Management: JSR 77 defines a management information model for the J2EE platform. The model is designed to be interoperable with many management systems and protocols.

In this chapter we have had a high-level overview of the various features available with JBoss. In the next chapter we will look into the details of installing JBoss and JBoss directory structure.

JBoss 3.0

Administration and Deployment

Handbook

2

Installing JBoss

In this chapter we will cover the installation process for JBoss and explore the installed files.

2.1 Installing JBoss

JBoss can be downloaded in both binary and source formats, from either the JBoss web site http://www.jboss.org, or from the JBoss page on Sourceforge at http://sourceforge.net/projects/jboss/. Version 3.x of JBoss comes in two flavors:

❑   With an integrated Jetty web container

❑   With an integrated Tomcat 4.x web container

All the files available from the download site, except the ones that are suffixed with-src, are binary archives. The latest binary archive for the JBoss-Jetty bundle will be something like jboss-3.0.X.tgz or jboss-3.0.X.zip and that of the JBoss-Tomcat bundle is jboss-3.0.X_tomcat-4.X.X.zip, depending on the latest release. These files can be exploded by any standard unzip tools like JDK JAR tool, WinZip, tar command on UNIX, etc. You can also find earlier versions along with more recent beta releases of JBoss on these web sites.

> **Before you install JBoss, make sure that you have installed JDK 1.3 (or higher) on your machine. Also make sure that the JAVA_HOME environment variable points to the JDK installation directory. JBoss uses this for adding tools.jar to the classpath.**

You can extract the contents of the archive file into any directory you wish. However, it is recommended that you install into a directory name without spaces as it may cause problems with some of the Sun VMs.

2.2 JBoss Directory Structure

Once you have extracted the contents of the binary archive, the directory structure for JBoss (for the JBoss-Jetty bundle) will look as follows:

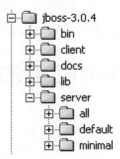

Obviously if you have a version other than 3.0.4 your root folder will be labeled slightly differently.

The directory structure for the JBoss-Tomcat bundle will look as shown below:

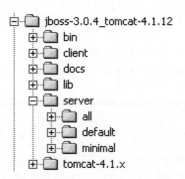

Again, if you have a version other than 3.0.4 your root folder will be labeled slightly differently.

The contents of the JBoss root directory are:

❑ The \bin directory contains the following files required for starting and stopping JBoss:

- run.bat/run.sh:
  These are the command files used for starting JBoss on Windows and *X systems respectively. This is covered in further detail in *Section 3.1: Starting JBoss.*

- run.jar
  This is the bootstrap JAR file used for starting JBoss.

- shutdown.sh/shutdown.bat:
  These are the command files used for shutting down JBoss on Windows and *X systems respectively. This is covered in further detail in *Section 3.2: Shutting Down JBoss.*

- shutdown.jar
  This is the bootstrap JAR file used for shutting down JBoss.

❑ The \client directory contains the JAR files required by the client applications for connecting to JBoss. The files contained in this directory are:

- auth.conf
  This is used for the JAAS client-side login module.

- cacerts
  This is the security file with root CA certificates.

- client-config.xml
  This is used for configuring Axis client-side handlers for accessing web services.

- concurrent.jar
  This is a third party library used by JBoss for collection-based classes.

- gnu-regexp.jar
  This JAR file contains classes for evaluating regular expressions.

- jaas.jar
  This file contains the JAAS classes.

- jacorb.jar
  This file contains the Jakarta Java-COM bridge classes.

- jboss-client.jar, and jboss-common-client.jar
  JBoss common client classes.

- jbossha-client.jar
  This contains the client classes for accessing clustered JBoss.

- jboss-iiop-client.jar
  This contains the client classes for using IIOP.

- jboss-j2ee.jar
  J2EE classes.

- `jbossjmx-ant.jar`
  Contains the classes and interfaces for the MBean server.

- `jboss-jsr77.jar`
  Classes for JSR 77: J2EE Management.

- `jbossmq-client.jar`
  This contains the client classes for using the JMS service.

- `jbossmqha.jar`
  This contains the client classes for using a clustered JMS service –
  although JBossMQ currently doesn't support clustering.

- `jboss-net-client.jar`
  This contains the client classes for using JBoss .NET for web services.

- `jboss-system-client.jar`
  Contains a couple of deployment exception classes.

- `jcert.jar`
  Classes that support public key certificates.

- `jmx-connector-client-factory.jar`
  This contains the factory classes for creating the connectors to access
  the JMX agent.

- `jmx-ejb-connector-client.jar`
  This contains the EJB-based connector for accessing the JMX agent.

- `jmx-rmi-connector-client.jar`
  This contains the RMI-based connector for accessing the JMX agent.

- `jnet.jar`
  This contains socket factories.

- `jnp-client.jar`
  This contains the JNDI initial context factory and related classes.

- `jsse.jar`
  This is the Java Secured Socket Extension classes.

- `log4j.jar`
  This contains the Log4J classes.

❑ The \docs directory contains the DTDs for the various JBoss-specific
deployment descriptors, standard J2EE deployment descriptor DTDs, and
examples for configuring datasources for the various DBMS vendors using
the JBoss JCA connection factories. Please note that this directory doesn't
contain any JBoss server documentation.

❑ The \lib directory contains the startup JAR files required for JBoss. The
directory from which the startup classes are loaded can be configured at
startup time using system properties. We will have a look at this in *Section
3.1.2: JBoss System Properties*, when we cover the standard system
properties used by JBoss. It is recommended that user JAR files are *not*
stored in this directory.

❑ The \server directory contains the various server configuration sets that can be used with JBoss. JBoss comes with three pre-configured sets – default, all, and minimal. JBoss server configuration sets are explained in detail in *Section 2.3: Server Configuration Sets*

❑ The \tomcat-4.1.2 directory contains Tomcat-specific files. We'll look at Tomcat configuration in *Section 12.1: Configuring Tomcat.*

2.3 Server Configuration Sets

JBoss comes with three server configuration sets: default, all, and minimal. A **server configuration set** is used to define the services that are available for the JBoss instance that is running. You can control the configuration set that is used by a JBoss instance during startup using command-line options. Keep in mind that:

❑ The minimal configuration set contains only the bare minimum services required to run JBoss.

❑ The default set that is used by default contains all the services except clustering, RMI-IIOP and Axis engine for web services.

❑ The all configuration set contains all the services.

You can also create your own configuration set by creating a new directory under the server directory and copying the contents of the default configuration set to it. We will create a new configuration set called petstore and use it throughout the book to store the petstore-specific services.

2.3.1 The Default Configuration Set

In this section, we look at the contents of the default configuration set. The contents of the default configuration set are depicted below:

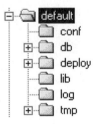

The directories present in the default configuration set are listed below:

❑   \conf
This directory contains the various configuration files. This includes the core JBoss configuration file called `jboss-service.xml` file. However, the location of the configuration directory, and the name of the core configuration file, can be controlled during startup using command-line options. This is covered in further detail in *Section 3.1.1: JBoss Startup Options.*

❑   \db
This directory is used to store all the persistent files. This directory will be used for storing a variety of information such as serialized EJB instances that are passivated, the default Hypersonic database that comes with JBoss, and persistent JMS messages that are stored to files. The location of this directory can also be specified at run time. This is covered in further detail in *Section 3.1.1: JBoss Startup Options*

❑   \deploy
This is the directory into which the various deployment components such as EAR, EJB JAR, WAR, RAR files as well as the JBoss-specific **Service Archive (SAR)** files are copied to be deployed. JBoss SAR files are covered in detail in *Section 4.2.1.2: JBoss SAR Components.*

This directory also contains configuration files with names that follow the pattern `"*-service.xml"`. Any of the aforementioned archives that are copied to this directory while JBoss is running, will be hot deployed to the server. We will have a detailed look at the contents of this and the \conf directories of the default configuration set, in *Section 4.2.2: The JBoss Root Configuration File.* You can configure the hot deployment behavior by editing some of the configuration files. We will cover this in detail in *Section 15.2: Hot Deployment.*

❑   \lib
This directory contains JAR files that are used by the server. JAR files located in this directory are automatically added into the server's class repository. You can use this directory for storing JAR files, such as JDBC driver classes, that are shared between your applications. The location of the server \lib directory may also be specified as a command-line option during server startup. This is covered in detail in *Section 3.1.1: JBoss Startup Options.*

❑   \log
This directory stores the log files. The two main log files are `boot log` and `server log`. JBoss also logs HTTP access messages. JBoss logging is based on Log4J and is on by default. Configuring logging in JBoss is explored in *Section 14.3: Configuring Logging.*

❑   \tmp
This directory is used by JBoss for storing temporary files during deploying applications. The location of this directory can be specified during server startup.

2.3.1.1 Default Configuration Set Contents

The JBoss architecture is based around the **Java Management Extension (JMX)** specification. The JBoss architecture and a brief overview of JMX will be covered in *Section 4.1: An Overview of JMX*. JBoss uses a variation of the standard **JMX Mlet syntax** for specifying the configuration information. A detailed coverage of the contents of the JBoss configuration files is provided in the next chapter.

In this section, we will have a look at the various configuration files that come with the default configuration set. These files are found in the \conf and \deploy directories. You can also author and store your own configuration files in the \deploy directory, following the pattern *-service.xml, compliant in the way JBoss configuration files are authored, and they will be deployed by the server. As mentioned earlier, files copied to the \deploy directory will be hot deployed on the server.

The contents of the \conf directory in the default configuration set are listed below:

❑　auth.conf
This file was used in the pre-3.x versions of JBoss for defining JAAS login modules. This file is now deprecated and is not used in 3.x versions.

❑　jboss-minimal.xml
This file contains the services that are available when JBoss is started with the minimal configuration set.

❑　jbossmq-state.xml
This file is used by the JMS implementation that comes with JBoss for storing usernames, passwords, roles, information regarding durable subscription, etc. This is covered in further detail in *Section 9.5: State Manager.*

❑　jboss-service.xml
This file is used for defining the core JBoss services. It contains core services such as class loading, system properties, transactions, naming, deployment, management, monitoring and administration, etc. This is covered in further detail in *Section 4.2.2: The JBoss Root Configuration File.*

❑　jndi.properties
This file contains the various JNDI properties such as initial context factory, provider URL, etc., used for connecting to the JBoss naming provider, within the JBoss server. This is covered in further detail in *Section 6.2.1: Initial Context Properties.*

❑　log4j.xml
This file is used for configuring Log4J for logging. By default, both, file and console logging, are enabled. The file logger uses a rolling log for midnight everyday. The threshold set for console messages is INFO, and this file also contains examples for logging messages to UNIX Syslogs daemon, JMS destinations, e-mails, etc. This is covered in further detail in *Section 14.3: Configuring Logging.*

❑ `login-config.xml`
This is the file used in JBoss 3.0 for storing JAAS based security. The login modules defined in this section can be used in your web applications, EJBs, etc. for enforcing declarative security. This is covered in further detail in *Section 7.3.3.2: XML Login Config.*

❑ `server.policy`
This is the Java security policy file used by JBoss.

❑ `standardjaws.xml`
This file contains the datasource mapping for the various DBMS vendors. The datasource mapping information are available for Interbase, DB2, Oracle, Sybase, PostgreSQL, Hypersonic SQL, PointBase, SOLID, MySQL, MS SQL Server, SAP DB, Cloudscape, and Informix. If the database you use is not in this file, you can append the mapping information for your database to this file. JBoss CMP (EJB 1.1) uses the contents of this file.

❑ `standardjboss.xml`
This file contains the default configuration for all the EJBs deployed on this server. The defaults can be overridden for each EJB by using JBoss-specific deployment descriptors. We will look at this in further detail in *Section 18.1: The JBoss EJB Deployment Descriptor.*

❑ `standardjbosscmp-jdbc.xml`
This file contains the CMP default configuration for all the CMP entity EJBs deployed on this server. The defaults can be overridden for each CMP entity EJB using JBoss-specific deployment descriptors. We will look at this in *Section 19.1: CMP Configuration Files.*

The \deploy directory contains the following files that follow the pattern `*-service.xml`. as well as the various SAR, RAR, and JAR files. The `*-service.xml` files contain the JMX MBean definitions used to configure various services. It also contains some standard J2EE JAR, WAR, and RAR components, which come with the JBoss installation. The contents of this directory are listed below:

❑ `jbossweb.sar`
This is an exploded service archive file for configuring the Jetty Servlet engine. Please note that this file won't be available for the Tomcat version. This file is covered in further detail in *Section 11.2: Configuring Jetty.*

❑ `jmx-console.war`
This is an exploded WAR file to access the JBoss JMX console through a web browser. You can use this web application to look at the MBean services that are installed on JBoss and set their properties and invoke methods (see *Section 4.3: Accessing the JMX Agent*).

❑ `http-invoker.sar`
This an exploded MBean services archive that allows HTTP/RMI for JNDI and EJBs. This is covered in detail in *Section 6.6: HTTP-based JNDI* and *Section 17.3.2: EJB Invoker.*

❑ `counter-service.xml`
This file contains the MBean service for an accumulating counter that can be used for diagnosing performance issues.

❑ `ejb-management.jar`
This is an EJB component that implements the JSR 77 for J2EE management specification.

❑ `jmx-ejb-adaptor.jar`
This is an EJB that exposes the JBoss JMX MBean server functionality for remote management. This also uses the MBean service archive `jmx-ejb-connector-server.sar`.

❑ `jboss-local-jdbc.jar`
This is a wrapper JCA resource adaptor for datasource connection factories for database drivers and doesn't support JCA. This is covered in detail in *Section 8.2: JBossCX and Datasources*.

❑ `jboss.xa.rar`
This is a JCA resource adaptor for datasource connection factories for JDBC drivers that support XA. This is covered in detail in *Section 8.2: JBossCX and Datasources*.

❑ `jms-ra.rar`
This is a wrapper JCA resource adaptor for JMS connection factories.

❑ `jmx-rmi-adaptor.sar`
This is an MBean service archive that exposes the JBoss JMX MBean server functionality for remote management through RMI.

❑ `hsqldb-service.xml`
This file contains the configuration information for the Hypersonic database that comes with JBoss, and the default datasource connection factory to the database.

❑ `jbossmq-destinations-service.xml`
This file is used for defining JMS destinations. JBoss comes with a set of pre-configured JMS queues and topics in this file. You can edit this for adding your own JMS destinations. This is covered in detail in *Section 9.7: Destinations*.

❑ `jbossmq-service.xml`
This file is used for configuring the JBoss JMS service. It also defines configuration information for persistent messages, message caches, connection factories, invocation layers, etc. This is covered in detail in *Chapter 9: Configuring JBossMQ*.

❑ `jca-service.xml`
This file contains the MBean services for the JBoss RAR deployer used for deploying resource archives. This file contains the MBean definition for the RAR deployer.

❑ `jms-service.xml`
This file contains the core MBean services for configuring JBoss JMS.

23

❏ mail-service.xml
This file contains the MBean used for configuring mail sessions. This is covered in detail in *Section 10.2: Configuring the Mail Service.*

❏ properties-service.xml
This file contains MBean services for defining system properties and JavaBean property editors. This is covered in detail in *Section 21.2: System Properties.*

❏ scheduler-service.xml
This file contains MBean services used for configuring scheduled services such as UNIX cron jobs and Windows scheduled tasks. This is covered in detail in *Section 21.1: Scheduling.*

❏ user-service.xml
This file can be used by the users as a template for defining their own MBean services.

❏ jmx-ejb-connector-server.sar
This file is used to register notification listeners for remote JAX agents.

2.3.2 Creating Configuration Sets

To create your own configuration set you need to create a directory by the name you want to call the configuration set in the \server directory and then copy the contents of the \default configuration set. This will contain all the services except IIOP, clustering, and Axis-based web services.

In order for JBoss to use this configuration set, you will need to configure its startup, as covered in *Section 3.1.1: JBoss Startup Options.*

In this chapter, we looked at JBoss installation, and how the various directories and files are organized. In the next chapter, we will have a look at JBoss operation, and will cover how to start and stop JBoss, JBoss startup options, system properties, running JBoss as a system service, etc.

JBoss 3.0

Administration and Deployment

Handbook

3

3.1 Starting JBoss

3.2 Shutting Down JBoss

3

Operating JBoss

Now that we have an overview of the JBoss directory structure, we will look at how to start and stop JBoss and also the various JBoss startup options.

> **By default, none of the ports used by JBoss-Jetty or JBoss-Tomcat listens on a port numbers between 0-1023, hence you don't need root access to start JBoss on UNIX systems.**

3.1 Starting JBoss

To start JBoss, you can run the following command on Windows systems:

```
run.bat
```

On UNIX systems, you need to run:

```
run.sh
```

Newer versions of JBoss 3.x also come with a specific startup file for RedHat Linux:

```
jboss_ini_redhat.sh start
```

You can also use the bootstrap JAR file as shown below:

```
java -jar run.jar
```

Make sure that you run the above commands from the \bin directory of your JBoss installation. If you are starting JBoss with the second option, please make sure that the JDK tools.jar file is available to the classloader. One way to do this is to copy tools.jar to the \lib directory of the configuration set you are using. The embedded web container within JBoss uses classes from this file for compiling JSP pages. If everything goes fine, you won't get any stack traces in the command window running JBoss, and you will have the output similar to the one shown below:

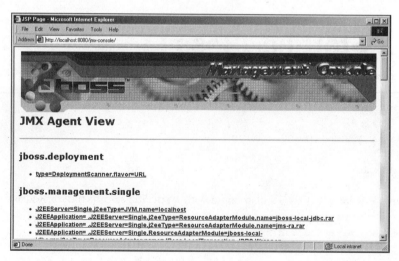

Neither JBoss-Jetty, nor the JBoss-Tomcat bundle comes with a default web application. Hence, to test whether JBoss is up and running, you can access the JMX console web application on http://localhost:8080/jmx-console. This will list all the MBeans registered with the JBoss JMX MBean server, as shown below:

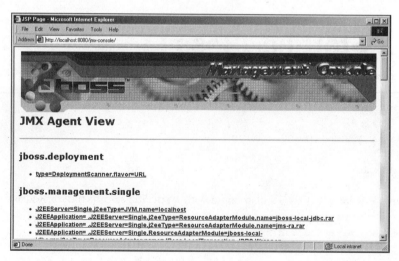

3.1.1 JBoss Startup Options

If you run JBoss without specifying any options, JBoss will use the default configuration set. However, if you run the command run -h, JBoss will print the various startup options. The various startup options available with JBoss are listed below:

Option	Description
-V	This will print the JBoss version.
-p	This option can be used for specifying the patch directory for any server updates. If the value specified is a directory URL, all the ZIP and JAR files present in the directory identified by the URL are added to the classpath. Otherwise, the URL itself is added to the classpath.
-h	This will print the various startup options.
-n	The URL specified by this option will be used as the base directory to boot remotely from the net.
-c	You can use this option to specify the configuration set to use. By default, JBoss uses the default configuration set. If you want to use the minimal configuration set, you can run the command run -c minimal. As explained in *Section 2.3.2: Creating Configuration Sets*, you can create your own configuration set, and use that to startup JBoss using the -c option. For example, if your configuration set resides in the directory petstore, you can issue the command run -c petstore.
-j	This option can be used to specify the JAXP parser to use. The allowed values are xerces or crimson. By default, JBoss uses crimson.
-L	This option can be used to add extra libraries to the JBoss classpath. All the archive files present in the filename specified by this option will be added to the class repository. JBoss class repositories are covered in detail in *Section 5.1.3: UnifiedClassLoader*.
-C	This option can be used to add extra libraries to the JBoss classpath. The archive URL specified by this option will be added to the class repository.
-P	This option can be used to specify a URL pointing to a file containing the system properties to be loaded.
-D	This option can be used to specify system properties, see *Section 3.1.2: JBoss System Properties*.

3.1.2 JBoss System Properties

You can specify the following properties using the -D option when you start JBoss to specify the system properties that are identified by JBoss:

29

❑ jboss.boot.library.list
This is used to specify a comma separated list of libraries required to boot the server. This defaults to all libraries specified by the jboss.lib.url property.

❑ jboss.server.type
This can be used to specify the JBoss server implementation class. The default is org.jboss.system.server.ServerImpl.

❑ jboss.server.root.deployment.filename
This can be used to specify the configuration file that contains the core MBean definitions. The default is the jboss-service.xml file present in the \conf directory of the configuration set that is used.

❑ jboss.home.dir
This is used to specify the JBoss home directory. The default value is the directory from which run.jar was loaded.

❑ jboss.home.url
This can be used to specify the net URL to be used as the base directory from where to start JBoss. The default is the value of the property jboss.home.dir.

❑ jboss.lib.url
This is used to specify the URL that contains the libraries for the server. The default is the \lib directory under the URL specified by the property jboss.home.url.

❑ jboss.patch.url
This is used to specify the URL points to the location that contains the patch libraries. If the value is a file URL, all the ZIP and JAR files in the location are added to the classpath. Otherwise the URL is added to the classpath.

❑ jboss.server.name
The value of this property is used to deduce the home directory for the configuration set that is used. The default value is default.

❑ jboss.server.base.dir
This property can be used to specify the base directory for deducing the configuration sets that are available. The default value is the path created using the values for jboss.home.url and the constant server.

❑ jboss.server.home.dir
This property can be used to specify the base directory for the configuration set that is used. The default value is the path created using the values for jboss.server.base.dir and jboss.server.name.

❑ jboss.server.temp.dir
This is used for specifying the temporary directory used in deployment. The default value is the path created using the values for jboss.server.home.dir and the constant tmp.

❏ jboss.server.data.dir
   This is used for specifying the directory used for storing persistent data. The
   default value is the path created using the values for
   jboss.server.home.dir and the constant db.

❏ jboss.server.temp.dir
   This is used for specifying the temporary directory used in deployment. The
   default value is the path created using the values for
   jboss.server.home.dir and the constant tmp.

❏ jboss.server.base.url
   This property can be used to specify the base URL for deducing the
   configuration sets that are available. The default value is the URL created
   using the values for jboss.home.url and the constant server.

❏ jboss.server.home.url
   This property can be used to specify the base directory for the
   configuration set that is used. The default value is the path created using
   the values for jboss.server.base.url and jboss.server.name.

❏ jboss.server.config.url
   This property can be used to specify the URL of the configuration directory
   for the configuration set. The default value is the URL created using the
   values for jboss.server.home.url and the constant conf.

❏ jboss.server.lib.url
   This property can be used to specify the URL of the lib directory for the
   configuration set. The default value is the URL created using the values for
   jboss.server.home.url and the constant lib.

❏ jboss.server.exitonshutdown
   This property specifies whether to exit the VM on server shutdown. The
   default value is false.

3.1.3 Enabling Remote Debugging

JBoss supports JPDA-based remote debugging. To enable this, you need to uncomment
the following line in run.sh/run.bat:

```
set JAVA_OPTS=-classic -Xdebug -Xnoagent -Djava.compiler=NONE
    -Xrunjdwp:transport=dt_socket,address=8787,server=y,suspend=y
    %JAVA_OPTS%
```

You can also run the debugger in shared memory by setting the following option:

```
set JAVA_OPTS=-classic  -Djava.compiler=NONE -Xnoagent -Xdebug
    -Xrunjdwp:transport=dt_shmem,server=y,address=jboss,suspend=n
    %JAVA_OPTS%
```

Now you can attach to the remote debugger through the specified port using and
supporting IDE.

31

3.1.4 Running JBoss as an NT Service

You can run JBoss as an NT service using any NT service wrapper for Java programs. When you choose a wrapper, you need to make sure it doesn't exit the VM on an NT logoff event. In this section, we will have a look at how to use the Wrapper utility available on http://sourceforge.net/projects/wrapper/ to run JBoss as an NT service. Wrapper allows Java applications to be installed and controlled like a native NT/Unix service, and also provides correction software to automatically restart crashed or frozen JVMs.

To use the Wrapper utility to install JBoss as an NT service, perform the following steps:

1. Download the latest version of the utility from Sourceforge.

2. Extract the contents of the ZIP file to a local directory.

3. Copy the file wrapper.exe from the \bin directory to the \bin directory of your JBoss home.

4. Copy wrapper.jar from the \lib directory to the JBoss \bin directory.

5. Save the following contents in a file called wrapper.conf in the JBoss \bin directory:

```
wrapper.java.command=java
wrapper.java.mainclass=com.silveregg.wrapper.WrapperSimpleApp
wrapper.app.parameter.1=org.jboss.Main
wrapper.java.classpath.1=./run.jar
wrapper.java.classpath.2=./wrapper.jar
wrapper.java.classpath.3=c:/Meeraj/Software/JDK/lib/tools.jar
wrapper.java.library.path=.
wrapper.port=1777
wrapper.startup.timeout=300
wrapper.ping.timeout=300
wrapper.shutdown.timeout=300
wrapper.disable_shutdown_hook=TRUE
wrapper.request_thread_dump_on_failed_jvm_exit=TRUE
wrapper.ntservice.name=JBoss
wrapper.ntservice.displayname=JBoss Server
wrapper.ntservice.description=JBoss J2EE Server
wrapper.ntservice.starttype=AUTO_START
wrapper.ntservice.process_priority=NORMAL
```

> *You will need to adjust the classpath setting to point to your JRE's* tools.jar *file as appropriate.*

6. Issue the following command from the JBoss \bin directory:

```
wrapper.exe -i wrapper.conf
```

This will install JBoss as an NT service. To make sure it has been installed properly, go to the Control Panel\Administrative Tools\Services on Windows 2000, and check whether the JBoss service is displayed in the list:

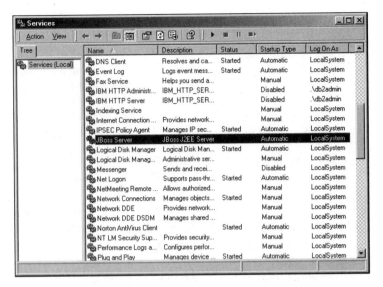

Make sure that the startup type is automatic so that the service is stated on system startup. You can manually start and stop the service by right-clicking on the service. You can also right-click on the service to edit the properties such as startup type, the system account that will run the service, etc. To uninstall the service, enter the following command:

```
wrapper.exe -r wrapper.conf
```

Some of the important properties supported in the Wrapper configuration file are listed below:

- ❏ `wrapper.java.command`
  This is the path to the Java executable.

- ❏ `wrapper.java.mainclass`
  This is used to specify the fully qualified name of the main class that should be executed if the class implements the interface. Otherwise, it should be `com.silveregg.wrapper.WrapperSimpleApp`, as in our case.

- ❏ `wrapper.java.classpath.<n>`
  This is used to specify an ordered list of classpath entries. We will specify the JBoss bootstrap JAR `run.jar`, JDK `tools.jar`, and the Wrapper-specific `wrapper.jar`.

- ❏ `wrapper.java.library.path`
  This is the path to the directory that contains `wrapper.dll`.

- ❏ `wrapper.java.additional.<n>`
  This is used to specify an ordered list of arguments to the Java executable. Note that this is *not* used to pass the application parameters.

- ❏ `wrapper.java.initmemory`
  This is used to specify the initial JVM heap size.

❏ `wrapper.java.maxmemory`
This is used to specify the maximum JVM heap size.

❏ `wrapper.app.parameter.<n>`
This is be used to specify an ordered list of arguments to the application. In our case, the first argument denoted by `wrapper.app.parameter.1` will be the JBoss main class `org.jboss.Main`. The class `com.silveregg.wrapper.WrapperSimpleApp` will internally call the main method on the JBoss main class.

❏ `wrapper.port`
This can be used to specify a port number used by the Wrapper executable to communicate with the Java application to monitor how it is running.

❏ `wrapper.startup.timeout`
This is the number of seconds to allow for the JVM to be launched and contact the wrapper before the wrapper should assume that the JVM is hung and terminate the JVM process.

❏ `wrapper.ping.timeout`
This can be used to specify the number of seconds to allow between the wrapper pinging the JVM and the response.

❏ `wrapper.startup.timeout`
This is the amount of time the service should wait after the wrapper halting the JVM before it gives a failed status.

❏ `wrapper.disable_shutdown_hook`
Disables JDK shutdown hook.

❏ `wrapper.request_thread_dump_on_failed_jvm_exit`
This is used to specify whether to dump the thread on JVM exit if the service failed.

❏ `wrapper.ntservice.name`
This is used to specify the NT service name.

❏ `wrapper.ntservice.displayname`
This is used to specify the service display name in the service window.

❏ `wrapper.ntservice.description`
This is to specify the service description.

❏ `wrapper.ntservice.dependency.<n>`
This is to specify the ordered list of services to be started, before this service can be started. This can be used for starting data servers, mail servers, etc. before starting JBoss.

❏ `wrapper.ntservice.starttype`
This is used to specify the startup mode. The allowed values are AUTO_START and ON_DEMAND_START to respectively indicate whether it should be started automatically or manually.

❏ `wrapper.ntservice.process_priority`
This is used to set process priority. The allowed values are NORMAL, LOW, HIGH, and REALTIME.

Along with the aforementioned properties, the configuration file also supports a wide variety of properties to specify the level and locations of logging. This can be used in the initial stages to debug, if the service is not working properly, or logging the JBoss console output. However, for the day-to-day operation, it is better to disable console logging and rely on the JBoss file logging. JBoss logging is covered in detail in *Section 14.2: Configuring Logging*.

3.1.5 Running JBoss as a *X Daemon

In this section we will have a look at how to run JBoss as Unix/Linux daemon. The example shown in this section used SuSE Linux v8.0. Make the necessary modification for your version of Unix/Linux. To run JBoss as a daemon you need to perform the following steps:

1. Create a script file called `jboss` that will be called during system startup and shutdown. This script is responsible for starting and shutting down JBoss. The contents of this script is shown below:

```
#!/bin/sh

. /etc/rc.status
. /etc/rc.config

export JAVA_HOME=/usr/lib/java
export JBOSS_HOME=/usr/local/jboss

export PATH=$JBOSS_HOME/bin:$JAVA_HOME/bin:/sbin:$PATH

case "$1" in
  start)
     echo "Starting JBoss"
     cd $JBOSS_HOME/bin
     startproc -l /var/log/jboss.log $JBOSS_HOME/bin/run.sh
     ;;
  stop)
     echo "Shutting down JBoss"
     cd $JBOSS_HOME/bin
     ./shutdown.sh
     rc_status -v
     ;;
  restart)
     echo "Restarting JBoss"
     cd $JBOSS_HOME/bin
     ./shutdown.sh
     sleep 10
     startproc -l /var/log/jboss.log $JBOSS_HOME/bin/run.sh
     ;;
  *)
     echo "Usage: $0 {start|stop|restart}"
     exit 1
     ;;
esac
rc_exit
```

2. Store the script shown above in a file called `jboss` in the `/etc/int.d` directory.

3. Make the file executable by running the command `chmod 751 jboss`.

4. Create soft links in /etc/init.d/rc3.d and /etc/init.d/rc5.d for starting the script during system startup. This can be done by the command ln -s /etc/init.d/jboss /etc/init.d/rc3.d/S10Jboss and ln -s /etc/init.d/jboss /etc/init.d/rc5.d/S10Jboss. Please note that the name of the symbolic link should start with the string 'SXX', where XX is a two-digit number indicating the order in which the startup script should be called during system startup.

5. Create soft links in /etc/init.d/rc3.d and /etc/init.d/rc5.d for stopping the script during system shutdown. This can be done by the command ln -s /etc/init.d/jboss /etc/init.d/rc3.d/K10Jboss and ln-s /etc/init.d/jboss /etc/init.d/rc5.d/K10Jboss. Please note that the name of the symbolic link should start with the string 'KXX', where XX is a two-digit number indicating the order in which the shutdown script should be called during system shutdown.

6. Now if you restart the system, JBoss will be run as a system service.

3.1.6 Startup Troubleshooting

In this section, we will have a look at some of the commonly encountered problems in running JBoss:

Problem	Solution
Exception in deploying Log4J service. Startup process throws DeploymentException stating no property editor found for attribute ConfigurationURL.	This happens only on the IBM JRE, and can be solved by upgrading to IBM JRE version 1.3.1.
Unable to access JMX console on port 8082 after starting JBoss.	From v3.01 onwards, the JMX console is available as a true J2EE application and can be accessed on the default port 8080 by accessing the context path /jmx-console.
Startup fails with JDom JAR file in the lib directory.	The JAR file contains an info.xml file in the META-INF directory; JBoss treats it as a deployment descriptor. Removing this JAR file will register the JDom JAR file in the class registry.
ClassCircularityError in starting JBoss.	This is due to a bug in Sun JVM that has not been fixed even in JDK 1.4. However, a delegation-based class-loading model since JBoss 3.0.1 has fixed this problem.

Problem	Solution
`FileNotFoundException` in trying to run JBoss as an NT service.	Give full access to the account used to run the service to the JBoss directories.
`BindException` when trying to start JBoss.	Make sure no other process is using ports used by JBoss.

3.2 Shutting Down JBoss

You can shut down JBoss in one of the following three ways:

❑ Press *Ctrl-C* from the command window that runs the server. JBoss will use a JDK shutdown hook to do a graceful shutdown.

❑ Use the `shutdown.sh/shutdown.bat` file to shut down the server. This will connect to the HTTP adaptor of the JBoss MBean server and issue a call to call the shutdown method on the server MBean. This batch file will try to connect to the JMX HTTP adaptor listening on localhost at port 8080. This can also used to issue a remote shutdown by specifying the host address and port number as shown below:

```
shutdown wombat.com 8000
```

❑ Use the following command to use the `shutdown.jar` file:

```
java -jar shutdown.jar
```

You can use the second and third options if the command window is not available, such as the JBoss server running on a remote server or as an NT service or a UNIX daemon.

JBoss 3.0

Administration and Deployment

Handbook

4

4

The JBoss Configuration Architecture

JBoss configuration is based on the **Java Management Extension (JMX)**. To understand JBoss' configuration options well, it is important to have a good grasp of the JMX architecture. In this chapter, we will have a brief overview of JMX and a detailed coverage of JBoss configuration architecture.

4.1 An Overview of JMX

In this section, we will provide a high-level overview of JMX (please note that a comprehensive coverage of JMX is beyond the scope of this chapter and the book; *JMX: Managing J2EE with Java Management Extensions (ISBN: 0-67232-288-9)* from *SAMS* may help).

Java Management Extensions is a specification that has evolved through the Java Community Process (JCP) with JSR #3. JMX primarily focuses on managing and monitoring applications. You can use JMX to manage resources within your application, such as connection factories, JMS destinations, mail sessions, etc. When you make a resource manageable, you need to provide the following pieces of information regarding the resource:

- ❑ Different ways the resource can be constructed
- ❑ Different properties the resource possesses
- ❑ Different behaviors exhibited by the resource

JMX provides a solution for this by defining a standard for representing manageable resources. It also defines:

❑ How these resources can be managed

❑ How the managed resources are made available to be managed

To address the aforementioned requirements, the JMX specification defines a management architecture that provides the following levels:

❑ An **instrumentation level** that exposes the resources managed using standard interfaces. In the JMX vocabulary, the instrumentation level components are called managed beans or **MBeans**. MBeans are very similar to the JavaBean component model. MBeans provide a wrapper around the application resources that are managed, to make them manageable.

❑ An **agent level** that provides the runtime in which the instrumentation level components can run. In the JMX vocabulary, the runtime in which the MBean components are run is called the **MBean server**. JMX implementations are required to provide MBean server implementations that will host all the MBean components that are managed. The JMX specification mandates the agent level to provide some MBean services for monitoring, timers, dynamic loading of MBeans, etc.

❑ A **distributed services level** that will provide the communication infrastructure for management applications to connect to the agent level and view the MBean components, alter their properties and invoke their methods. The management applications can be browser-based or thick client applications.

The JMX architecture explained above is depicted in the diagram below:

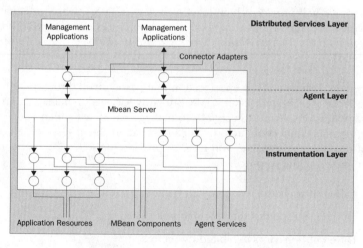

*Please note that the resource that is being managed, and the MBean
component that exposes the resource for management, do not need to
be separate components; they can very well be implemented in the
same component.*

4.1.1 Instrumentation Level

The instrumentation level constitutes the MBean components that represent the managed
resources. In the last section, we also saw the information we need about a resource
before it can be managed. From a Java perspective, this information comprises of:

❑   The resource properties that represent the state of the resource. For
    example, if you were exposing a JDBC connection pool as a managed
    resource, you would want information (such as pool size, initial capacity,
    increment size, shrink size, etc.) regarding the resource.

❑   The information on the constructors you can use to create the resources. In
    the case of the JDBC connection pool, these may include operations to get
    and release connections.

❑   Information regarding the various parameters that are passed to the
    constructors, and operations of the managed resources.

❑   Notifications that are sent by MBean bean components through the JMX
    notification infrastructure. In a connection pool, the resource may need to
    send a notification when the data server goes down.

JMX defines a standard way of defining MBean components, so that the MBean server
can gather information about the MBean components. For this, JMX defines four types
of MBean components:

❑   Standard MBean Components
❑   Dynamic MBean Components
❑   Model MBean Components
❑   Open MBean Components

> **Currently the JBoss JMX implementation only supports
> standard and dynamic MBean components.**

4.1.1.1 Standard MBeans

Standard MBeans are the most primitive form of JMX MBeans. They provide
information about their attributes and operations using plain Java interfaces. The
interfaces that describe the properties of the MBeans are required to have names
ending with the string MBean.

4.1.1.2 Dynamic MBeans

The difference between standard and dynamic MBeans is that in standard MBeans, the JMX implementation extracts the metadata about the MBean attributes and operations from the MBean interface, whereas in dynamic MBeans, the MBean provider provides this metadata using some standard JMX classes for describing the metadata. This provides more flexibility to the MBean provider for defining the manageable behavior of the MBean.

4.1.1.3 Model MBeans

Model MBeans are very similar to dynamic MBeans. Every JMX implementation is required to provide an implementation of this interface called `RequiredModelMBean`. The only thing the instrumentation developer needs to do for using model MBeans, is to provide the required metadata classes.

4.1.1.4 Open MBeans

The dynamic and model MBeans are used when the metadata provided, as pertains to the behavior of the MBean components, can be described by primitive data types, strings, or arrays of strings, or primitive types. Open MBeans are used when the metadata information is more complex. Open MBeans provide a set of generic classes to describe complex metadata so that the management applications don't need to worry about the complex data types used within the JMX system to describe the metadata for the MBeans, thus avoiding tight coupling between the management applications and the JMX system.

4.1.2 The Agent Level

The agent level provides the runtime in which the MBean components operate. At the heart of the agent level is the MBean server that acts as repository of all the MBean components running within the JMX system. This is represented by the JMX interface `MBeanServer`. The attributes and operations of every MBean registered with an MBean server are available for remote management through the distributed services layer.

Each MBean component registered with an MBean server is uniquely identified by a name represented by the JMX class `ObjectName`. Object names take the format of a domain name, separated from zero or more key-value pairs by a colon:

```
domainName:[key=value,key=value,….]
```

The key-value pairs are mainly used in querying the MBean server for MBean components. An example of an object name used in JBoss configuration for the transaction manager MBean is shown below:

```
jboss:service=TransactionManager
```

In the example above, the domain is jboss and it contains one key by the name service and value TransactionManager.

The MBean server interface defines a variety of methods for the following purposes:

- ❑ Creating MBean instances

- ❑ Removing MBean instances

- ❑ Registering MBean instances with the MBean server

- ❑ Querying MBean instances registered in the server

- ❑ Viewing and changing the various MBean attributes

- ❑ Invoking operations on the MBean instances

MBean server instances are created using the factory class MBeanServerFactory.

4.1.2.1 Agent Level Services

The JMX specification mandates the implementations to provide the following MBean services that are themselves MBeans, as part of the agent level:

- ❑ **MLet Service**

    MLet is the short form of Management Applet and this service is used to load MBean components defined in an XML-like format into the MBean server. The MBean that represent the MLet service provides methods to load MBean information from remote URLs. JBoss uses a variation of the MLet services to load the various configuration information and components as MBeans. We will have a look at that in detail in *Section 4.2: JMX in JBoss.*

    The snippet below shows the syntax of how an MLet service is defined:

    ```
    <MLET
      CODE="" | OBJECT=""
      ARCHIVE=""
      [CODEBASE=""]
      [NAME=""]
      [VERSION=""]
      [ARG TYPE="" VALUE=""]
    </MLET>
    ```

    An MLET tag is used for each MBean that is dynamically loaded. The CODE attribute defines the fully qualified class of the MBean that needs to be loaded. Alternatively, you can specify a file that contains the serialized MBean object using the OBJECT attribute. The ARCHIVE attribute is used to define the list of JAR files that will contain the definitions for MBean class and any dependent classes.

The CODEBASE attribute can be used to define the relative path to the archives. The NAME attribute is used to define the unique object name for the MBean. The VERSION attribute is used to define an optional version number. The ARG tag is used to define the arguments that are passed to the MBean constructor.

❑ **Monitoring Services**
This service is used to monitor MBean attributes at pre-defined intervals. This service will send a notification to registered listeners if the attribute value changes above a pre-defined limit during successive observations. The services provide different types of monitors such as counter monitors for monitoring a non-negative integer, increasing MBean attribute, gauge monitors for monitoring arbitrarily changing integer values, string monitors for monitoring string attributes, etc.

❑ **Timer Service**
This is for sending timer-based notifications.

❑ **Relation Service**
This is used to associate MBean instances with each other.

4.1.3 Distributed Service Level

The distributed services level is used to enable management applications to connect to the agent level and manipulate the MBean components registered with the MBean server. Most of the distributed service layer details are standardized in a separate JSR (#160) on JMX Remoting 1.2. This provides a client-side API for management applications to discover both, local and remote JMX agent levels, and interact with them.

4.2 JMX in JBoss

The JBoss server uses a JMX-based configuration architecture. It provides an MBean server implementation that acts as a repository for all the JBoss components. All the JBoss components, including the JBoss server, are written as JMX MBean components. The JBoss server, when it starts up, creates an MBean server instance. All the JBoss components are then registered with this MBean server. The default domain name used by the JBoss MBean server instance is jboss.

It then registers both the server and the server configuration instances as MBean components with the MBean server. As we have seen in *Section 2.3: Server Configuration Sets*, the server configuration instance defines various properties such as the JBoss home directory, server configuration set, boot library path, root configuration file, etc.

Then JBoss creates and registers the following MBean components:

❏ A service controller MBean that controls the lifecycle of other MBean components registered with the server.

❏ An MBean component that represents the main deployer within JBoss. This component will deploy all the MBeans specified in the root configuration file identified by the `jboss.server.root.deployment.filename` system property. This defaults to `jboss-service.xml` file found in the `\conf` directory of the configuration set that is used. JBoss configuration sets are covered in detail in *Section 2.3: Server Configuration Sets*. The MBeans defined in this file control the behavior of the JBoss instance that is running. The contents of this file use an XML format similar to the one used by the standard JMX MLet service.

❏ MBean components capable of deploying various types of components such as EAR, JAR, and SAR. **SAR** is the acronym for **service archive**, which is a component model JBoss introduces for packaging MBean components. See *Section 4.2.1.2: JBoss SAR Components* for more details.

4.2.1 MBeans in JBoss

In JBoss, you can write two different types of MBeans:

❏ The first one is either one of JMX standard or dynamic MBean types. These MBeans are not dependent on any of the JBoss services. You can use these MBeans if you don't expect JBoss to manage the lifecycle for the MBean.

❏ You can also write MBeans that are dependent on the JBoss services. These MBeans are written in a format specific to JBoss MBean services. JBoss MBean services expose methods that can be used to manage the lifecycle of the MBean instances to notify the MBean when it can create, destroy, and start itself. You can use these MBeans if your MBeans are dependent on other MBeans and you want to define lifecycle dependencies. The service lifecycle of every JBoss service MBean is controlled by the following MBeans:

- MBean responsible for SAR deployment
- A service configurator MBean
- A service controller MBean

4.2.1.1 JBoss Service MBeans

MBean components that utilize JBoss services are required to implement the `org.jboss.system.Service` interface. The service controller MBean will call the methods defined in this interface on various MBean components at appropriate times:

❑ create()
  The service controller MBean calls the create() method on MBean components on occurrence of an event that affects the state of the MBean component. This will also trigger the invocation of the create() method on all other MBean components that this MBean is dependent on. MBean dependencies are covered in detail in *Section 4.2.1.2: JBoss SAR Components*.

❑ start()
  The start() method is invoked on the MBean when it is ready to start its service. This will be called only after calling the start() method on all other MBeans on which this MBean is dependent.

❑ stop()
  The stop() method is called when the service controller requires the MBean to stop its service. This method can be used for cleaning up resources.

❑ destroy()
  The destroy() method is called when the service controller requires to destroy the MBean. This method can be used for cleaning up resources.

4.2.1.2 JBoss SAR Components

JBoss introduces the notion of **SAR (Service Archive)** components for packaging and deploying MBeans. The SAR deployer MBean is responsible for the deployment of SAR components. SAR components can be deployed either in packaged or exploded formats.

When a SAR component is deployed in the packaged format, it should be a JAR file with the extension sar. The META-INF directory of the JAR file should contain an XML file called jboss-service.xml. This file uses an XML syntax similar to the one used by the JMX MLet service for defining MBean definitions. The JAR file should also contain the MBean class as well as any other dependent classes. In the exploded format, the MBean definitions should be stored in a file with name ending with the string -service.xml.

The structure of the SAR deployment descriptor is shown below:

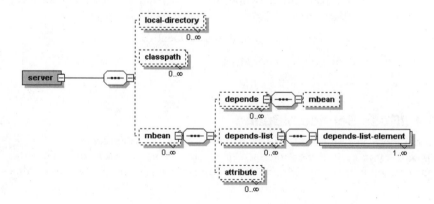

It is important that you understand the structure of the SAR deployment descriptor DTD, as you will be using it often for configuring the various MBean services that come with JBoss as well as writing your own MBean services.

The root element of the deployment descriptor is called `server`. This element can have one or more `local-directory` and `classpath` elements. The `local-directory` element has a `path` attribute that describes the path within the SAR file that should be copied to the directory within the server that is used for persistent storage. The `classpath` element is used to define external JAR files that should be deployed with the MBean components defined in the SAR. The `classpath` element has `archives` attribute used to define a comma separated list of JAR files and the `codebase` attribute used to define a URL that contains the JAR files.

4.2.1.2.1 Defining MBeans

MBeans are defined using **mbean** elements within the `server` element. The mandatory `code` attribute defines the class that represents the MBean component. The `name` attribute defines the unique object name that is used to identify the MBean within the MBean server. The `mbean` element may contain zero or more `attribute` elements to define the MBean attributes. The `name` attribute of the `attribute` element defines the attribute name and the text content of the element defines the attribute value. The element content may be any arbitrary XML, if the type of the attribute is `org.w3c.dom.Element`.

An example of an MBean definition is shown below:

```
<mbean code="org.jboss.naming.NamingService"
       name="jboss:service=Naming">
  <attribute name="Port">1099</attribute>
</mbean>
```

The snippet above defines an MBean by the name `jboss:service=Naming` and class `org.jboss.naming.NamingService` with an attribute `Port` set to the value `1099`.

4.2.1.2.2 Defining Dependencies

When you define MBean services, the service you define may depend on other services. This means you want to make sure all those services on which your service is dependent are deployed and started before your service is started. For example, if you define an MBean service that uses JNDI lookup, you would want to make sure that the JBoss naming MBean service is started before your service is started.

Dependencies are resolved by the service configuration and service controller MBeans by using the lifecycle callbacks defined for the MBean services and the dependencies defined in the SAR deployment descriptor for the MBean. The SAR deployment descriptor defines two ways of defining dependencies:

47

❏ The mbean element may contain zero or more depends elements to define dependencies on other MBean services. The text content of this element may be used for defining the object name of an MBean on which this MBean ID is dependent. The snippet below shows how the depends element is used to define dependencies:

```
<mbean code="org.jboss.deployment.cache.DeploymentCache"
       name="jboss.deployment:type=DeploymentCache">
    <depends optional-attribute-name="Deployer">
       jboss.system:service=MainDeployer
    </depends>
    <depends optional-attribute-name="Store">
       jboss.deployment:type=DeploymentStore,flavor=File
    </depends>
</mbean>
```

The optional-attribute-name attribute can be used to bind the service depended upon, to an attribute of the dependent service. You can also use the nested mbean element to define the MBean that this MBean is dependent on:

```
<mbean
    ...
        <depends optional-attribute-name="someAttribute">
           <mbean code="someCode" name="someName">
              <attribute name="attrib">value</attribute>
              ...
           </mbean>
        </depends>
</mbean>
```

❏ Alternatively, you can use the depends-list element to define multiple object names for the MBean service on which this MBean service is dependent:

```
<mbean
    ...
        <depends-list optional-attribute-name="someName">
           <depends-list-element>
              someDomain:key1=value1
           </depends-list-element>
           <depends-list-element>
              someDomain:key2=value2
           </depends-list-element>
        </depends-list>
</mbean>
```

4.2.2 The JBoss Root Configuration File

When JBoss starts up, the main deployer deploys the MBean services defined in the root configuration file. By default, this file is the `jboss-service.xml` file in the `\conf` directory of the configuration set that is used. However, the location of this file can be controlled using the system property `jboss.server.root.deployment.filename`.

The MBean services specified in this file define the behavior of the server instance that is running. In this section, we will have a look at the core services that are defined in the root configuration file for the default configuration set. The listing below shows the MBean services defined in the `jboss-service.xml` file present in the `%JBOSS_HOME%\server\default\conf` directory:

```
<?xml version="1.0" encoding="UTF-8"?>

<server>

  <!-- Load all jars from the JBOSS_DIST/server/<config>/ -->
  <classpath codebase="lib" archives="*"/>
```

This is a service to access `java.beans.PropertyEditorManager`. Property managers are used in JavaBeans to locate bean property editors for a given types:

```
<mbean code="org.jboss.varia.property.PropertyEditorManagerService"
    name="jboss:type=Service,name=BootstrapEditors">
  <attribute name="BootstrapEditors">
    java.math.BigDecimal=
        org.jboss.util.propertyeditor.BigDecimalEditor
    java.lang.Boolean=org.jboss.util.propertyeditor.BooleanEditor
    java.lang.Class=org.jboss.util.propertyeditor.ClassEditor
    java.util.Date=org.jboss.util.propertyeditor.DateEditor
    java.io.File=org.jboss.util.propertyeditor.FileEditor
    java.net.InetAddress=
        org.jboss.util.propertyeditor.InetAddressEditor
    java.lang.Integer=org.jboss.util.propertyeditor.IntegerEditor
    javax.management.ObjectName=
        org.jboss.util.propertyeditor.ObjectNameEditor
    java.util.Properties=
        org.jboss.util.propertyeditor.PropertiesEditor
    [Ljava.lang.String;=
        org.jboss.util.propertyeditor.StringArrayEditor
    java.net.URL=org.jboss.util.propertyeditor.URLEditor
  </attribute>
</mbean>
```

A system property service for loading system properties:

```
<!-- System Properties -->
<mbean
    code="org.jboss.varia.property.SystemPropertiesService"
    name="jboss:type=Service,name=SystemProperties">
  <attribute name="Properties">
```

```
    invokerServletPath=
    http://localhost:8080/invoker/JMXInvokerServlet
  </attribute>
</mbean>
```

The service to enable logging using Log4J. This service supports attributes for specifying the Log4J configuration file and the refresh period for reloading Log4J configuration. We'll look at this MBean more closely in *Section 14.1: The Logging MBean*:

```
<!-- Log4j Initialization -->
<mbean
  code="org.jboss.logging.Log4jService"
  name="jboss.system:type=Log4jService,service=Logging">
  <attribute name="ConfigurationURL">resource:log4j.xml</attribute>
</mbean>
```

The service to enable dynamic class loading:

```
<!-- Class Loading -->
<mbean
  code="org.jboss.web.WebService"
  name="jboss:service=Webserver">
  <attribute name="Port">8083</attribute>
  <attribute name="DownloadServerClasses">true</attribute>
</mbean>
```

An MBean used for implementing JSR 77, Java Management specification:

```
<!-- JSR-77 Single JBoss Server Management Domain  -->
<mbean
  code="org.jboss.management.j2ee.SingleJBossServerManagement"
  name="jboss.management.single:j2eeType=J2EEDomain,name=Manager" >
</mbean>
```

The JNDI service to enable naming and directory lookup. We'll look at these MBean more closely in *Section 6.1: The JBoss Naming Service* and *Section 6.3: JNDI View*:

```
<!-- JNDI -->
<mbean
  code="org.jboss.naming.NamingService"
  name="jboss:service=Naming">
  <attribute name="Port">1099</attribute>
</mbean>

<mbean
  code="org.jboss.naming.JNDIView"
  name="jboss:service=JNDIView"/>
```

Services to enable JAAS-based security. We'll look at this MBean more closely in *Section 7.3.2: Configuring the JAAS Security Manager.*

```
<!-- Security -->
<mbean
  code="org.jboss.security.plugins.SecurityConfig"
  name="jboss.security:name=SecurityConfig">
  <attribute name="LoginConfig">
    jboss.security:service=XMLLoginConfig
  </attribute>
</mbean>
<mbean
  code="org.jboss.security.auth.login.XMLLoginConfig"
  name="jboss.security:service=XMLLoginConfig">
  <attribute name="ConfigResource">login-config.xml</attribute>
</mbean>

<!-- JAAS security manager and realm mapping -->
<mbean
  code="org.jboss.security.plugins.JaasSecurityManagerService"
  name="jboss.security:service=JaasSecurityManager">
  <attribute name="SecurityManagerClassName">
    org.jboss.security.plugins.JaasSecurityManager
  </attribute>
</mbean>
```

MBean services for transactions:

```
<!-- Transactions -->
<mbean
  code="org.jboss.tm.XidFactory"
  name="jboss:service=XidFactory">
</mbean>

<mbean
  code="org.jboss.tm.TransactionManagerService"
  name="jboss:service=TransactionManager">
  <attribute name="TransactionTimeout">300</attribute>
  <depends optional-attribute-name="XidFactory">
    jboss:service=XidFactory
  </depends>
</mbean>

<mbean
  code="org.jboss.tm.usertx.server.ClientUserTransactionService"
  name="jboss:service=ClientUserTransaction">
</mbean>

<!-- The CachedConnectionManager -->
<mbean
  code=
  "org.jboss.resource.connectionmanager.CachedConnectionManager"
  name="jboss.jca:service=CachedConnectionManager">
</mbean>
```

MBean service for the EJB deployer. We'll look at this MBean more closely in *Section 17.2.1: The EJB Deployer*.

```
<!-- EJB deployer -->
<mbean
  code="org.jboss.ejb.EJBDeployer"
  name="jboss.ejb:service=EJBDeployer">
  <attribute name="VerifyDeployments">true</attribute>
  <attribute name="ValidateDTDs">false</attribute>
  <attribute name="MetricsEnabled">false</attribute>
  <attribute name="VerifierVerbose">true</attribute>
  <depends>
    jboss.mq:service=JMSProviderLoader,name=JBossMQProvider
  </depends>
  <depends>
    jboss.mq:service=ServerSessionPoolMBean,name=StdJMSPool
  </depends>
</mbean>
```

MBean service for the EAR deployer. We'll look at this MBean more closely in *Section 20.1: The EAR Deployer*.

```
<!-- EAR deployer -->
<mbean
  code="org.jboss.deployment.EARDeployer"
  name="jboss.j2ee:service=EARDeployer">
</mbean>
```

MBean for JMX invocation:

```
<!-- Invokers to the JMX node -->

<!-- RMI/JRMP invoker -->
<mbean
  code="org.jboss.invocation.jrmp.server.JRMPInvoker"
  name="jboss:service=invoker,type=jrmp">
  <attribute name="RMIObjectPort">4444</attribute>
</mbean>

<mbean
  code="org.jboss.invocation.local.LocalInvoker"
  name="jboss:service=invoker,type=local">
</mbean>
```

MBeans for hot deployment. We'll look at these MBeans more closely in *Section 15.2: Hot Deployment*:

```
<!-- Deployment Scanning -->
<mbean
  code="org.jboss.deployment.scanner.URLDeploymentScanner"
  name="jboss.deployment:type=DeploymentScanner,flavor=URL">
  <depends optional-attribute-name="Deployer">
    jboss.system:service=MainDeployer
  </depends>
  <attribute name="URLComparator">
```

```
        org.jboss.deployment.DeploymentSorter
    </attribute>
    <attribute name="Filter">
        org.jboss.deployment.scanner.DeploymentFilter
    </attribute>
    <attribute name="ScanPeriod">5000</attribute>

    <attribute name="URLs">./deploy</attribute>

  </mbean>

</server>
```

4.3 Accessing the JMX Agent

In this section, we will have a look at how to access the JBoss JMX agent level and manipulate the registered MBeans. The JBoss JMX agent can be accessed using the JMX HTML adaptor provided with JBoss. This is provided as a standard J2EE web application and can be accessed using the context path /jmx-console. The console web application is available as an exploded WAR in the \deploy directory of the default configuration set. The home page for the console displays all the MBean services registered with JBoss sorted by domain name. The screenshot below displays the initial page of the JMX console:

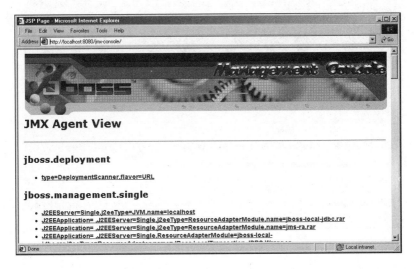

From the Agent View page, you can view any of the MBean services by clicking on the link representing the service. The screenshot below displays the MBean service for viewing the JNDI tree:

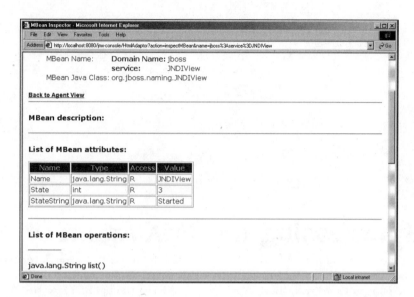

From this page, you can set the attributes on the MBean as well as invoke operations on the MBean. The screenshot below displays the results of invoking the `list()` method on the `JNDIView` Mbean:

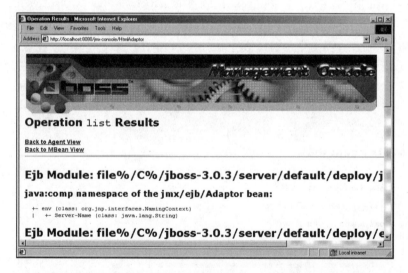

JBoss also provides an RMI adaptor for connecting to the JMX agent level. This allows remote clients to connect to the JMX agent and invoke MBean operations. This can be useful if you have clients that rely on MBeans deployed within the JBoss server instances. However, for pure administration of the server it is best to connect to the browser-based interface for invoking MBean operations.

4.3.1 Securing the JMX Console

JBoss installation provides anonymous access to the JMX console application. However, you may want to permit access to the console only to authorized users. To do this, you need to secure the console by specifying a security domain in the `jboss-web.xml` JBoss web deployment descriptor for the console web applications. Security domains are covered in detail in *Section 7.2: The JBoss Security Layer*, and the JBoss-specific web deployment descriptor is covered in *Section 16.1: The JBoss Web Deployment Descriptor.*

You can enable security by editing the `jboss-web.xml` file in the `\deploy\jmx-console.war\WEB-INF` directory in the `\deploy` directory. Add the following code to the XML file:

```
<jboss-web>
    <security-domain>java:/jaas/jmx-console</security-domain>
</jboss-web>
```

You'll probably find this line is already present but commented so all you'll need to do is uncomment it.

This will use a pre-configured security domain and use basic authentication for the console application allowing access only to username `admin` and password `admin`. You may have to restart the server. This domain uses the `user.properties` and `role.properties` files available in the `\WEB-INF\classes` directory. You also need to uncomment the `security-constraint` defined in the `web.xml` file in the `\jmx-console.war\WEB-INF` directory in the `\deploy` directory:

```
<security-constraint>
  <web-resource-collection>
    <web-resource-name>HtmlAdaptor</web-resource-name>
    <description>
        An example security config that only allows users with the
        role JBossAdmin to access the HTML JMX console web
        application
    </description>
    <url-pattern>/*</url-pattern>
    <http-method>GET</http-method>
    <http-method>POST</http-method>
  </web-resource-collection>
  <auth-constraint>
    <role-name>JBossAdmin</role-name>
  </auth-constraint>
</security-constraint>
```

Now if you try to access the console, the browser will prompt you for user name and password:

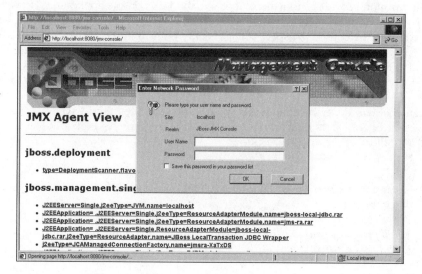

JBoss 3.0

Administration and Deployment

Handbook

5

Runtime Properties

Application servers generally adopt different classloading strategies to resolve dependencies between various classes used in an enterprise application as well as their dependencies on external libraries. Even though J2EE defines standards on classloading issues, such as using the classpath manifest attribute and Servlet 2.3 classloading model, etc., it is extremely important that you understand the classloading model adopted by your application server as it significantly influences how you package your various components.

In this chapter we will have a detailed look at the JBoss classloading architecture. We will also cover how to configure various runtime properties such as the JVM heap, profiling, setting the classpath, etc.

5.1 JBoss Classloading

Before we delve into the intricacies of the JBoss classloading architecture, we will have a look at how JBoss loads the system classes on startup. As we saw in *Section 3.1: Starting JBoss*, JBoss is started using the bootstrap JAR file `run.jar`. This JAR file contains the bare minimum classes required to gain an entry point to the JBoss system classes.

5.1.1 Classloading During JBoss Startup

The class with the `main()` method in the `run.jar` file is `org.jboss.Main`. This `main()` method creates a thread group called `jboss` and adds a thread called `main` and starts the thread. This thread will call the `boot()` method on the `org.jboss.Main` class by passing the command-line arguments passed to the `main()` method. This series of steps is depicted in the sequence diagram below:

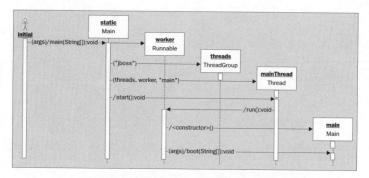

The boot() method will first parse the command-line arguments to identify the various pieces of information such as the library URL, patch directory, etc., and add them as system properties. The various command-line options are covered in detail in *Section 3.1.1: JBoss Startup Options*. The boot() method will then create an instance of org.jboss.system.server.ServerLoader and add the libraries specified by the -L and -C options (as well as the JAXP, JMX, and concurrent library JAR files present in the \lib directory at the root of the JBoss home) to the list of libraries maintained by the server loader.

> **The JAR files present in the \lib directory are hard-coded within JBoss and hence copying user-defined JAR files to this directory won't make them available to the classloader.**

The server loader is a helper class to load the JBoss server instance. Then it will ask this instance to load the server by passing the thread context classloader. This is depicted in the following sequence diagram:

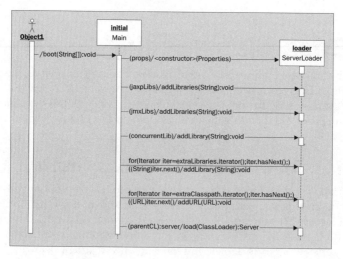

The server loader will first create an instance of the URLClassLoader with the thread context classloader as the parent, passing the following libraries:

❑ The URLs specified by the jboss.boot.library.list system property. The default value is the \lib directory under JBoss home.

❑ The JAXP JAR (crimson.jar or xerces.jar depending on the -j option). The default is crimson.jar.

❑ The JMX JAR jboss-jmx.jar.

❑ Oswego Concurrent JAR (concurrent.jar) – a third-party collections library used by JBoss.

❑ JARs specified as libraries via -L command-line options.

❑ JARs or directories specified via -C command-line options.

It then sets the newly created classloader as the thread context classloader and creates an instance of the server by creating the class org.jboss.system.server.ServerImpl. The init() method is called on the server instance by passing the list of properties created from the command-line options and system properties and the start() method is called. Once the start() method returns, the server loader resets the thread context classloader to the old thread context classloader.

The start() method of the server first starts an MBean server and registers the server configuration and server instance itself as MBean services. It will then register the service controller MBean. After this it creates and registers the main deployer MBean. This MBean is responsible for orchestrating the deployment process. This deployer will delegate the deployment process to sub-deployers responsible for deploying specific types of deployment units. JBoss provides different sub-deployers for EAR, JAR, WAR, EJB, SAR, etc. Refer to *Section 15.1: Deployers* for more information on deployers in JBoss.

5.1.2 Classloading Architecture

The JBoss 3.0 classloading architecture allows the sharing of classes across multiple application components. This classloading architecture introduces the concept of an MBean service that acts as a **shared repository** of classes. The classloaders used within JBoss will first look into this repository before loading a class. To implement this strategy JBoss introduces the UnifiedClassLoader as the primary classloader within JBoss. This class extends the JDK URLClassLoader class.

5.1.3 UnifiedClassLoader

The UnifiedClassLoader is an MBean service that is responsible for loading classes from a single URL in conjunction with a centralized class repository. This class is initialized with the URL from which to load the classes. The classloader will look into a global shared repository whether the requested class is available, before loading the class from the URL.

JBoss creates a unified classloader for each deployment unit that is deployed. The deployed units include WARs, EJBs, EARs, SARs, and RARs. Each time an instance of the unified classloader is created, it is registered with the central loader repository. The loader associated with the deployed unit will be responsible for loading all the classes from that deployed unit.

The diagram below depicts the typical classloading strategy in an EAR deployment scenario:

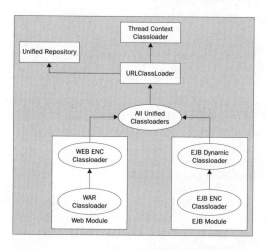

As with any other classloading scenario, the scheme depicted above uses a hierarchical scheme. Whenever a classloader is asked to load a class, it will ask its parent classloader for the class before loading it. The diagram above depicts the following classloaders:

- ❑ The thread context classloader is the system classloader.

- ❑ The URLClassLoader created by the server loader loads classes from the boot library path as explained in *Section 5.1.1: Classloading During JBoss Startup*.

- ❑ A pool of unified classloaders contains a classloader each for every deployed unit. The relevant deployers will create a unified classloader and register it with the loader repository when it deploys a component. These classloaders will consult with loader repository for a class before loading the class.

- ❑ The EJB dynamic classloader, which is an instance of org.jboss.web.WebClassLoader (a simple subclass of URLClassLoader), is used in conjunction with the WebService MBean to allow dynamic loading of resources and classes from deployed EARs, EJB JARs and WARs. A WebClassLoader is associated with a container and must have a UnifiedClassLoader as its parent.

❏ The EJB ENC (Environment Naming Context) classloader is a URLClassLoader, used solely for the deployed EJB's `java:comp` JNDI context.

❏ The WEB ENC (Environment Naming Context) classloader, is a URLClassLoader, used solely for the deployed WAR component's `java:comp` JNDI context.

❏ The WAR classloader that loads classes from the `\WEB-INF\lib` and `\WEB-INF\classes` directories of the WAR.

! **Please note that if you are using Servlet 2.3 classloading, the WAR loader will try to load the classes from the `\WEB-INF` directories before consulting with the parent classloader. This can cause a `ClassCastException` if you have EJB client views in your `\WEB-INF` directories as the class that is looked up the WAR loader is different from the dynamic proxy class that implements the EJB client view. This is because JBoss uses dynamic reflection proxies to implement EJBs. A possible solution to this is not to include the EJB client view in the `\WEB-INF` directories.**

5.1.3.1 Advantages and Disadvantages

The main advantage of this classloading scheme is that the classes are shared across multiple components without the need to replicate them across the components.

> **One major disadvantage is that it is impossible to have multiple versions of the same class across different EAR files, as JBoss will always use the first version that is loaded.**

This means that if you have a JAR file in the `\lib` directory of the server, JBoss will use that JAR file to load the classes even if you package a different version of the JAR file with your application. This is because the URLClassloader used by the server loader is the parent classloader for all the unified classloaders. Hence whenever a unified classloader is asked to load a class, it will ask its parent classloader to load the class before trying it itself. Hence, if the library were present in the `\lib` directory, the URL classloader would load it before the unified classloader would get a chance to load it from the EAR file.

For example, imagine an EAR X uses v 1.0 of library A and EAR Y uses v1.1 of the same library. EAR X has v1.0 bundled with it and EAR Y has v1.1 bundled with it. If EAR X is deployed first, even if EAR Y contains v1.1 of the library, JBoss will use v1.0 whenever EAR Y tries to use the library. This is because the classes from v1.0 of the library are already available in the loader repository, and when a component in EAR Y asks the classloader to load the class, it will look in the repository first before loading it from the v1.1 JAR file packaged with EAR Y.

However, you can circumvent this problem using scoped classloading in EAR files. This is achieved using the following entry in the JBoss-specific application deployment descriptor, `jboss-app.xml`, present in the `\META-INF` directory of the EAR file:

```
<jboss-app>
   <loader-repository>MyLoaderRepository</loader-repository>
</jboss-app>
```

This EAR will use its own loader repository, and looks into this repository before falling back to the default repository. See *Section 20.2.2: Loader Repository* for more details on this feature.

5.2 Setting the Classpath

By default the JBoss startup script uses only the JDK `tools.jar` file and the JBoss bootstrap `run.jar` JAR file in the classpath. After that, as explained in *Section 5.1.1. Classloading During JBoss Startup*, JBoss will add the necessary archives and paths to the classloaders as specified by the command-line options. All the JAR files in the `\lib` directory of the configuration set you use will be available to the classloaders. Hence, rather than modifying the classpath during startup, it is recommended to copy the JAR files containing shared classes to the `\lib` directory of your configuration set.

> **Copying the JAR files to the `\lib` directory of the JBoss home won't make them available to the classloaders, as these JARs are hard-coded in JBoss.**

If your class files are remote, then you can use the −L and −C options during startup to make them available to the classloaders.

5.3 Setting JVM Options

By default, the startup script doesn't use any JVM options. This means the JVM uses all the default values. You can set JVM options by editing the `run.bat` file. These options include:

❑ −Xmixed
   Mixed mode execution (default)

❑ −Xint
   Interpreted mode execution only

❑ −Xbootclasspath <directories and zip/JAR files separated by ;>
   Set the search path for bootstrap classes and resources

- ❑ -Xbootclasspath/a <directories and zip/JAR files separated by ; >
  Append to end of bootstrap classpath

- ❑ -Xbootclasspath/p <directories and zip/jar files separated by ; >
  Prepend in front of bootstrap classpath

- ❑ -Xnoclassgc
  Disable class garbage collection

- ❑ -Xincgc
  Enable incremental garbage collection

- ❑ -Xbatch
  Disable background compilation

- ❑ -Xms<size>
  Set initial Java heap size

- ❑ -Xmx<size>
  Set maximum Java heap size

- ❑ -Xss<size>
  Set Java thread-stack size

- ❑ -Xprof
  Output CPU profiling data

- ❑ -Xrunhprof
  Perform JVMPI heap, CPU, or monitor profiling

- ❑ -Xdebug
  Enable remote debugging

- ❑ -Xfuture
  Enable strictest checks, anticipating future default

- ❑ -Xrs
  Reduce use of OS signals by Java/VM

The snippet below shows the excerpt from run.bat file to start JBoss by specifying initial and maximum JVM heap size of 128 megabytes:

```
%JAVA% %JAVA_OPTS% -classpath "%JBOSS_CLASSPATH%" -Xmx128m -Xms128m
org.jboss.Main %ARGS%
```

Please to the JDK tools documentation for an exhaustive coverage of standard and non-standard JVM options.

JBoss 3.0

Administration and Deployment

Handbook

6

6

Configuring Naming

In this chapter, we will have a look at the JBoss naming architecture and how to configure the JBoss naming service on both server and client sides.

6.1 The JBoss Naming Service

JBoss provides an RMI-based implementation for the **Java Naming and Directory Interface (JNDI)**. The clients use the Java RMI protocol for connecting to the naming service provider and performing naming and directory operations. The RMI-based implementation uses optimized invocation to use call-by-reference for in-VM lookups. At the core of the JBoss naming implementation is the naming service MBean that is normally declared in the `jboss-service.xml` root configuration file available in the `\conf` directory of the configuration set you use. The MBeans definition is:

```
<mbean
   code="org.jboss.naming.NamingService"
   name="jboss:service=Naming">
```

This MBean supports the following attributes:

Attribute	Function
Port	The port on which the **JBoss Naming Provider (JNP)** server listens. The default value for this is 1099.
RmiPort	The RMI port on which the RMI naming implementation is exported. The default value of 0 means any available port is used.

Table continued on following page

Attribute	Function
BindAddress	Used on a multi-IP host to specify the address on which the JNP server listens.
Backlog	To define the maximum number of connection requests that can be queued.
ClientSocketFactory	To specify an optional RMI client socket factory to be used. The default is `java.rmi.server.RMIClientSocketFactory`.
ServerSocketFactory	To specify an optional RMI server socket factory to be used. The default is `java.rmi.server.RMIServerSocketFactory`.
JNPServerSocketFactory	Optionally used to specify a factory for creating server sockets.

The listing below shows the definition of the naming service MBean in the root configuration file:

```
<mbean
   code="org.jboss.naming.NamingService"
   name="jboss:service=Naming">
   <attribute name="Port">1099</attribute>
</mbean>
```

6.2 JNDI Client Configuration

In this section, we will have a look at the configuration required on the client side to connect to the JNP server. Two important things to keep in mind are the properties required for creating the JNDI initial context, and the required client side JAR files.

6.2.1 Initial Context Properties

You don't need to specify any of the properties when you connect to the JNDI provider from within JBoss. In such scenarios, JBoss reads the properties from the file jndi.properties in the \conf directory. This file doesn't specify the provider URL enabling JBoss RMI-based context implementation to use an in-VM call. The contents of the jndi.properties file, available in the \conf directory of the default configuration set, are shown below:

```
java.naming.factory.initial=org.jnp.interfaces.NamingContextFactory
java.naming.factory.url.pkgs=org.jboss.naming:org.jnp.interfaces
# Do NOT uncomment this line as it causes in VM calls to go over
# RMI!
#java.naming.provider.url=localhost
```

The properties that are required when a client outside the JBoss VM connects to the JNP server are listed below:

Property	Value
Context.INITIAL_CONTEXT_FACTORY	org.jnp.interfaces.NamingContextFactory
Context.PROVIDER_URL	jnp://<your server>:port. If you don't specify the protocol, it defaults to jnp; if you don't specify the port, it defaults to 1099.
Context.URL_PKG_PREFIXES	org.jboss.naming:org.jnp.interfaces
jnp.socketFactory	This should specify an implementation of javax.net.SocketFactory. The default value is org.jnp.interfaces.TimedSocketFactory
jnp.timeout	This is used to specify the connection timeout in milliseconds. A default value of 0 means the connection will wait for the underlying transport to timeout.
jnp.sotimeout	This is used to specify the read timeout for a connected socket. The default value of zero will perform a blocking read.

So, for example, to configure a client to call into the JBoss JNDI namespace you would use code such as this.

Create the properties required to connect to the JBoss naming provider:

```
Properties prop = new Properties();

prop.put(Context.INITIAL_CONTEXT_FACTORY,
    "org.jnp.interfaces.NamingContextFactory");
prop.put(Context.PROVIDER_URL,
    "jnp://localhost:1099");
prop.put(Context.URL_PKG_PREFIXES,
    "org.jboss.naming:org.jnp.interfaces");
```

Create an initial context connecting to the JBoss naming provider:

```
InitialContext jbossContext = new InitialContext(prop);
```

6.2.2 Client JAR Files

To connect to the JNP server, at bare minimum, you need the following JAR files available in the client directory of your JBoss installation:

❑   `jnp-client.jar`

❑   `log4j.jar`

❑   `jboss-common-client.jar`

However, depending on the type of object you are looking up, you may need extra JAR files. For example, if you are looking up JMS administered objects, you will need `jbossmq-client.jar` file in the client classpath. See *Section 2.2: The JBoss Directory Structure* for a complete run-down of the client JAR files.

6.3 JNDI View

JBoss provides an MBean that is configured in the root configuration file to view the objects bound in its JNDI namespace. The MBean definition is shown below:

```
<mbean
    code="org.jboss.naming.JNDIView"
    name="jboss:service=JNDIView">
```

If you access the MBean from the JMX console and invoke the `list()` method, it will list all the contexts and objects in the JNDI namespace:

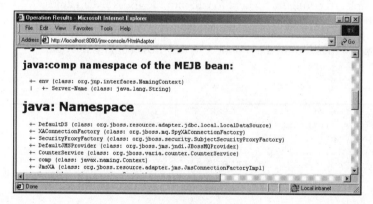

This page is very useful in troubleshooting problems that occur in performing naming and lookup operations. The page lists all the contexts and sub-contexts within the naming provider and all the objects that are bound within the naming provider showing the JNDI name and type of the object that is exported.

6.4 External JNDI Namespaces

JBoss provides an MBean for incorporating external namespaces into the JBoss namespace. This means that you can lookup objects bound in JNDI namespaces defined outside JBoss, through the JBoss naming provider. The MBean definition is:

```
<mbean
  code="org.jboss.naming.ExternalContext"
  name="jboss.jndi:service=ExternalContext">
```

This MBean supports the following attributes:

Attribute	Function
JndiName	This is the JNDI name under which the external namespace is bound.
RemoteAccess	This is a flag to indicate whether the initial context of the external namespace should be bound as a serializable object. This will allow a client running outside the JBoss VM to create the external initial context. The external initial context is looked up using the standard JNDI lookup calls through the JBoss initial context.
CacheContext	A flag to state whether the external initial context should be created and cached when the MBean is started.
InitialContext	The fully qualified name of the class that implements the JNDI initial context.
Properties	This is to specify a standard properties file that contains the initial context properties required to connect to the external naming provider.

An example is shown below:

```
<mbean
  code="org.jboss.naming.ExternalContext"
  name="jboss.jndi:service=ExternalContext, jndiName=WLSContext">

  <attribute name="JndiName">WLSContext</attribute>
  <attribute name="InitialContext">
    weblogic.jndi.internal.WLInternalContext
  </attribute>
  <attribute name="RemoteAccess">true</attribute>
  <attribute name="RemoteAccess">weblogic.properties</attribute>

</mbean>
```

The example above defines an external naming provider running within a BEA WebLogic environment. You can lookup the initial context for the WebLogic JNDI namespace through the JBoss initial context. To do this, you need to first create an initial context that connects to the JBoss naming provider. Then you should use that initial context to lookup the WebLogic initial context.

The code to use the external context may look as follows:

```
Properties prop = new Properties();

prop.put(Context.INITIAL_CONTEXT_FACTORY,
    "org.jnp.interfaces.NamingContextFactory");
prop.put(Context.PROVIDER_URL,
    "jnp://localhost:1099");
prop.put(Context.URL_PKG_PREFIXES,
    "org.jboss.naming:org.jnp.interfaces");


InitialContext jbossContext = new InitialContext(prop);
```

Look up the external initial context using the JBoss initial context:

```
InitialContext wlsContext =
    (InitialContext)jbossContext.lookup("WLSContext");
```

6.5 JNDI Link References

JBoss provides an MBean for creating JNDI link references. JNDI link references allow you to create symbolic links to existing JNDI names. The MBean definition is:

```
<mbean
   code="org.jboss.naming.NamingAlias"
   name="myDomain:service=myService">
```

This MBean supports the following attributes:

Attribute	Function
FromName	Specifies the original JNDI name
ToName	The alias name

An example is shown below:

```
<mbean
   code="org.jboss.naming.NamingAlias"
   name="myDomain:service=myService">
   <attribute name="ToName">newName</attribute>
   <attribute name="FromName">oldName</attribute>
</mbean>
```

This MBean will link the oldName mapping to the new mapping of newName.

6.6 HTTP-based JNDI

JBoss provides an HTTP-based implementation for using JNDI contexts. As mentioned earlier the JNDI implementation provided by JBoss uses RMI for communication between the JNDI clients and the naming provider. However, this can pose problems if the clients that connect to the naming provider sit outside a firewall. Firewalls allow communication to a set of pre-defined ports. In such cases, communication based on RMI may not be possible. HTTP is one of the protocols passed through by most firewalls and they allow remote clients to connect to port 80 of the internal servers. In such cases, rather than using RMI-based initial context factories, you can use the alternative HTTP-based JNDI implementation provided by JBoss.

This is available as a SAR component called `http-invoker.sar` in the `\deploy` directory. To use this, you need to use the following code:

```
Properties prop = new Properties();

prop.put(Context.INITIAL_CONTEXT_FACTORY,
    "org.jboss.naming.HttpNamingContextFactory");
prop.put(Context.PROVIDER_URL,
    "http://localhost:8080/invoker/JNDIFactory");
InitialContext context = new InitialContext(prop);
```

Please note that the initial context factory is different from the one mentioned earlier, and the protocol for the provider URL is HTTP rather than JNP. To use this you need to have `jboss-client.jar` file in the client classpath.

JBoss 3.0

Administration and Deployment

Handbook

7

7

Configuring Security

Security is a key aspect of enterprise application development; it should be addressed with utmost importance. J2EE provides a simple yet powerful means of defining role-based security in both programmatic and declarative manners. J2EE web applications are secured by defining, in the web deployment descriptor, the roles required by the subjects for accessing secured URLs. As for EJBs, the security constraints are defined at method level for the home and remote interface methods in the EJB deployment descriptor.

JBoss provides a security mechanism independent of the implementation technology. JBoss security caters for standard J2EE role-based security as well as custom security requirements. In this chapter, we will cover the JBoss security architecture and look at how to configure and extend the various JBoss security features.

7.1 JBoss Security Features

In this chapter, we will be covering the security features provided by JBoss in further detail:

❑ **Pluggable Security Layer**
JBoss provides a set of interfaces that define the behavior of the JBoss security layer. These interfaces define the contract between the other JBoss core modules for performing various security related tasks such as authentication, authorization, security realm mapping, etc. These interfaces provide an implementation-independent way of integrating the security layer to the rest of the JBoss core modules. This means you can write your own security layer compliant with the JBoss security interfaces, and configure JBoss to use it.

❑ **JBossSX Implementation**
JBossSX is an out-of-the-box security extension that implements the JBoss security layer. JBossSX is implemented based on **Java Authentication and Authorization Service (JAAS)**. JBoss also comes with a set of built-in JAAS login modules that enable you to store security information such as principals, credentials, and roles, in a variety of sources such as database servers, directory services, text files, etc. It also allows you to write custom login modules to integrate with specialized security applications.

❑ **Security Proxy**
J2EE provides a very simplified form of enforcing security using users and roles mapping. However, this scheme may not solve complex security requirements where security policies are influenced by domain data. For example, in an employee information system, you may want to allow an employee to change only their address and nobody else's. Requirements like this one are obviously difficult to implement using J2EE user-role-based security. One obvious option is to implement this security requirement in your business components. However, JBoss provides a powerful scheme of externalizing security functionality from business components, using the security proxy architecture. Security proxies are covered in detail in *Section 18.3.7.4: Security Proxy.*

❑ **Secure Remote Password (SRP) Protocol**
SRP protocol is an Internet standard working group specification for public key exchange handshake. JBossSX provides an implementation of the SRP protocol.

❑ **Secure Sockets**
JBoss supports EJB invocation using secure sockets. This is covered in detail in *Section 18.3.7.3: EJB SSL Invocation.*

7.2 The JBoss Security Layer

In this section, we look at the JBoss security layer, which is comprised mainly of the following three interfaces:

❑ org.jboss.security.AuthenticationManager
Defines methods for validating credentials against principals.

❑ org.jboss.security.RealmMapping
Defines methods for mapping principals and roles to security information stored in a datasource such as a database or directory service.

❑ org.jboss.security.SecurityProxy
Used for implementing custom security requirements.

It's important that security implementations implement the aforementioned interfaces. In addition to the interfaces listed above, the security layer also defines the following interfaces:

❏ org.jboss.security.SubjectSecurityManager
Extends the authentication manager interface, and defines extra methods for accessing the security domain associated with the security manager and the authenticated subject associated with the current thread.

❏ org.jboss.security.SecurityDomain
Extends the subject security manager and realm mapping interfaces, and defines methods to provide support for secure invocations, keystore interactions, etc.

> **Please note that the functionality offered by the SecurityDomain interface is still in development and will provide comprehensive security architecture in the future versions of JBoss that support multiple domains.**

Both the web and EJB containers delegate the actual task of authentication and authorization to the security layer implementation, through the interfaces defined in the security layer. At run time, JBoss uses the security layer implementation with which it has been configured. In most cases, you will be using the default JBossSX implementation that comes with JBoss. The class diagram below depicts how the JBoss web and EJB containers interact with the security implementation through the security layer. Please note that the security layer is accessed through an interceptor-based framework that is explained in detail in *Section 7.3.1: Security Interceptor Architecture*.

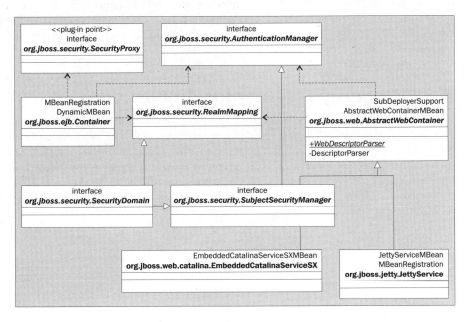

> **Enforcing declarative security constraints for web components using the JBoss security layer and JBoss-specific web deployment descriptor is covered in detail in *Section 16.1.1: The JBoss Web Deployment Descriptor*, and that for EJBs is covered in detail in *Section 18.3.7: EJB Security*.**

7.3 JBossSX Implementation

JBossSX provides an implementation to the security layer explained in the last section, using JAAS. The `org.jboss.security.plugins.JaasSecurityManager` class, which implements the authentication manager and realm mapping interfaces, is at the core of JBossSX. The security implementation layer that should be used within JBoss is usually defined using the security manager MBean service in the `jboss-service.xml` JBoss root configuration file available in the \conf directory of the configuration set you use.

In the JBoss-specific deployment descriptors for EJB and web components, `jboss.xml` and `jboss-web.xml` respectively, you can specify the security domain to be used for authenticating and authorizing threads when they access secure methods and URIs. The EJB and web containers interface with the JAAS security manager to perform authentication and authorization checks. The security domain normally defines the JAAS login module to use for authentication and authorization and any information specific to the login module used. JBoss comes with a set of pre-built login modules that can interface with security information stored in databases, LDAP directory services, etc.

7.3.1 Security Interceptor Architecture

Both JBoss EJB and web containers use an interceptor-based architecture similar to the GoF Decorator pattern. This framework allows interceptors to be inserted between the originator of the invocation and the invocation target to add additional functionality. In JBoss, interceptors are used for a wide variety of purposes, such as imposing security, transactions, etc. The security interceptors access the underlying security implementation through the contract exposed by the security layer, to perform various security-related tasks.

The diagram below depicts how the JBoss security interceptors use the JBossSX implementation for performing security-related tasks:

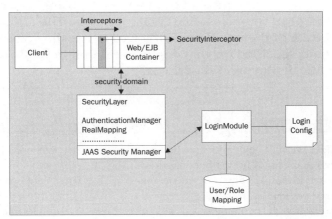

J2EE web components are secured by specifying the roles used to access URIs in the web deployment descriptor. In the same way, EJB components are secured by specifying the roles required to invoke the home and component interface methods, in the EJB deployment descriptors. Please refer to *Professional Java Server Programming – J2EE 1.3 Edition (ISBN: 1-86100-537-7)* from *Wrox Press* for more information on J2EE declarative security.

However, to map these roles to the security policies in the operational environment, you need to use the JBoss-specific web and EJB deployment descriptors. These descriptors provide a `security-domain` element that is used to map the security policies defined in the JBoss environment to the declarative security specified in the standard deployment descriptors. The value of this element should be in the format `java:jaas/<domain_name>`, where `domain_name` is the name used to define the login configuration for the domain.

During the deployment of web and EJB components, JBoss creates an instance of the security manager for the component and sets its security domain name to the value specified by the `security-domain` element. When a client accesses a secure web resource or invokes a secure EJB method, the container delegates the process of authentication and authorization to the security manager instance.

Here, the JAAS security manager instance will use the standard JAAS API to use an appropriate login module to perform the necessary security tasks. The JAAS security manager creates an instance of the JAAS `LoginContext` class by passing the security domain value to the login context, and uses the methods defined on the login context to perform authentication and authorization. Login modules are configured in external resources against the same value specified for the `security-domain` element. JBoss comes with a set of pre-built login modules. The pre-built login modules that come with JBoss are explained in *Section 7.3.4: Pre-built Login Modules.*

> **Please note that if you are using JAAS security manager in different components, all of them will be using different instances of the JaasSecurityManager class. The difference is that each of them will be configured to use the security domain specified for that deployment unit in its JBoss-specific deployment descriptor.**

7.3.2 Configuring the JAAS Security Manager

In this section, we will have a look at how to configure the JAAS security manager. The JAAS security manager is normally configured using the JaasSecurityManagerService MBean service in the JBoss root configuration file, jboss-service.xml, in the \conf directory of the configuration set you use. Please note that even though the name of the MBean is JaasSecurityManagerService, it has got nothing specific to do with JAAS. It can be used for defining any security manager implementation for the JBoss abstract security layer. The MBean definition is:

```
<mbean
    code="org.jboss.security.plugins.JaasSecurityManagerService"
    name="jboss.security:service=JaasSecurityManager">
```

The security manager MBean provides a variety of attributes for configuring the various security related properties, such as security manager implementation, security proxy factory, caching policy, etc.

An example of using the security manager MBean for defining the security layer implementation to be used is shown below:

```
<mbean
    code="org.jboss.security.plugins.JaasSecurityManagerService"
    name="jboss.security:service=JaasSecurityManager">
    <attribute name="SecurityManagerClassName">
        org.jboss.security.plugins.JaasSecurityManager
    </attribute>
</mbean>
```

The security manager implementation service defined above defines the JAAS security manager as the security layer implementation to use. Please note that the class identified by the content for the SecurityManagerClassName attribute should implement the AuthenticationManager and RealmMapping interfaces.

> *This service also provides a JNDI SPI object factory implementation for creating objects in the context java:/jaas. This is to make sure that any lookup for objects in the java:/jaas context will always return instances of the JaasSecurityManager class. The EJB and web containers will lookup the security manager associated with the EJB or web application to perform a security check.*

The security manager MBean service supports the following attributes:

Attribute	Function
SecurityManagerClassName	Used for defining the class that implements the org.jboss.security.AuthenticationManager and org.jboss.security.RealmMapping interfaces. If not supplied it defaults to org.jboss.security.plugins.JaasSecurity Manager.
SecurityProxyFactory ClassName	Used for defining the class that implements the org.jboss.security.SecurityProxyFactory class used for creating security proxies. The default value is org.jboss.security. SubjectSecurityProxyFactory. Security proxies are used for implementing custom security.
AuthenticationCache JndiName	Used for defining the security credential caching policy. Caching policies are defined per security domain. By default, JBoss uses a timed caching policy. CachePolicy is a generic JBoss interface used for defining caching policies. Several implementations are available based on different logics such as LRU replacement, timed caching, etc. The value defined in this attribute is appended to the security domain name to lookup the cache policy for the domain.
DefaultCacheTimeout	Used for defining the timeout value, in seconds, for the timed cache policy. The default value is 1800 seconds. This attribute is only applicable when the AuthenticationCacheJndiName attribute is not set. A small timeout value means that changes made to the user-role mapping information made in the underlying security store will be available to the security manager in a shorter period of time, at the cost of performance.
DefaultCache Resolution	Used for defining the interval, in seconds, at which the cache is checked for resolution. The default value is 60 seconds. This attribute is only applicable when the AuthenticationCacheJndiName attribute is not set.

The listing below shows a more exhaustive example of using the security manager service MBean to define the security layer implementation to be used:

```
<mbean
  code="org.jboss.security.plugins.JaasSecurityManagerService"
  name="jboss.security:service=JaasSecurityManager">
  <attribute name="SecurityManagerClassName">
    org.jboss.security.plugins.JaasSecurityManager
  </attribute>
  <attribute name="DefaultCacheTimeout">
    60
  </attribute>
  <attribute name="DefaultCacheResolution">
    15
  </attribute>
</mbean>
```

Shorter values defined for the timed cache policy configuration values mean that the JAAS security manager will be revalidating the cached principal, roles, and credentials information, at relatively short intervals of time. This will make sure that the cached information reflects the security store information more accurately.

7.3.3 Login Configuration

In the last section, we saw that the JAAS security manager used the login modules configured for the security domains for performing authentication and authorization. We have also seen that the information specific to the login modules are stored against the security domain names in external resources. In this section, we will see how these external resources can be configured within JBoss.

7.3.3.1 Security Config MBean

The security config MBean is used to define a reference to another MBean that is used for reading login configuration information. JBoss 3.0 uses an implementation of the JAAS Configuration interface, and uses an XML file for storing the login configuration information. This information contains the mapping of security domain values to login module definitions. The snippet below shows the definition of the security config MBean in the JBoss root configuration file:

```
<mbean
  code="org.jboss.security.plugins.SecurityConfig"
  name="jboss.security:name=SecurityConfig">
  <attribute name="LoginConfig">
    jboss.security:service=XMLLoginConfig
  </attribute>
</mbean>
```

The LoginConfig attribute is used to define the MBean object name of the MBean that provides access to the security configuration information. If this is not specified, JBoss will use the default implementation of the javax.security.auth.login.Configuration class. The default format used by this class is shown below:

```
1 -> identityModule {
2 ->    org.jboss.security.auth.spi.IdentityLoginModule required
```

```
3 ->    principal=Meeraj
4 ->    roles=admin,author
5 -> }
```

In the above example, line 1 defines the security domain name. If this login module is used to define the security domain for your web or EJB components, the value that should be used is java:/jaas/identityModule. Line 2 defines the login module to be used, and whether the login module is required, requisite, sufficient, or optional. The significance of these attributes is explained in *Section 7.3.3: Login Configuration*. The class defined on line 2 should implement the JAAS LoginModule interface. Lines 3 to 5 are used to specify properties specific to the login module that is used.

7.3.3.2 XML Login Config MBean

The XML login config MBean extends the JAAS Configuration interface to provide the security configuration functionality based on an XML structure. The definition of this MBean in the JBoss root configuration file is shown below:

```
<mbean
    code="org.jboss.security.auth.login.XMLLoginConfig"
    name="jboss.security:service=XMLLoginConfig">
    <attribute name="ConfigResource">login-config.xml</attribute>
</mbean>
```

The ConfigResource attribute defines the name of the XML file containing the security configuration information. JBoss comes with a sample file called login-config.xml in the \conf directory of the default configuration set that contains some simple definitions for JAAS login modules.

The diagram below depicts the organization of the security MBeans and the login configuration file:

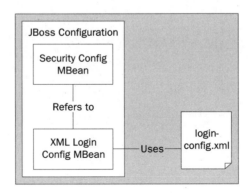

7.3.3.3 Login Configuration Data

In this section, we will have a look at the structure of the XML file used for storing login configuration. The structure for the XML is shown in the figure below:

Element	Function	Attributes
policy	The root element of the security policy configuration. It can contain one or more application-policy elements.	None.
application-policy	Defines the security configuration for an application domain and may contain one authentication element.	name is a mandatory attribute for the application-policy element, and is used to link the login modules defined for the application policy to the security domain defined in the JBoss-specific deployment descriptors for the web and EJB components.
authentication	Used to define one or more login modules that should be used to perform authentication.	

Element	Function	Attributes
login-module	Defines the details of the login module that should be used for authentication.	The flag attribute controls how a login module participates in the overall authentication procedure: ❑ Required means the login module is required to succeed. Irrespective of whether it succeeds or fails, the authentication continues to proceed down the login module list. ❑ Requisite means the login module is required to succeed. If it succeeds, authentication continues down the login module list. If it fails, control immediately returns to the application. ❑ Sufficient means the login module is not required to succeed. If it does succeed, control immediately returns to the application. If it fails, authentication continues down the login module list. ❑ Optional means the login module is not required to succeed. If it succeeds or fails, authentication continues to proceed down the login module list. The overall authentication succeeds only if all required and requisite login modules succeed. If a sufficient login module is configured and it succeeds, only the required and requisite login modules *prior* to that sufficient login module need to have succeeded for the success of the overall authentication. If no required or requisite login modules are configured for an application, then at least *one* sufficient or optional login module must succeed.

Table continued on following page

85

Element	Function	Attributes
		code is a mandatory attribute used to define the name of the class that implements the JAAS LoginModule interface.
module-option	Used to define any options that are specific to the configured login module. For example, it can be used for defining the datasource JNDI name, user ID, password, etc., for a database login module. The value of the text content defines the value of the option and the value of the name attribute defines the name of the option.	The name attribute is used to define the name of the module option.

The snippet below shows how the login configuration explained in the last section can be defined using the XML structure:

```
<policy>
  <application-policy name="identityModule">
    <authentication>
      <login-module
        flag="true"
        code="org.jboss.security.auth.spi.IdentityLoginModule">
        <module-option name="principal">Meeraj</module-option>
        <module-option name="roles">admin,author</module-option>
      </login-module>
    </authentication>
</policy>
```

We'll look at these options in more detail the following sections.

7.3.4 Pre-built Login Modules

JBoss comes with a set of pre-built login modules as well as some abstract login module implementations, which can be used for writing your own custom login module. The important pre-built login modules that come with JBoss are:

❑   Identity login module

❑   Users/Roles login module

❑   LDAP login module

❑   Database login module

❑   Client login module

In this section, we see how to configure each of these login modules in detail.

7.3.4.1 Identity Login Module

The identity login module is very primitive, and can be used for testing your security behavior of your application. The implementation class is `org.jboss.security.auth.spi.IdentityLoginModule`. The users and roles information are stored in the login module configuration itself. This module supports the following module options:

Module option	Function
principal	To define the value against which the identities of all subjects are authenticated.
roles	To specify a list of comma-separated roles that the principals are assigned to.
password-stacking	If the value of this option is set to true, the module will look for a property by the name javax.security.auth.login.name in its shared state map. If found, it will use that value for authenticating the user. If not, it will store the value specified by the principal option in the shared state map against the same name. Login modules use shared state for sharing information.

An example of configuring identity login modules is shown below:

```
<policy>
  <application-policy name="myIdentityModule">
    <authentication>
      <login-module
        flag="true"
        code="org.jboss.security.auth.spi.IdentityLoginModule">
        <module-option name="principal">Meeraj</module-option>
        <module-option name="roles">admin,author</module-option>
      </login-module>
    </authentication>
</policy>
```

The example above defines a login module that will authenticate a user only if the user name is `Meeraj` and assigns the roles `admin` and `author` to the authenticated user.

87

7.3.4.2 Users Roles Login Module

The Users Roles login module is based on two properties files that store the users and roles information. The user names and passwords are stored in a file called users.properties, and the roles assigned to users are stored in roles.properties. These files can be placed in any location available to the thread context classloader. This means you can place the files in the system or server classpath, including deployment units, configuration directory, etc.

The code attribute is org.jboss.security.auth.spi.UsersRolesLoginModule, which supports the following module options:

Module option	Function
unauthenticated-identity	This is used to specify the identity for requests without any authentication information. This can be used for getting the name of the authenticated principal in unsecured EJB methods and servlet URIs.
password-stacking	If the value of this option is set to true, the module will look in its shared state map for a property by the name javax.security.auth.login.name. If found, it will use that value for authenticating the user. If not found it will store the value specified by the principal option in the shared state map against the same name. Login modules use shared state for sharing information amongst them.
hashAlgorithm	This is the message digest algorithm to be used to hash the password. If hashing is enabled, the passwords stored in the properties file should be hashed. The password obtained from the caller is hashed before they are compared to those stored in the properties file. Unless specified, hashing is not used. The valid hashing algorithms are MD5, SHA-1, etc.
hashEncoding	This is used to define the string format for the hashed password and should be either hex or base64. The default is base64. This is only used if a hash algorithm is specified.
hashCharset	This is used to define the character set to transform the hashed password to a byte array. If not specified, this uses the platform's default character set.
usersProperties	This is used to define name of the file that contains the users-to-passwords mapping and the default value is users.properties.
rolesProperties	This is used to define name of the file that contains the users-to-roles mapping and the default value is roles.properties.

7.3.4.2.1 Properties File Format

The properties file that stores the users-to-passwords mapping stores it in the format user_name=password as shown below:

```
Meeraj=batoutofhell
Waheeda=barkatthemoon
Fiza=hitthelights
```

The roles properties file stores the users-to-roles mapping in the format user_name=role1,role2,... . The users-to-roles mapping can optionally use a role group value. The role group is used to define a named group of roles assigned to the user. The JAAS security manager expects the standard Roles role group to define the permissions defined for the user. An example is shown below:

```
meeraj=admin,author
meeraj.Roles=admin,author
```

An example of using the users/roles login module is shown below:

```
<policy>
   <application-policy name="myUsersRolesModule">
     <authentication>
       <login-module
         flag="true"
         code="org.jboss.security.auth.spi.UsersRolesLoginModule">
         <module-option name="hashAlgorithm">MD5</module-option>
       </login-module>
     </authentication>
</policy>
```

The above login module reads the user and role mapping information from the default users.properties and roles.properties file to perform authentication/authorization. The passwords are hashed using MD5 algorithm.

7.3.4.3 Database Login Module

The database login module is used to authenticate the users and roles against the security information stored in a JDBC compliant database. The login module implementation class used is org.jboss.security.auth.spi.DatabaseServerLoginModule. This login module uses SQL to get the users-to-passwords mapping and users-to-roles mapping information.

The query for the users-to-passwords mapping should return a result set of the format shown below:

```
Principal          Password
*********************************
Meeraj             nightcrawler
```

89

The names of the columns are not important. However, the number and order of columns are important. The SQL for returning user information should return two columns representing the user names and passwords respectively. The query for the users-to-roles mapping should return the result set in the following format:

```
Principal            Role        RoleGroup
*************************************************
Meeraj               admin       Roles
Meeraj               author      Roles
```

Please note that for the JAAS security manager, the roles assigned to the user should be defined in rows for which the RoleGroup value is Roles. The names of the columns are not important, but the number and order of columns are. The SQL for returning roles mapping should return three columns representing user name, role, and role group respectively.

A simple database table creation script for storing users-to-passwords mapping may look like:

```
CREATE TABLE users (
    user_id VARCHAR(30) NOT NULL PRIMARY KEY,
    password VARCHAR(30) NOT NULL)
```

The query for getting the users-to-passwords information may look like:

```
SELECT user_id, password FROM users WHERE user_id = ?
```

A simple database table creation script for storing users-to-roles mapping may look like:

```
CREATE TABLE roles (
    user_id VARCHAR(30) NOT NULL,
    role VARCHAR(30) NOT NULL,
    role_group VARCHAR(30) NOT NULL)
```

The query for getting the users-to-roles information may look like:

```
SELECT user_id, roles, role_group FROM roles WHERE user_id = ?
```

The database server login module supports the following module options in addition to unauthenticated-identity, password-stacking, hashAlgorithm, hashEncoding, and hashCharset options, as seen in *Section 7.3.4.2: User Roles Login Module*.

Module option	Function
dsJndiName	The JNDI name of the datasource used to get connections to the database that stores the security information. The default value is java:/DefaultDS.
principalsQuery	To define the query used for getting the principals-to-passwords mapping information. This query expects the subject identity as known in the operational environment as an input argument.
rolesQuery	To define the query used for getting the principals-to-roles mapping information. This query expects the subject identity as known in the operational environment as an input argument.

An example of using the database login module is shown below:

```
<policy>
  <application-policy name="myDatabaseModule">
    <authentication>
      <login-module
        flag="true"
        code="org.jboss.security.auth.spi.DatabaseServerLoginModule">
        <module-option name="dsJndiName">java:/MyDS</module-option>
        <module-option name="principalsQuery">
          SELECT * FROM users WHERE user_id = ?
        </module-option>
        <module-option name="rolesQuery">
          SELECT * FROM roles WHERE user_id = ?
        </module-option>
      </login-module>
    </authentication>
</policy>
```

The example above defines a login module that will read the users and roles mapping information from database tables.

7.3.4.4 LDAP Login Module

The LDAP login module retrieves the security information from an LDAP directory server. The login module implementation class used is org.jboss.security.auth.spi.LDAPLoginModule. The LDAP login module supports the following module options in addition to unauthenticated-identity, password-stacking, hashAlgorithm, hashEncoding, and hashCharset options as seen in *Section 7.3.4.2: User Roles Login Module*:

Module Option	Function
java.naming.factory.initial	The JNDI initial context factory used to connect to the LDAP server.
java.naming.provider.url	The JNDI provider URL used to connect to the LDAP server.
java.naming.security.authentication	The security level to use to connect to the LDAP server. The allowed values are none (for using no authentication, binding anonymously) and simple (for weak authentication, using a clear text password).
java.naming.security.protocol	Optionally used to define the wire protocol for secure access to the LDAP server.
java.naming.security.principal	The principal used to connect to the LDAP server.
java.naming.security.credentials	The credentials used to connect to the LDAP server.
principalDNPrefix	To specify a string that should be prefixed to the passed user name to construct the fully distinguished LDAP name of the user.
principalDNSuffix	To specify a string that should be suffixed to the passed user name to construct the fully distinguished LDAP name of the user.
useObjectCredential	A flag is used to define whether JBoss should use an opaque object for the password, or a plain char array.
rolesCtxDN	To specify the distinguished name of the context that is used to store the users-to-roles mapping.
roleAttributeId	To specify the name of the attribute that contains the user's roles. The default value is roles.
uidAttributeID	To specify the attribute name used to identify the object containing the roles for a user ID.
matchOnUserDN	If this flag is true, the search for user roles should match the users fully distinguished name.

An example of using the LDAP login module for getting users and roles mapping information is shown below:

```
<policy>
  <application-policy name="myLDAPModule">
    <authentication>
      <login-module
        flag="true"
        code="org.jboss.security.auth.spi.LDAPLoginModule">
        <module-option name="java.naming.factory.initial">
          com.sun.jndi.ldap.LdapCtxFactory
        </module-option>
        <module-option name="java.naming.provider.url">
          ldap://Scooby-doo:1389
        </module-option>
        <module-option name="java.naming.security.authentication">
          simple
        </module-option>
        <module-option name="principalDNPrefix">
          uid=
        </module-option>
        <module-option name="uidAttributeID">
          user_id
        </module-option>
        <module-option name="roleAttributeID">
          role
        </module-option>
        <module-option name="principalDNSuffix">
          ou=I Solutions, o=EDS
        </module-option>
        <module-option name="rolexCtxDN">
          cn=Roles, ou=Roles, o=EDS
        </module-option>
      </login-module>
    </authentication>
  </application-policy>
</policy>
```

In the above example, users-to-roles mapping will be stored in a context identified by the DN "cn=Roles, ou=Roles, o=EDS" under the attribute named role. The login module uses the JNDI properties specified as the module option to connect to the LDAP server. The LDAP module will set the JNDI principal property by concatenating the values specified for principalDNPrefix and principalDNSuffix around the subject ID passed to the login module. In this case, if the passed subject identity is meeraj, the principal that is set will be "uid=meeraj,ou=I Solutions, o=EDS". The JNDI credentials property will be set to the password passed to the login module. The login to succeed the passed password should match the userPassword attribute stored in the principal context.

To perform authorization, the login module will get the list of attributes by the name role in the sub-contexts with an attribute named user_id matching the subject identity passed in any sub-contexts of the roles context. An example of the context organization is shown below:

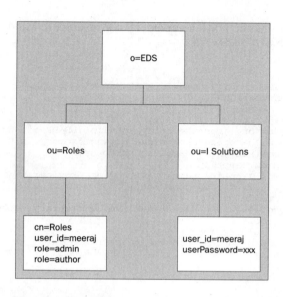

7.3.4.5 Client Login Modules

JBoss EJB clients can use client modules for authenticating themselves. An example of the client login module configuration is shown below:

```
<policy>
    <application-policy name="myClientModule">
        <authentication>
            <login-module
                flag="true"
                code=" org.jboss.security.auth.spi.ClientLoginModule">
            </login-module>
        </authentication>
</policy>
```

This login module doesn't perform any authentication. It simply copies the authentication information to the client-side EJB invocation layer, which sends it to the server during EJB invocation. This login module supports the following module options:

Module Option	Function
password-stacking	If the value of this option is set to `true`, the module will look in its shared state map for a property by the name `javax.security.auth.login.name`. If found, it will use that value for authenticating the user. If not found, it will store the value specified by the principal option in the shared state map against the same name. Login modules use shared state for sharing information amongst them.
multi-threaded	If this flag is set to `true`, each thread will have its own copy of principal and credentials information.

The \client directory under JBoss installation contains a sample login config file called auth.conf based on the standard JAAS configuration format that can be used for client login. The snippet below shows the excerpt from this file for configuring client login module:

```
other {
    // JBoss LoginModule
    org.jboss.security.ClientLoginModule required
        ;
};
```

To use the client login module in your applications, you need to perform the following steps:

1. Write an implementation of the JAAS CallbackHandler interface:

```
public class MyCallbackHandler implements CallbackHandler {

    private String userId;
    private char[] passwd;

    public MyCallbackHandler(String arg0, String arg1) {
        userId = arg0;
        passwd = arg1.toCharArray();
    }

    public void handle(Callback[] callbacks)
        throws IOException, UnsupportedCallbackException {

        for(int i = 0; i < callbacks.length; i++) {
            if(callbacks[i] instanceof NameCallback) {
                ((NameCallback)callbacks[i]).setName(userId);
            } else if(callbacks[i] instanceof PasswordCallback) {
                ((PasswordCallback)callbacks[i]).setPassword(passwd);
            }
        }
    }
}
```

2. In the client code set the path to the JBoss login configuration file should be set as the system property java.security.auth.login.config:

```
System.setProperty("java.security.auth.login.config", c:\\auth.conf");
```

3. Create a JAAS login() context by passing an instance of your callback handler and the name of the login module to use:

```
MyCallbackHandler handler = new MyCallbackHandler("meeraj",
                                                  password");
```

4. Call the login() method on the login context:

```
ctx.login();
```

7.3.5 Custom Login Modules

To write custom login modules that can work with the JAAS security manager, we need to understand how the JAAS security manager identifies subject identities and roles. The JAAS security manager uses the `javax.security.auth.Subject` class to store subject identities and roles. JAAS security manager expects user identities to be stored using `java.security.Principal` instances in the set of principals for the `Subject`. JBoss provides an implementation of `java.security.Principal`, called `org.jboss.security.SimplePrincipal`.

The roles assigned to a user are also stored as set of principals. They are grouped as a set of `java.security.acl.Group` instances. This interface extends the `Principal` interface and models an aggregation of principals. The JAAS security manager expects a group called `Roles` that contains the list of roles assigned to the user.

JBoss provides two abstract login modules that provide the implementation of the subject usage pattern. You can extend these classes to write a custom login module. These are:

- ❑ `AbstractServerLoginModule`
- ❑ `UserNamePasswordLoginModule`

7.3.5.1 AbstractServerLoginModule

The `AbstractServerLoginModule` class is the base class of all the JBoss login modules, and implements the JAAS SPI interface `LoginModule`. If you are using this as your base class, you need to override and provide implementation to the following methods:

```
public void initialize(Subject subject,
                       CallbackHandler handler,
                       Map sharedSate,
                       Map options);
```

This method initializes the login module. Normally you would call `super.initialize()` and extract any module options you have specified for your module in the login module configuration from the options map. For example, in the database login module you would extract the module options like datasource JNDI name.

```
public boolean login();
```

This method will implement the logic for verifying the subject's identity. The superclass provides convenience methods for getting subject identity in the operational environment and the credentials that are passed. This method should look for the following properties in the shared state map if the `useFirstPass` option is set:

- ❑ `javax.security.auth.login.name` for the subject identity that is passed
- ❑ `javax.security.auth.login.password` for the credentials that is passed

```
abstract protected Principal getIdentity();
```

This method should return the subject identity in the underlying security information store corresponding the identity that is passed in.

```
abstract protected Group[] getRoleSets();
```

This method should return the groups that correspond to the roles that are assigned to the users. The JAAS security manager expects a group called Roles that contains all the roles assigned to the user.

7.3.5.2 UserNamePasswordLoginModule

The UserNamePasswordLoginModule class extends the AbstractServerLoginModule, and provides convenience methods that return user identity as a string and password as a char array. If you are using this class as your base class, you need to override and provide implementation to the following methods:

```
public void initialize(Subject subject,
                       CallbackHandler handler,
                       Map sharedSate,
                       Map options);
```

This method initializes the login module. Normally you would call super.initialize() and extract any module options you have specified for your module in the login module configuration from the options map. For example, in the database login module you would extract the module options like datasource JNDI name.

```
abstract protected String getUsersPassword();
```

This method should return the password of the subject identity in the underlying security information store.

```
abstract protected Group[] getRoleSets();
```

This method should return the groups that correspond to the roles that are assigned to the users. The JAAS security manager expects a group called Roles that contains all the roles assigned to the user.

7.3.5.3 Writing a Login Module

In this example, we look at a UsersRolesLoginModule class, which extends the UsernamePasswordLoginModule, to see how to write custom login modules:

```
package org.jboss.security.auth.spi;

import java.io.InputStream;
import java.io.IOException;
```

```
import java.net.URL;
import java.util.*;

import java.security.acl.Group;
import javax.security.auth.Subject;
import javax.security.auth.callback.*;
import javax.security.auth.login.*;
import javax.security.auth.spi.LoginModule;

import org.jboss.security.*;
import org.jboss.security.auth.spi.UsernamePasswordLoginModule;

public class UsersRolesLoginModule
extends UsernamePasswordLoginModule {
```

The instance variables store the users-to-passwords and users-to-roles mapping:

```
private String usersRsrcName = "users.properties";
private String rolesRsrcName = "roles.properties";
private Properties users;
private Properties roles;
```

The initialize() method calls the same on the superclass and parses the module options. It also loads the security information stored in the files:

```
public void initialize(Subject subject,
    CallbackHandler callbackHandler, Map sharedState, Map options) {

    super.initialize(subject, callbackHandler, sharedState, options);
    try {
        String option = (String) options.get("usersProperties");
        if(option != null) usersRsrcName = option;
        option = (String) options.get("rolesProperties");
        if(option != null) rolesRsrcName = option;

        loadUsers();
        loadRoles();
    } catch(Exception e) {
        super.log.error("Failed to load users/passwords/role files", e);
    }

}
```

The login() method calls the same method on the superclass:

```
public boolean login() throws LoginException {

    if(users == null) {
        throw new LoginException("Missing users.properties file.");
    }
    if(roles == null) {
        throw new LoginException("Missing roles.properties file.");
    }
    return super.login();

}
```

The following method iterates through the roles defined for the users and returns the roles as an array of groups. Each group in the array is a named role set:

```
protected Group[] getRoleSets() throws LoginException {

    String targetUser = getUsername();
    Enumeration users = roles.propertyNames();
```

This group is important for the JAAS security manager, as it should contain all the roles that are allowed to the user:

```
    SimpleGroup rolesGroup = new SimpleGroup("Roles");

    ArrayList groups = new ArrayList();
    groups.add(rolesGroup);
    while(users.hasMoreElements() && targetUser != null) {

        String user = (String) users.nextElement();
        String value = roles.getProperty(user);

        int index = user.indexOf('.');
        boolean isRoleGroup = false;
        boolean userMatch = false;

        if(index > 0 && targetUser.regionMatches(0, user, 0, index)
            == true) {
          isRoleGroup = true;
        } else {
          userMatch = targetUser.equals(user);
        }
        if(isRoleGroup == true ) {
          String groupName = user.substring(index+1);
          if( groupName.equals("Roles")) {
            parseGroupMembers(rolesGroup, value);
          } else {
            SimpleGroup group = new SimpleGroup(groupName);
            parseGroupMembers(group, value);
            groups.add(group);
          }
        } else if(userMatch == true) {
          parseGroupMembers(rolesGroup, value);
        }
    }
    Group[] roleSets = new Group[groups.size()];
    groups.toArray(roleSets);

    return roleSets;
}
```

The following method returns the user's password. This method is used from the superclass for performing the login:

```
protected String getUsersPassword() {

    String username = getUsername();
    String password = null;
    if(username != null) {
       password = users.getProperty(username , null);
    }
    return password;
}
```

A utility method for parsing the roles has been presented below:

```
private void parseGroupMembers(Group group, String value) {

    StringTokenizer tokenizer = new StringTokenizer(value, ",");
    while(tokenizer.hasMoreTokens()) {
      String token = tokenizer.nextToken();
      SimplePrincipal p = new SimplePrincipal(token);
      group.addMember(p);
    }
  }
}
```

The next three methods are utility methods for loading the security information:

```
private void loadUsers() throws IOException {
  users = loadProperties(usersRsrcName);
}

private void loadRoles() throws IOException {
  roles = loadProperties(rolesRsrcName);
}

private Properties loadProperties(String propertiesName)
      throws IOException {

  Properties bundle = null;
  ClassLoader loader =
  Thread.currentThread().getContextClassLoader();

  URL url = loader.getResource(propertiesName);
  if(url == null) {
      throw new IOException("Properties file " + propertiesName +
      " not found");
  }
  super.log.trace("Properties file=" + url);
  InputStream is = url.openStream();
  if(is != null) {
    bundle = new Properties();
    bundle.load(is);
  } else {
    throw new IOException("Properties file " +
      propertiesName + " not avilable");
  }
  return bundle;
  }
}
```

To use your login module within JBoss, you need to first make the login module class available to the classloader. An easy way to do this is to package this into a JAR and copy to the \lib directory of the configuration set you use. Once you have done that, you can use it in login-config.xml by specifying the class name of your login module as the value for the class attribute for the login module you are configuring.

7.3.6 JAAS Security Domain

The JAAS security domain extends the JAAS security manager that provides, in addition to the functionality already provided by the JAAS security manager, support for SSL and cryptographic functionalities. You need to use the JAAS security domain if you want to setup SSL for accessing the JBoss embedded web container or invoke EJBs over SSL, as explained in detail in *Section 18.3.7.3: EJB SSL Invocation*. The JAAS security domain supports the following MBeans:

- ❏ `KeyStoreType`
  The type of the keystore that is used.

- ❏ `KeyStoreURL`
  The location of the keystore that should be used.

- ❏ `KeyStorePass`
  The keystore password.

- ❏ `LoadSunJSEProvider`
  A flag to indicate whether the Sun JSSE provider should be loaded.

- ❏ `ManagerServiceName`
  To set the object name of the security manager service MBean. The default value is `jboss.security:service=JaasSecurityManager`.

Configuring the JAAS security domain is covered in *Section 18.3.7.3: EJB SSL Invocation* and *Sections 11.2.3.3.3: Enabling SSL on Jetty* and *12.3.3.2: Enabling SSL on Tomcat.*

7.4 Security Proxies

Security proxies provide a mechanism of externalizing custom security code from the business components on a per-method basis. Security proxy works alongside the security proxy interceptor. In the JBoss-specific EJB deployment descriptor, you can specify a security proxy class that will implement the custom security logic for that EJB. The interceptor architecture will use the proxy to execute the custom security code before invoking the bean methods. These classes are required to implement the `org.jboss.security.SecurityProxy` interface. The interface defines the following methods:

```
public void init(Class beanHome,
                 Class beanRemote,
                 Object securityMgr)
      throws InstantiationException;
```

This method can be used to perform any initialization like caching method references for the home and remote classes.

```
public void setEJBContext(EJBContext ctx);
```

This method is called prior to any method invocation to set the current EJB context.

```
public void invokeHome(Method m, Object[] args)
    throws SecurityException;
```

This method is called to allow the security proxy to perform any custom security checks required for the EJB home interface method.

```
public void invoke(Method m, Object[] args, Object bean)
    throws SecurityException;
```

This method is called to allow the security proxy to perform any custom security checks required for the EJB remote interface method.

You can use the security-proxy element in the JBoss EJB deployment descriptor for configuring a security proxy with a bean.

> **Security proxies are covered in further detail in *Section 18.3.7.4: Security Proxy*.**

7.5 Enabling SSL

JBoss allows you to use RMI over SSL for invoking EJBs and the web container allows SSL for secure access to web components. JBoss uses **Java Secure Socket Extension (JSSE)** for enabling SSL-based invocation. To enable SSL-based invocation, you need to perform the following steps:

1. Install JSSE:

    If you are using JDK 1.4, you don't need to do this as JSSE bundles with JDK. If you are using an earlier version, follow the steps explained below:

JSSE can be downloaded from the Javasoft web site (http://www.javasoft.com/products/jsse/). The latest version is 1.0.3. Please follow the following steps to install JSSE:

❑   Unpack the downloaded file to your local drive. This will create a directory called \jsse1.0.3 that will contain a \lib directory. The \lib directory will contain the files jcert.jar, jnet.jar and jsse.jar.

❑   Install these files as installed extensions. For this, copy these files to the \lib\ext directory of your JRE.

❑   Register the JSSE provider in the java.security file in the \lib\security directory of your JRE by adding the following entry. Depending on the number of registered providers, the number following the string security.provider will vary.

```
security.provider.3=com.sun.net.ssl.internal.ssl.Provider
```

2. Install a keystore entry for the key pair to use.

Now we need to generate the key pair. For testing, we will use a self-signed certificate. In production, you may need to get your certificate signed by a CA like Verisign or RSA. To do this, use the following command:

```
keytool -genkey -keyalg RSA -storepass password -keypass password
        -keystore ssl.keystore
```

This will create a new keystore by the name `ssl.keystore` with the store password and the default key `password` as password using the RSA key algorithm. Now create a directory called \ssl under the JBoss \bin directory and copy the keystore to the newly created directory.

Using SSL with the EJB and web containers is covered more specifically in *Sections 11.2.3.3: Enabling SSL on Jetty, 12.3.3.2: Enabling SSL on Tomcat,* and *18.3.7.3: EJB SSL Invocation.*

JBoss 3.0

Administration and Deployment

Handbook

8

8.1 JCA in JBossCX

8.2 JBossCX and Datasources

Configuring JCA and Datasources

The Java Connector Architecture (JCA) is a J2EE API for enabling J2EE applications to interface with external resource managers, such as databases, legacy mainframe systems, ERP systems, etc. **JBossCX** is a JCA implementation that comes with JBoss. Internally JBoss uses the JCA implementation for connecting to JDBC databases.

The Java Connector Architecture is based on resource adapters that are used for connecting to external resource managers. Resource managers provide standard resource adapters that are used to connect them. These resource adapters run within any application server that supports JCA, to make use of the various services provided by the applications, such as resource pooling, transactions, and security.

The diagram below depicts an overview of the Java Connector Architecture:

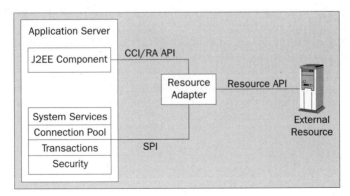

The resource adapter uses a resource-specific API to communicate to the external resource manager. J2EE components can communicate with the external resource through the resource adapter. For this they can either use the resource adapter-specific API or the loosely typed Common Client Interface (CCI). Visual development tools provided by the resource manager normally use CCI. In most cases, application developers will use a resource-specific API for communicating with the resource manager.

For example, JBoss provides JCA adapters for communicating with JDBC databases. In this case rather than using CCI, you will be using JDBC to communicate with the database.

JCA resource adapters are packaged as JAR files with `.rar` extensions. They contain a file called `ra.xml` in the `\META-INF` directory that describes the resource adapter. The resource adapter deployment descriptor provides information on handling connection pooling, security, transactions, etc.

> *Please note that a comprehensive coverage of JCA is beyond the scope of this book. Please refer to Professional Java Server Programming – J2EE 1.3 Edition from Wrox Press (ISBN: 1-86100-537-7) for a detailed coverage of JCA.*

8.1 JCA in JBossCX

JBossCX implements the application server side of the Java Connector Architecture. The JBossCX implementation makes use of several MBean components for enabling the use of JCA resource adapters within the JBoss environment. These MBean components expose the connection factory that is used to create connections to the resource manager in the JNDI namespace. The location in the JNDI namespace is defined as one of the MBean attributes.

Before you deploy the MBean services that are used to expose the resource adapter connection factory in the JNDI namespace, you need to make sure that the RAR representing the resource adapter is deployed within JBoss. The MBean services get relevant information on the managed connection factory and other details from the RAR deployment descriptor of the deployed resource adapter.

The diagram below depicts the main MBeans that are used to create the resource adapter connection factory in the JNDI namespace and their dependencies:

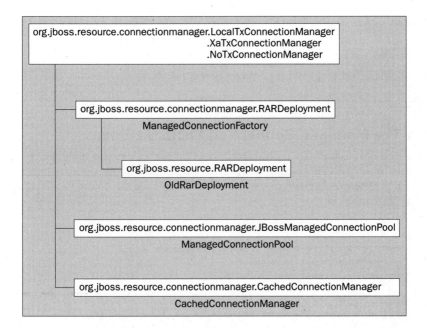

8.1.1 The Connection Manager MBean

The connection manager MBean is the main MBean that decides the level of transaction support you require from the JCA resource adapter. JBoss provides three connection managers that extend `org.jboss.resource.connectionmanager.BaseConnectionManager2`. These connection managers are (all located in the `org.jboss.resource.connectionmanager` package):

❏ `NoTxConnectionManager`
   Use this if your connection factory doesn't support transactions.

❏ `LocalTxConnectionManager`
   Use this if your connection factory supports only local transactions.

❏ `XATxConnectionManager`
   Use this if your connection factory supports distributed transactions.

The example below shows a connection manager MBean definition that supports local transactions:

```
<mbean
   code=
   "org.jboss.resource.connectionmanager.LocalTxConnectionManager"
   name="jboss.jca:service=LocalTxCM,name=OracleDS">
</mbean>
```

This MBean mainly depends on the following MBeans:

❑ Managed connection factory (*Section 8.1.1.1*)

❑ Managed connection pool (*Section 8.1.1.2*)

❑ Cached connection manager (*Section 8.1.1.3*)

8.1.1.1 The Managed Connection Factory MBean

The managed connection factory MBean is responsible for creating an instance of the connection factory and exposing it in the JNDI namespace by the specified JNDI name. Normally this MBean is defined as an embedded MBean of the connection manager MBean as shown below:

```
<mbean
   code="org.jboss.resource.connectionmanager.
        LocalTxConnectionManager"
   name="jboss.jca:service=LocalTxCM,name=OracleDS">
   ...
   <depends
     optional-attribute-name="ManagedConnectionFactoryName">
     <mbean
       code="org.jboss.resource.connectionmanager.RARDeployment"
       name="jboss.jca:service=LocalTxDS,name=OracleDS">
       ...
     </mbean>
   </depends>

</mbean>
```

This MBean gathers information about the resource adapter from the actual RAR that is deployed. Each time a RAR is deployed, the RAR deployer starts an MBean that exposes an MBean of type `org.jboss.resource.connectionmanager.RARDeployment` that encapsulates the deployment descriptor information present in `ra.xml`. The object name of this MBean takes the format `jboss.jca:service=RARDeployment,name=<Display Name>`, where `<Display Name>` represents the display name of the resource adapter specified in the RAR deployment descriptor.

The managed connection factory MBean should use the `depends` element with the `optional-attribute-name` attribute to define the object name of the MBean that encapsulates the RAR deployment descriptor as shown below. The value of the `optional-attribute-name` attribute should be `OldRarDeployment`.

```
<mbean
   code="org.jboss.resource.connectionmanager.RARDeployment"
   name="jboss.jca:service=LocalTxDS,name=OracleDS">
```

```
<depends optional-attribute-name="OldRarDeployment">
   jboss.jca:service=RARDeployment,name=JBoss LocalTransaction
   JDBC Wrapper
</depends>
   ...
</mbean>
```

The above MBean supports two MBean attributes:

❑   The first one called `JndiName` specifies the JNDI name to which the resource manager connection factory is bound

❑   The second called `ManagedConnectionFactoryProperties` is an XML fragment required to specify the configuration information required for the connection factory

The XML fragment for the `ManagedConnectionFactoryProperties` attribute has the following format:

```
<properties>
   <config-property name="name" type="type"></config-property>
   <config-property name="name" type="type"></config-property>
   ...
<properties>
```

The root element is `properties`, which can contain zero or more `config-property` elements. Each `config-property` element has a `name` attribute identifying the name of the property and a `type` attribute specifying the type of the property. The text content of this element defines the value of the property. The properties are passed to the resource manager connection factory by the managed connection factory MBean.

The connection factory properties for a local transaction connection factory are:

❑   `ConnectionURL`

❑   `DriverClass`

❑   `UserName`

❑   `Password`

Whereas for a XA connection factory the properties expected are:

❑   `XADataSourceProperties`

❑   `XADataSourceClass`

❑   `UserName`

❑   `Password`

The following example shows the properties required to create a local transaction-based connection to an Oracle database:

```
<mbean
  code="org.jboss.resource.connectionmanager.RARDeployment"
  name="jboss.jca:service=LocalTxDS,name=OracleDS">
  ...
  <attribute name="JndiName">OracleDS</attribute>

  <attribute name="ManagedConnectionFactoryProperties">
    <properties>
      <config-property name="ConnectionURL" type="java.lang.String">
        jdbc:oracle:thin:@youroraclehost:1521:yoursid
      </config-property>
      <config-property name="DriverClass" type="java.lang.String">
        oracle.jdbc.driver.OracleDriver
      </config-property>
      <config-property name="UserName" type="java.lang.String">
        megadeath
      </config-property>
      <config-property name="Password" type="java.lang.String">
        euthanasia
      </config-property>
    </properties>
  </attribute>

</mbean>
```

8.1.1.2 The Managed Connection Pool MBean

The managed connection pool MBean is responsible for providing connection pooling functionality. JBoss provides a managed connection pool implemented by the class `org.jboss.resource.connectionmanager.JbossManagedConnectionPool`. This MBean supports the following attributes:

Attribute	Function
MinSize	Minimum size of the pool.
MaxSize	Maximum size of the pool.
BlockingTimeoutMillis	Indicates the maximum time to block while waiting for a connection before throwing an exception.
IdleTimeoutMinutes	Indicates the maximum time a connection may be idle before being closed.
Criteria	Indicates whether to use container-managed security for this connection. The possible values are: ByContainerAndApplication ByContainer ByApplication ByNothing

The managed connection pool MBean is defined as an embedded MBean within the connection manager MBean using the depends element with the optional-attribute-name attribute set to ManagedConnectionPool:

```
<mbean
    code="org.jboss.resource.connectionmanager.LocalTxConnectionManager"
    name="jboss.jca:service=LocalTxCM,name=OracleDS">
    ...
    <depends optional-attribute-name="ManagedConnectionPool">
      <mbean
        code="org.jboss.resource.connectionmanager.
            JBossManagedConnectionPool"
        name="jboss.jca:service=LocalTxPool,name=OracleDS">

        <attribute name="MinSize">0</attribute>
        <attribute name="MaxSize">50</attribute>
        <attribute name="BlockingTimeoutMillis">5000</attribute>
        <attribute name="IdleTimeoutMinutes">15</attribute>
    </mbean>
    </depends>
    ...
</mbean>
```

8.1.1.3 The Cached Connection Manager MBean

The connection manager uses this for handling connections across transaction and method boundaries. The connection manager uses the optional attribute name CachedConnectionManager to get a reference to the object name of the cached connection manager as an MBean attribute. The cached connection manager MBean is normally defined in the JBoss root configuration file jboss-service.xml defined in the \conf directory of the configuration set:

```
<mbean
    code="org.jboss.resource.connectionmanager.LocalTxConnectionManager"
    name="jboss.jca:service=LocalTxCM,name=OracleDS">
    ...
    <depends optional-attribute-name="CachedConnectionManager">
      jboss.jca:service=CachedConnectionManager
    </depends>
    ...
</mbean>
```

8.1.1.4 Other Dependencies and Attributes

The connection manager may also define the following attributes and dependencies:

❑ JaasSecurityManagerService
   This is defined as a depends element with the optional-attribute-name attribute. This refers to the object name of the JAAS security manager MBean.

❑ TransactionManager
This is defined as a plain MBean attribute and refers to the JNDI name of
the transaction manager.

❑ RARDeployer
This is defined as a depends element that refers to the object name of the
RAR deployer MBean. This is actually a hack to get the RAR deployer
MBean started and all the RARs deployed, before the MBeans used for
exposing the RAR connection factory in the JNDI namespace and providing
connection pooling to the resource manager are started.

The following code is an example of these three dependencies:

```
<mbean
    code="org.jboss.resource.connectionmanager.LocalTxConnectionManager"
    name="jboss.jca:service=LocalTxCM,name=OracleDS">
    ...
    <depends optional-attribute-name="JaasSecurityManagerService">
      jboss.security:service=JaasSecurityManager
    </depends>

    <attribute name="TransactionManager">
      java:/TransactionManager
    </attribute>

    <depends>jboss.jca:service=RARDeployer</depends>

</mbean>
```

8.2 JBossCX and Datasources

JBoss uses JCA to interface with relational databases. For databases that support JCA,
JBoss directly use the resource adapters provided by the database. However, for
databases that don't support JCA, JBoss provides two resource adapters that are present
in the \deploy directory of the default configuration set:

❑ jboss-local-jdbc.rar
This resource adapter should be used for configuring datasources that
support only local transactions.

❑ jboss-xa.rar
This should be used for configuring datasources that support
distributed transactions.

One thing you need to keep in mind about these resource adapters is their display
names in the resource deployment descriptor, as we need this when we configure the
managed connection factory MBean. The display name for the local RAR is JBoss
LocalTransaction JDBC Wrapper and that for the XA RAR is Minerva JDBC
XATransaction ResourceAdapter.

To configure a datasource, you need to configure the MBeans that are explained in the previous sections. JBoss provides example MBean configurations for many mainstream databases in the \docs\examples\jca\ directory of the JBoss installation. These examples include:

- ❑ db2-service.xml
  Datasources supporting local transactions for DB2

- ❑ firebird-service.xml
  Firebird provides a JCA-compliant adapter

- ❑ hsqldb-service.xml
  Datasources supporting local transactions for HSQL DB

- ❑ informix-service.xml
  Datasources supporting local transactions for Informix

- ❑ informix-xaservice.xml
  Datasources supporting distributed transactions for Informix

- ❑ jdatastore-service.xml
  Datasources supporting local transactions for Borland JDataStore

- ❑ lido-versant-service.xml
  LIDO provides a JCA-compliant adapter

- ❑ msaccess-service.xml
  Datasources supporting local transactions for Microsoft Access

- ❑ mssql-service.xml
  Datasources supporting local transactions for Microsoft SQL Server

- ❑ mssql-xa-service.xml
  Datasources supporting distributed transactions for Microsoft SQL Server

- ❑ oracle-service.xml
  Datasources supporting local transactions for Oracle

- ❑ oracle-xa-service.xml
  Datasources supporting distributed transactions for Oracle

- ❑ postgres-service.xml
  Datasources supporting local transactions for PostgreSQL

- ❑ sapdb-service.xml
  Datasources supporting local transactions for SAP DB

- ❑ solid-service.xml
  Datasources supporting local transactions for Solid

- ❑ sybase-service.xml
  Datasources supporting local transactions for Sybase SQL Server

8.2.1 Configuring Datasources

Configuring datasources within JBoss involves the same steps as configuring any JCA resource adapter connection factory explained in *Section 8.1.1: The Connection Manager MBean*. In this section, we'll summarize the steps involved once again, whilst constructing a datasource to connect to an Oracle database using local transactions for the PetStore application:

1. Configure the connection manager MBean. This is normally defined as the root MBean of a SAR deployment descriptor. The code for this MBean should be one of `NoTxConnectionManager`, `LocalTxConnectionManager` or `XaTxConnectionManager` depending on the level of transaction support you need:

```
<mbean
    code="org.jboss.resource.connectionmanager.
        LocalTxConnectionManager"
    name="jboss.jca:service=LocalTxCM,name=jdbc/petstore/PetStoreDB">
```

2. Define an embedded MBean within the connection manager MBean using the depends element to define the connection factory MBean. The depends element should have an `optional-attribute-name` attribute with value set to `ManagedConnectionFactoryName`:

```
<depends optional-attribute-name="ManagedConnectionFactoryName">
    <mbean
        code="org.jboss.resource.connectionmanager.RARDeployment"
        name="jboss.jca:service=LocalTxDS,
            name=jdbc/petstore/PetStoreDB">
```

3. Use the `ManagedConnectionFactoryProperties` MBean attribute of the connection factory MBean to define an XML fragment containing the configuration information for the connection factory. The local JDBC-JCA wrapper provided by JBoss expects `DriverClass`, `ConnectionURL`, `UserName`, and `Password` whereas XA JDBC-JCA wrapper provided by JBoss expects `XADataSourceProperties`, `XADataSourceClass`, `UserName`, and `Password`:

```
<attribute name="ManagedConnectionFactoryProperties">
    <properties>
        <config-property name="ConnectionURL"
                        type="java.lang.String">
            jdbc:oracle:thin:@youroraclehost:1521:yoursid
        </config-property>
        <config-property name="DriverClass"
                        type="java.lang.String">
            oracle.jdbc.driver.OracleDriver
        </config-property>
        <config-property name="UserName" type="java.lang.String">
```

```
          megadeath
       </config-property>
       <config-property name="Password" type="java.lang.String">
         euthanasia
       </config-property>
     </properties>
   </attribute>
```

> **Of course, the driver class needs to be loaded onto the JBoss classpath. See *Section 5.2: Setting the Classpath* on how to do this.**

4. Use the JndiName MBean attribute of the connection factory MBean to define the JNDI name used lookup the datasource:

```
<attribute name="JndiName">
   jdbc/petstore/PetStoreDB
</attribute>
```

5. Define an embedded MBean within the connection factory MBean using the depends element to define the RAR deployment MBean that encapsulates the RAR deployment information. For the local JDBC-JCA wrapper this content should be jboss.jca:service=RARDeployment,name=JBoss LocalTransaction JDBC Wrapper and for XA JDBC-JCA wrapper it should be jboss.jca:service=RARDeployment,name=Minerva JDBC XATransaction ResourceAdapter:

```
<depends optional-attribute-name="OldRarDeployment">
   jboss.jca:service=RARDeployment,
   name=JBoss LocalTransaction JDBC Wrapper
</depends>
```

6. Define an embedded MBean within the connection manager MBean using the depends element to define the connection factory MBean. The depends element should have an optional-attribute-name attribute with value set to ManagedConnectionPool. Use the embedded MBean's attributes to define pool initial size, maximum size, etc.:

```
<depends optional-attribute-name="ManagedConnectionPool">
  <mbean
   code="org.jboss.resource.connectionmanager.
       JBossManagedConnectionPool"
   name="jboss.jca:service=LocalTxPool,
       name=jdbc/petstore/PetStoreDB">

   <attribute name="MinSize">1</attribute>
```

```
        <attribute name="MaxSize">50</attribute>
        <attribute name="BlockingTimeoutMillis">5000</attribute>
        <attribute name="IdleTimeoutMinutes">15</attribute>
        <attribute name="Criteria">ByContainer</attribute>
    </mbean>
</depends>
```

7. Define a depends element within the connection manager MBean with content as the object name of the cached connection manager MBean. The depends element should have an optional-attribute-name attribute with value set to CachedConnectionManager:

```
<depends optional-attribute-name="CachedConnectionManager">
   jboss.jca:service=CachedConnectionManager
</depends>
```

8. Define a depends element within the connection manager MBean with content as the object name of the JAAS security manager MBean:

```
<depends optional-attribute-name="JaasSecurityManagerService">
   jboss.security:service=JaasSecurityManager
</depends>
```

9. Define an attribute element within the connection manager MBean with content pointing to the JNDI name of the transaction manager:

```
<attribute name="TransactionManager">
   java:/TransactionManager
</attribute>
```

10. Define a depends element within the connection manager MBean with content as the object name of the RAR deployer to force the RAR deployer to deploy all the RAR components:

```
<depends>jboss.jca:service=RARDeployer</depends>
```

8.2.2 Using Container-Managed Resource Security

When you connect to a resource manager from your application, you can either manage the security in the application, or let the container handle the security. Examples for this are the getConnection() and getConnection(user, passwd) methods on the javax.sql.DataSource class. If you use the first method the *container* should manage the security, and in the second instance the *application* manages security.

When you configure datasources in JBoss, it can manage the security for you. To enable this:

1. Set the `Criteria` attribute of your connection pool to `ByContainer`:

```
<mbean
    code="org.jboss.resource.connectionmanager.
        JBossManagedConnectionPool"
    name="jboss.jca:service=LocalTxPool,
        name=jdbc/petstore/PetStoreDB">

    <attribute name="MinSize">1</attribute>
    <attribute name="MaxSize">50</attribute>
    <attribute name="BlockingTimeoutMillis">5000</attribute>
    <attribute name="IdleTimeoutMinutes">15</attribute>
    <attribute name="Criteria">ByContainer</attribute>
</mbean>
```

2. Next, you will have to configure a login module that is an instance of the `org.jboss.resouce.security.AbstractPasswordCredentialLoginModule` class. This login module expects a module option called `managedConnectionFactoryName`, which should be set to the connection manager object name. JBoss provides two subclasses of the aforementioned login module. They are:

❏ `ConfiguredIdentityLoginModule`
This will use the principal and credentials specified as the module options for connecting to the resource manager.

❏ `CallerIdentityLoginModule`
This login module will use the principal and credentials of the user authenticated by the application for connecting to the resource manager.

You can configure the login module either embedded in the connection manager MBean or in the `login-config.xml` file. Here we use the embedded MBean:

```
<mbean
    code="org.jboss.resource.connectionmanager.
        LocalTxConnectionManager"
    name="jboss.jca:service=LocalTxCM,name=jdbc/petstore/PetStoreDB">
    ...
    <application-policy name="DbRealm">
      <authentication>
        <login-module
          code="org.jboss.resource.security.
              ConfiguredIdentityLoginModule"
          flag="required">
          <module-option name="principal">dba</module-option>
          <module-option name="userName">sql</module-option>
          <module-option name="password">sql</module-option>
```

```
            <module-option name="managedConnectionFactoryName">
                jboss.jca:service=LocalTxCM,name=jdbc/petstore/PetStoreDB
            </module-option>
          </login-module>
        </authentication>
      </application-policy>
    ...
  </mbean>
```

Please refer to Section 7.3.3.3: Login Configuration Data for a guideline to the elements configured above.

The module option `managedConnectionFactoryName` should match the object name of the connection manager. You can also define the login module inside the `login-config.xml` file, as discussed in *Section 7.3.3.3: Login Configuration Data*.

3. Next, you need to specify the name of the login module as the value for the `SecurityDomainJndiName` of the connection manager:

```
<mbean
  code="org.jboss.resource.connectionmanager.
      LocalTxConnectionManager"
  name="jboss.jca:service=LocalTxCM,name=jdbc/petstore/PetStoreDB">
  ...
    <attribute name="SecurityDomainJndiName">DbRealm</attribute>
</mbean>
```

The MBean attribute `SecurityDomainJndiName` should match the login module that should be used for authentication.

In the example above, the container passes the user name and password specified by the configured identity login module for getting connections from the database.

JBoss 3.0

Administration and Deployment

Handbook

9

9

Configuring JBossMQ

In this chapter, we look at how to configure JBossMQ, a fully compliant JMS 1.0.2 implementation from JBoss for building message-oriented enterprise-class applications. JBossMQ supports both point-to-point and publish/subscribe messaging. To begin with, let's look at the JBossMQ architecture.

9.1 JBossMQ Architecture

JBossMQ is comprised of multiple submodules as depicted in the diagram below:

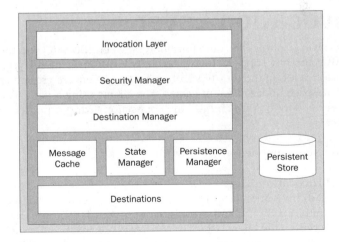

The submodules of JBossMQ are:

❑ **Invocation Layer**
The invocation layer handles the communication between JBossMQ and messaging clients, for sending and receiving JMS messages

❑ **Security Manager**
The security manager is used to control access to the JMS destinations defined with JBossMQ

❑ **Destination Manager**
The destination manager is responsible for managing destinations, message cache, state manager, and persistence manager

❑ **Message Cache**
JMS messages within JBossMQ are stored in memory caches for performance enhancement

❑ **State Manager**
The state manager is used by JBossMQ to keep track of users and their durable subscriptions

❑ **Persistence Manager**
The persistence manager is used by JBossMQ to persist the JMS messages that are marked as persistent to a **Persistent Store**

❑ **Destinations**
Destinations are the topics and queues to which JMS messages are sent and consumed

9.2 Invocation Layer

The invocation layer controls the communication between JBossMQ and the messaging clients. JBossMQ currently supports four different types of invocation layers. Connection factories for all the four types of invocation layers are created and bound in the JNDI namespace under different names. The clients using a particular type of invocation layer need to look up and use the connection factory associated with that invocation layer.

The invocation layers supported by JBossMQ are:

❑ **RMI Invocation Layer**
The RMI invocation layer uses the Java RMI protocol for handling the communication. The RMI invocation layer uses TCP/IP sockets to connect the server to the client, which can cause problems by stopping the clients in a restricted environment from opening server sockets. RMI invocation layer is useful in scenarios where the JMS clients and JBoss run in an intranet environment.

❏ **Optimized Invocation Layer (OIL)**
The optimized invocation layer uses a custom TCP/IP protocol for handling communication to enhance performance. However, this invocation layer is restricted in ways similar to the RMI invocation layer.

❏ **Unified Invocation Layer (UIL)**
The unified invocation layer allows clients sitting within a firewall to send and receive JMS messages. However, this invocation layer is slower than the OIL.

❏ **JVM Invocation Layer**
The JVM invocation layer is used when both the client and the server reside within the same VM. It doesn't have the overheads associated with TCP/IP socket-based communication.

All the four invocation layers use a full duplex channel for communication. This enables the clients to simultaneously send and receive messages. Invocation layers are normally configured as MBean services in the `jbossmq-service.xml` file available in the `\deploy` directory of the configuration set you use.

9.2.1 RMI Invocation Layer

The RMI invocation layer is implemented using an MBean service. Here's the MBean definition:

```
<mbean
    code="org.jboss.mq.il.rmi.RMIServerILService"
    name="jboss.mq:service=InvocationLayer,type=RMI">
```

This MBean supports the following configurable attributes:

Attribute	Function
Invoker	The object name of the MBean that passes the client requests to the JBossMQ destination manager.
ConnectionFactoryJNDIRef	The JNDI name that the RMI invocation layer will bind its connection factory to.
XAConnectionFactoryJNDIRef	The JNDI name that the RMI invocation layer will bind its XA connection factory to.
PingPeriod	The interval, in milliseconds, which the client should ping the server to ensure that the connection is not lost. The value zero is used for disabling pinging.

The snippet below shows the MBean definition for the RMI invocation layer:

```
<mbean
    code="org.jboss.mq.il.rmi.RMIServerILService"
    name="jboss.mq:service=InvocationLayer,type=RMI">
    <depends optional-attribute-name="Invoker">
      jboss.mq:service=Invoker
    </depends>
    <attribute name="ConnectionFactoryJNDIRef">
      RMIConnectionFactory
    </attribute>
    <attribute name="XAConnectionFactoryJNDIRef">
      RMIXAConnectionFactory
    </attribute>
    <attribute name="PingPeriod">60000</attribute>
</mbean>
```

JBoss comes pre-configured with the RMI invocation layer in the `jbossmq-service.xml` file in the `\deploy` directory of the `default` configuration set. Clients intending to use the RMI invocation layer should name `RMIConnectionFactory` or `RMIXAConnectionFactory` to look up the JMS connection factory depending on whether they need XA transaction support or not.

9.2.2 Optimized Invocation Layer

The optimized invocation layer is implemented using an MBean service. The MBean definition is:

```
<mbean
    code="org.jboss.mq.il.oil.OILServerILService"
    name="jboss.mq:service=InvocationLayer,type=OIL">
```

In addition to the attributes supported by the RMI invocation layer, this MBean supports the following configurable attributes:

Attribute	Function
ServerBindPort	The attribute used for defining the listen port on the server.
BindAddress	The attribute used to define the listen address on the server.
EnableTcpNoDelay	This flag indicates whether the TcpNoDelay option should be used. If it is set to true, TCP/IP packets will not be buffered.

The snippet below shows the MBean definition for the OIL:

```
<mbean
    code="org.jboss.mq.il.oil.OILServerILService"
    name="jboss.mq:service=InvocationLayer,type=OIL">
    <depends optional-attribute-name="Invoker">
      jboss.mq:service=Invoker
    </depends>
```

```
  <attribute name="ConnectionFactoryJNDIRef">
    ConnectionFactory
  </attribute>
  <attribute name="XAConnectionFactoryJNDIRef">
    XAConnectionFactory
  </attribute>
  <attribute name="ServerBindPort">8090</attribute>
  <attribute name="PingPeriod">60000</attribute>
  <attribute name="EnableTcpNoDelay">true</attribute>
</mbean>
```

JBoss comes pre-configured with the optimized invocation layer in the jbossmq-service.xml file in the \deploy directory of the default configuration set. Clients intending to use the optimized invocation layer should use the JNDI name ConnectionFactory or XAConnectionFactory to look up the JMS connection factory depending on whether they need XA transaction support or not.

9.2.3 Unified Invocation Layer

The UIL is also configured as an MBean, and supports all the attributes supported by the MBean for OIL.

The snippet below shows an MBean definition for the UIL:

```
<mbean
    code="org.jboss.mq.il.uil.UILServerILService"
    name="jboss.mq:service=InvocationLayer,type=UIL">
    <depends optional-attribute-name="Invoker">
       jboss.mq:service=Invoker
    </depends>
    <attribute name="ConnectionFactoryJNDIRef">
       UILConnectionFactory
    </attribute>
    <attribute name="XAConnectionFactoryJNDIRef">
       UILXAConnectionFactory
    </attribute>
    <attribute name="ServerBindPort">8091</attribute>
    <attribute name="PingPeriod">60000</attribute>
    <attribute name="EnableTcpNoDelay">true</attribute>
</mbean>
```

JBoss comes pre-configured with the unified invocation layer in the jbossmq-service.xml file in the \deploy directory of the default configuration set. Clients intending to use the unified invocation layer should use the JNDI name UILConnectionFactory or UILXAConnectionFactory to look up the JMS connection factory depending on whether they need XA transaction support or not.

9.2.4 JVM Invocation Layer

The JVM invocation layer is also implemented as an MBean and supports all the attributes supported by the RMI invocation layer.

The snippet below shows the MBean definition for the JVM invocation layer:

```
<mbean
   code="org.jboss.mq.il.jvm.JVMServerILService"
   name="jboss.mq:service=InvocationLayer,type=JVM">
   <depends optional-attribute-name="Invoker">
      jboss.mq:service=Invoker
   </depends>
   <attribute name="ConnectionFactoryJNDIRef">
      java:/ConnectionFactory
   </attribute>
   <attribute name="XAConnectionFactoryJNDIRef">
      java:/XAConnectionFactory
   </attribute>
   <attribute name="PingPeriod">0</attribute>
</mbean>
```

Note that the ping period is set to zero for JVM invocation layer as the JMS client and the provider both run in the same VM. JBoss comes pre-configured with the JVM invocation layer in the file jbossmq-service.xml file in the \deploy directory of the default configuration set. Clients intending to use the JVM invocation layer should use the JNDI name java:/ConnectionFactory or java:/XAConnectionFactory to lookup the JMS connection factory depending on whether they need XA transaction support or not.

9.3 Destination Manager

The destination manager is responsible for keeping track of all the destinations and managing the message cache, state manager, and the persistence manager. The destination manager is configured in the jbossmq-service.xml file as an MBean service. The MBean definition is as follows:

```
<mbean
   code="org.jboss.mq.server.jmx.DestinationManager"
   name="jboss.mq:service=DestinationManager">
```

The service supports the following attributes:

Attribute	Function
PersistenceManager	The object name of the MBean that configures the persistence manager
StateManager	The object name of the MBean that configures the state manager

The snippet below shows an example of the destination manager MBean configuration:

```
<mbean
  code="org.jboss.mq.server.jmx.DestinationManager"
  name="jboss.mq:service=DestinationManager">
  <depends optional-attribute-name="PersistenceManager">
    jboss.mq:service=PersistenceManager
  </depends>
  <depends optional-attribute-name="StateManager">
    jboss.mq:service=StateManager
  </depends>
</mbean>
```

The destination manager is part of an interceptor chain that passes the message from the invocation layer through to the destinations. The destination manager is required to be the last interceptor in that chain.

The diagram below depicts the interceptor chain that is pre-configured in the file jbossmq-service.xml:

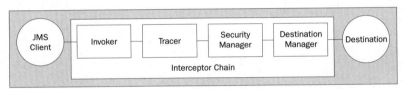

The interceptor chain shown above contains the following components:

❑ **Invoker**

The invoker passes the invocation layer requests to the destination manager through the interceptor chain.

❑ **Tracer**

The tracer traces all the requests that go through the interceptor chain. To improve performance, you may remove this interceptor from the chain.

❑ **Security Manager**

Security manager controls access to the destinations. If you don't want to secure your destinations, you may remove this interceptor from the chain to improve performance.

❑ **Destination Manager**

The destination manager is responsible for keeping track of all the destinations, and managing the message cache, state manager, and the persistence manager.

The listing below shows how the interceptor chain is configured in the jbossmq-service.xml file:

```
<mbean
  code="org.jboss.mq.server.jmx.Invoker"
  name="jboss.mq:service=Invoker">
```

127

```
        <depends
          optional-attribute-name="NextInterceptor">
          jboss.mq:service=TracingInterceptor
        </depends>
      </mbean>

      <mbean
        code="org.jboss.mq.server.jmx.InterceptorLoader"
        name="jboss.mq:service=TracingInterceptor">
        <attribute
          name="InterceptorClass">
          org.jboss.mq.server.TracingInterceptor
        </attribute>
        <depends
          optional-attribute-name="NextInterceptor">
          jboss.mq:service=SecurityManager
        </depends>
      </mbean>

      <mbean
        code="org.jboss.mq.security.SecurityManager"
        name="jboss.mq:service=SecurityManager">
        <depends
          optional-attribute-name="NextInterceptor">
          jboss.mq:service=DestinationManager
        </depends>
      </mbean>

      <mbean
        code="org.jboss.mq.server.jmx.DestinationManager"
        name="jboss.mq:service=DestinationManager">
        <depends
          optional-attribute-name="PersistenceManager">
          jboss.mq:service=PersistenceManager
        </depends>
        <depends
          optional-attribute-name="StateManager">
          jboss.mq:service=StateManager
        </depends>
      </mbean>
```

Each interceptor defines the next interceptor in the chain by referring to the next interceptor's JMX object name as a depended MBean.

9.4 Message Cache

JBossMQ uses an in-memory cache to store the messages that are created. However, when the JVM runs short of resources, JBossMQ may decide to swap the messages in the cache to a persistent storage, based on a least recently used algorithm. The two MBeans (MessageCache and CacheStore) explained below, control the behavior of the message cache.

The first MBean, `MessageCache`, decides where to put JBossMQ messages waiting to be consumed by a client. Once the JVM memory usage hits the high memory mark, the old messages in the cache will start getting stored in a persistent store. As memory usage gets closer to the `MaxMemoryMark`, the number of messages kept in the memory cache approaches 0. The MBean's definition is:

```
<mbean
    code="org.jboss.mq.server.MessageCache"
    name="jboss.mq:service=MessageCache">
```

The `MessageCache` MBean supports the following attributes:

Attribute	Function
CacheStore	Defines the object name of the MBean that configures the persistent store to which the messages are written.
HighMemoryMark	The JVM heap, in megabytes, that should be used before the messages are swapped to secondary storage. The default value when not specified is 16 MB.
MaxMemoryMark	The maximum amount of JVM heap that the message cache can use in megabytes. The default value when not specified is 32 MB.

The snippet below shows the message cache MBean definition pre-configured in the `jbossmq-service.xml` file:

```
<mbean
    code="org.jboss.mq.server.MessageCache"
    name="jboss.mq:service=MessageCache">
    <attribute name="HighMemoryMark">16</attribute>
    <attribute name="MaxMemoryMark">32</attribute>
    <depends optional-attribute-name="CacheStore">
      jboss.mq:service=CacheStore
    </depends>
</mbean>
```

The second MBean that controls the behavior of the message cache, the `CacheStore` MBean, decides where to store JBossMQ messages that the `MessageCache` has decided to move to the secondary storage. This MBean has the following definition, stored in the `jbossmq-service.xml` file:

```
<mbean
    code="org.jboss.mq.pm.file.CacheStore"
    name="jboss.mq:service=CacheStore">
    <attribute name="DataDirectory">tmp/jbossmq</attribute>
</mbean>
```

It supports only one attribute, `DataDirectory`, which specifies the directory to which the messages are stored.

9.5 State Manager

The state manager is responsible for keeping track of the users who access the JBossMQ server, and their durable subscriptions. The state manager is configured in the `jbossmq-service.xml` file as an MBean service. The service supports a single attribute called `StateFile`, which stores the users and durable subscriptions. The example below shows the state manager MBean configuration:

```
<mbean
    code="org.jboss.mq.sm.file.DynamicStateManager"
    name="jboss.mq:service=StateManager">
    <attribute name="StateFile">jbossmq-state.xml</attribute>
</mbean>
```

The state file is stored in XML format in the `\conf` directory with the following format:

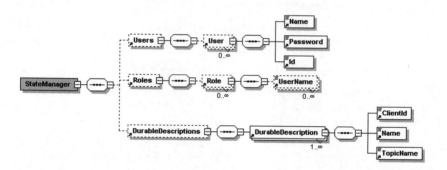

The XML contains three main elements:

❑ `Users`:
Contains zero or more `User` elements used to define the user name, password, and ID. The `User` element contains the following sub-elements:

- `Name`
Used to specify the name of the user

- `Password`
Used to define the password of the user

- `Id`:
The client ID assigned for JMS connections. The client id is used for setting durable subscriptions

❑   Roles
    Contains zero or more Role elements. Each Role element has a name
    attribute identifying the role name, and zero or more UserName elements
    defining the users that have this role. The UserName element content
    should be one of the users defined within the User element.

❑   DurableSubscriptions
    This element may contain one or more DurableSubscription elements
    representing the durable subscription properties. This element contains the
    following sub-elements:

    •   ClientID
        Used to specify the client Id used for durable subscriptions

    •   Name
        Used to define the durable subscription name

    •   TopicName
        Used to specify the topic for which the durable subscription is defined

The snippet below shows an example of the state file:

```xml
<?xml version="1.0" encoding="UTF-8"?>
<StateManager>
  <Users>
    <User>
      <Name>meeraj</Name>
      <Password>hitthelights</Password>
      <Id>DurableSubscriberExample</Id>
    </User>
    <User>
      <Name>guest</Name>
      <Password>guest</Password>
    </User>
    <User>
      <Name>nobody</Name>
      <Password>nobody</Password>
    </User>
  </Users>
  <Roles>
    <Role name="guest">
      <UserName>guest</UserName>
      <UserName>meeraj</UserName>
    </Role>
    <Role name="subscriber">
      <UserName>meeraj</UserName>
    </Role>
    <Role name="publisher">
      <UserName>meeraj</UserName>
      <UserName>dynsub</UserName>
    </Role>
    <Role name="durpublisher">
      <UserName>meeraj</UserName>
      <UserName>dynsub</UserName>
    </Role>
    <Role name="noacc">
      <UserName>nobody</UserName>
    </Role>
  </Roles>
```

```
<DurableSubscriptions>
  <DurableSubscription>
    <ClientID>DurableSubscriberExample</ClientID>
    <Name>myDurableSub</Name>
    <TopicName>TestTopic</TopicName>
  <DurableSubscription>
</DurableSubscriptions>
</StateManager>
```

9.6 Persistence Manager

The persistence manager is responsible for storing persistent messages to a secondary storage device. JBossMQ supports three different types of persistence managers:

❑ **File Persistence Manager**
   This persistence manager stores persistent messages in a file system. It creates one directory per destination for storing persistent messages. Each message is stored as a file in the directory that corresponds to its respective destination.

❑ **Rolling Logged Persistence Manager**
   This is similar to the file persistence manager, but stores multiple messages in a single file. This file is rolled every day.

❑ **JDBC2 Persistence Manager**
   This stores persistent messages in a JDBC database.

Persistence managers are normally configured in the `jbossmq-service.xml` file, and you can only define one persistence manager.

9.6.1 File Persistence Manager

The MBean for configuring the file persistence manager has the following definition:

```
<mbean
  code="org.jboss.mq.pm.file.PersistenceManager"
  name="jboss.mq:service=PersistenceManager">
```

It supports the following attributes:

Attribute	Function
MessageCache	The object name of the message cache to use
DataDirectory	The directory used to store the persistent messages

The snippet below shows an example configuration of the file persistence manager MBean:

132

```
<mbean
  code="org.jboss.mq.pm.file.PersistenceManager"
  name="jboss.mq:service=PersistenceManager">
  <attribute name="DataDirectory">db/jbossmq/file</attribute>
  <depends optional-attribute-name="MessageCache">
    jboss.mq:service=MessageCache
  </depends>
</mbean>
```

9.6.2 Rolling Logged Persistence Manager

The rolling logged persistence manager supports the same attributes as the file persistence manager. The snippet below shows an example configuration of the rolling logged persistence manager MBean:

```
<mbean
  code="org.jboss.mq.pm.rollinglogged.PersistenceManager"
  name="jboss.mq:service=PersistenceManager">
  <attribute name="DataDirectory">db/jbossmq/file</attribute>
  <depends optional-attribute-name="MessageCache">
    jboss.mq:service=MessageCache
  </depends>
</mbean>
```

9.6.3 JDBC2 Persistence Manager

The JDBC2 persistence manager MBean has the definition:

```
<mbean
  code="org.jboss.mq.pm.jdbc2.PersistenceManager"
  name="jboss.mq:service=PersistenceManager">
```

This MBean supports the following attributes:

Attribute	Function
MessageCache	The object name of the message cache.
DataSource	The JNDI name of the datasource pointing to the data store used for storing messages.
SqlProperties	Defines the SQL statements for creating, selecting from and inserting into tables that store persistent messages, and handling JMS transactions. The JDBC-based persistence manager uses two tables, JMS_MESSAGES for storing messages and JMS_TRANSACTIONS for keeping track of transactions.

The snippet below shows an example configuration of the JDBC2 persistence manager MBean:

```
<mbean
  code="org.jboss.mq.pm.jdbc2.PersistenceManager"
  name="jboss.mq:service=PersistenceManager">
  <depends optional-attribute-name="MessageCache">
    jboss.mq:service=MessageCache
  </depends>
  <depends optional-attribute-name="DataSource">
    jboss.jca:service=LocalTxDS,name=hsqldbDS
  </depends>
  <depends>
    jboss.jca:service=LocalTxCM,name=hsqldbDS
  </depends>
  <attribute name="SqlProperties">
    BLOB_TYPE=OBJECT_BLOB
    INSERT_TX = INSERT INTO JMS_TRANSACTIONS (TXID) values(?)
    INSERT_MESSAGE = INSERT INTO JMS_MESSAGES (MESSAGEID, \
      DESTINATION, MESSAGEBLOB, TXID, TXOP) VALUES(?,?,?,?,?)
    SELECT_ALL_UNCOMMITED_TXS = SELECT TXID FROM JMS_TRANSACTIONS
    SELECT_MAX_TX = SELECT MAX(TXID) FROM JMS_MESSAGES
    SELECT_MESSAGES_IN_DEST = SELECT MESSAGEID, MESSAGEBLOB \
      FROM JMS_MESSAGES WHERE DESTINATION=?
    SELECT_MESSAGE = SELECT MESSAGEID, MESSAGEBLOB FROM \
    JMS_MESSAGES WHERE MESSAGEID=? AND DESTINATION=?
    MARK_MESSAGE = UPDATE JMS_MESSAGES SET (TXID, TXOP) \
      VALUES(?,?) WHERE MESSAGEID=? AND DESTINATION=?
    DELETE_ALL_MESSAGE_WITH_TX = DELETE FROM JMS_MESSAGES \
      WHERE TXID=?
    DELETE_TX = DELETE FROM JMS_TRANSACTIONS WHERE TXID = ?
    DELETE_MARKED_MESSAGES = DELETE FROM JMS_MESSAGES WHERE \
      TXID=? AND TXOP=?
    DELETE_MESSAGE = DELETE FROM JMS_MESSAGES WHERE MESSAGEID=? \
      AND DESTINATION=?
    CREATE_MESSAGE_TABLE = CREATE TABLE JMS_MESSAGES \
      ( MESSAGEID INTEGER NOT NULL, \
      DESTINATION VARCHAR(50) NOT NULL, TXID INTEGER, TXOP CHAR(1), \
      MESSAGEBLOB OBJECT, PRIMARY KEY (MESSAGEID, DESTINATION) )
    CREATE_TX_TABLE = CREATE TABLE JMS_TRANSACTIONS ( TXID INTEGER )
  </attribute>
</mbean>
```

9.7 Destinations

Destinations are also configured as MBeans, normally in the jbossmq-destinations-service.xml file in the \deploy directory of the configuration set. The MBean has the following definition for defining queues:

```
<mbean
  code="org.jboss.mq.server.jmx.Queue"
  name="jboss.mq.destination:service=Queue,name=queue">
```

While defining topics, this MBean has the following definition:

```
<mbean
  code="org.jboss.mq.server.jmx.Topic"
  name="jboss.mq.destination:service=Topic,name=testDurableTopic">
```

It supports the following attributes:

Attribute	Function
DestinationManager	The object name of the destination manager used.
SecurityManager	The JNDI name of the security manager used to control access to the destinations.
SecurityConf	Contains an XML element that defines the roles required to read, write, and create destinations.
JNDIName	Defines the JNDI name of the destination. If the JNDI name is not specified the JNDI name defaults to queue|topic/queue-name|topic-name, where queue-name|topic-name identifies the name attribute of the object name of the MBean.

The format of the SecurityConf XML fragment is:

```
<security>
  <role name="name" read="true/false" write="true/false"
       create="true/false"></role>
  <role name="name" read="true/false" write="true/false"
       create="true/false"></role>
  ...
</security>
```

The root element is security which is used to define the roles required for reading from, writing to, and creating durable subscriptions to the destination. Roles and the permissions available for each role are defined using zero or more role child elements of the security element. The role element contains the attributes name which specifies the role, and read, write, and create can take either true or false to indicate that the user, having the role identified by the name attribute, can read, write, and create durable subscriptions to the destination, respectively. The default value for read, write, and create when not specified is false.

The snippet below shows an example of a queue definition:

```
<mbean
  code="org.jboss.mq.server.jmx.Queue"
  name="jboss.mq.destination:service=Queue,name=queue">
  <depends optional-attribute-name="DestinationManager">
    jboss.mq:service=DestinationManager
  </depends>
  <depends optional-attribute-name="SecurityManager">
    jboss.mq:service=SecurityManager
  </depends>
  <attribute name="SecurityConf">
    <security>
      <role name="guest" read="true" write="false"/>
      <role name="publisher" read="true" write="true"/>
```

```
        <role name="noacc" read="false" write="false" create="false"/>
      </security>
    </attribute>
    <attribute name="JNDIName">
      opc/MailOrderApprovalQueue
    </attribute>
  </mbean>
```

The example above defines a queue that can be accessed by the opc/MailOrderApprovalQueue JNDI name. Users with guest role can read from the queue and not write to it. Users with publisher role can read from and write to the queue.

The snippet below shows an example of a topic definition:

```
<mbean
  code="org.jboss.mq.server.jmx.Topic"
  name="jboss.mq.destination:service=Topic,name=testDurableTopic">
  <depends optional-attribute-name="DestinationManager">
    jboss.mq:service=DestinationManager
  </depends>
  <depends optional-attribute-name="SecurityManager">
    jboss.mq:service=SecurityManager
  </depends>
  <attribute name="SecurityConf">
    <security>
      <role name="guest" read="true" write="true"/>
      <role name="publisher" read="true" write="true" create="true"/>
    </security>
  </attribute>
  <attribute name="JNDIName">
    opc/InvoiceTopic
  </attribute>
</mbean>
```

The example above defines a topic that can be accessed by the opc/InvoiceTopic JNDI name. Users with guest role can read from and write to the topic. Users with publisher role can read from, write to, and create durable subscriptions to the queue.

9.8 Security Manager

The security manager is used to control access to the JMS destinations. The security manager refers to the jbossmq-state.xml file to identify the user and the role assigned to the user and the file in which the addressed destination is configured to identify the roles required to read, write, and create the destination. The destinations are normally configured in jbossmq-destinations-service.xml file in the \deploy directory. You can remove the security manager from the interceptor chain if you do not wish to secure your destinations.

The MBean that configures the security manager is an intermediate interceptor in the chain that passes the messages from the invocation layer. The `NextInterceptor` attribute defines the object name of the MBean that acts as the next interceptor in the chain. Normally, the next interceptor configured in the chain, after the security manager, is the destination manager. The example below shows the MBean definition for the security manager in the `jbossmq-service.xml` file:

```
<mbean
    code="org.jboss.mq.security.SecurityManager"
    name="jboss.mq:service=SecurityManager">
    <depends optional-attribute-name="NextInterceptor">
        jboss.mq:service=DestinationManager
    </depends>
</mbean>
```

9.9 Administering JMS

Most of the JBossMQ subsystems are configured as MBean services, and thus can be efficiently monitored and administered using the JMX console.

The destination manager MBean can be used to create and destroy destinations at run time. To do this, click on the destination manager MBean's object name (`service=DestinationManager`) under the `jboss.mq` domain in the JMX console. This will display the window shown below:

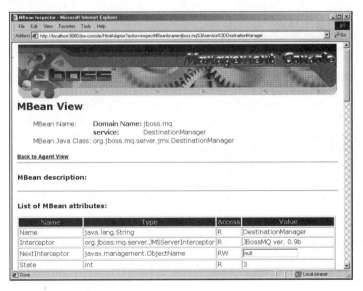

The destination manager MBean provides the operations to create and destroy queues and topics at run time. Please note that the destinations added during run time are *not* available until after a server restart. The following operations are available for managing destinations at run time:

- `createQueue(String name, String jndiName)`
  Creates a queue dynamically

- `destroQueue(String name)`
  Removes a previously created queue

- `createTopic(String name, String jndiName)`
  Creates a topic dynamically

- `destroTopic(String name)`
  Removes a previously created topic

The message cache MBean can be used for useful information regarding the message cache (such as the number of messages in the cache, the number of messages that have been swapped to the secondary storage, cache hits, cache misses, etc.) as shown below:

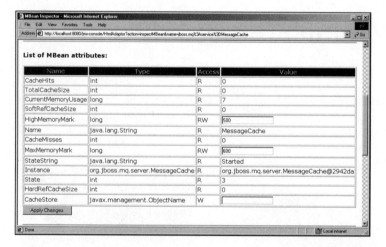

You can manage destinations by clicking on the object name for the destination in the JMX console. The MBean object names for JMS destinations normally have the domain set to `jboss.mq.destination`. The screenshot below shows the destinations that are configured within a JBoss server instance:

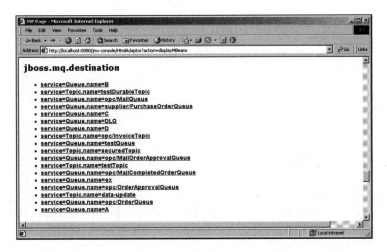

If you click on the object name for the destination, `opc/OrderQueue`, for example, the JMX console will display the attributes for that destination:

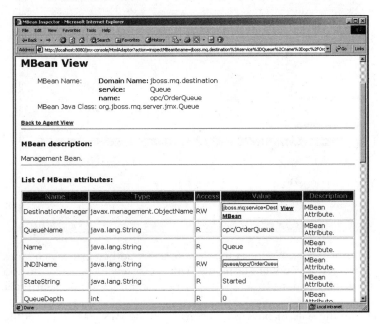

Both the MBean classes for queues and topics provide an MBean operation called `removeAllMessages()` as shown in the screenshot below. This operation can be invoked from the JMX console to remove all the messages in the destination:

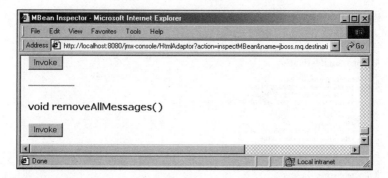

You can click on the persistence manager's object name in the JMX console to set the properties for the persistence manager. By default this can be found under the domain `jboss.mq` with the attribute `service=PersistenceManager`. Below is the screen for configuring the persistence manager:

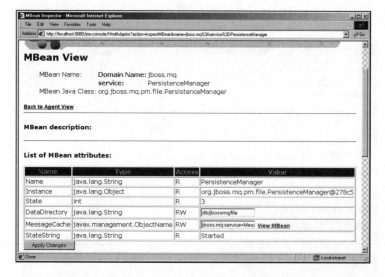

You can use the screen above to set the data directory and message cache for the file persistence manager. If you were using the JDBC persistence manager, the above screen would display options to set the properties for the JDBC persistence manager.

You can click on the state manager's object name in the JMX console to set the properties for the state manager. By default, this can be found under the domain `jboss.mq` with the attribute `service=StateManager`. Seen below is the screen for configuring the state manager:

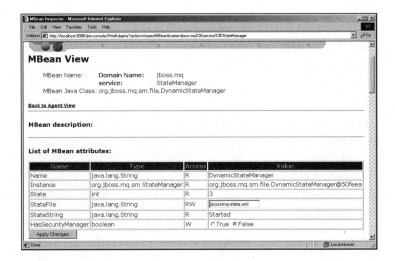

The state manager MBean allows you to set the file that stores the state information. The MBean also allows you to invoke the following operations, through the JMX console, which are displayed in the screen below:

❑ saveConfig()
Saves the current configuration to the backing state file. The default is
jbossmq-state.xml. Note that you need to invoke this operation to
persist any of the following operations you invoke on the state manager.

❑ addUser(String user, String passwd, String clientId)
Adds a new user.

❑ removeUser(String user)
Removes the user.

❑ addRole(String name)
Adds a new role.

❑ removeRole(String name)
Removes the role.

❑ addUserToRole(String user, String role)
Adds the specified user to the role.

❑ removeUserFromRole(String user, String role): Removes the user
from the role.

JBoss 3.0

Administration and Deployment

Handbook

10

10

Configuring JavaMail

In this chapter, we look at how to configure JavaMail sessions in JBoss.

10.1 The Mail Service MBean

JBoss provides an MBean for configuring mail connection factories. This MBean is normally defined in the `mail-service.xml` file in the `\deploy` directory of your configuration set. The MBean definition is:

```
<mbean
    code="org.jboss.mail.MailService"
    name="jboss:service=Mail">
```

The MBean supports the following attributes:

Attribute	Function
JNDIName	The JNDI name of the mail session that is configured.
User	The User ID for connecting to the mail server.
Password	The Password for connecting to the mail server.

Table continued on following page

Attribute	Function

Configuration	This attribute accepts an XML element that defines the configuration information for connecting to the mail server and sending e-mails. This MBean accepts an XML structure of the following format:
	
	`<configuration>`
	  `<property name="" value=""/>`
	  `<property name="" value=""/>`
	  `...`
	`</configuration>`

The `configuration` attribute is used for specifying the properties required by the mail session according to the JavaMail specification. The mail session properties are:

❑ `mail.transport.protocol`
This is the transport protocol to use.

❑ `mail.store.protocol`
This is the store protocol to use.

❑ `mail.host`
This is the default host for transport and store protocol.

❑ `mail.user`
Default user for both store and transport.

❑ `mail.from`
User's return e-mail address.

❑ `mail.protocol.host`
The host specific to the protocol. For example to specify an SMTP host you would use `mail.smtp.host`.

❑ `mail.protocol.user`
The user specific to the protocol. For example to specify an SMTP user you would use `mail.smtp.user`.

❑ `mail.debug`
The debug setting.

A comprehensive coverage of JavaMail API is beyond the scope of this book. Refer to Professional Java Server Programming: J2EE 1.3 Edition *from the Wrox Press (ISBN 1-86100-537-7) for a more exhaustive coverage.*

10.2 Configuring the Mail Service

1. To configure a mail service you need to configure the
   `org.jboss.mail.MailService` MBean in the `mail-service.xml` file of the
   `\deploy` directory of your configuration set.

First we add the JavaMail JAR files to the classpath:

```
<server>

  <classpath
    codebase="lib"
    archives="mail.jar, activation.jar, mail-plugin.jar"/>
```

Then we define the MBean for the mail service:

```
  <mbean
    code="org.jboss.mail.MailService"
    name="jboss:service=Mail">
  </mbean>
```

2. Next we need to define the JNDI name by which the mail Session object is
   looked up:

```
  <mbean
    code="org.jboss.mail.MailService"
    name="jboss:service=Mail">
      <attribute name="JNDIName">java:/Mail</attribute>
  </mbean>
```

3. Then we define the username and password for the mail server:

```
  <mbean
    code="org.jboss.mail.MailService"
    name="jboss:service=Mail">
      <attribute name="JNDIName">java:/Mail</attribute>
      <attribute name="User">fred</attribute>
      <attribute name="Password">flintstone</attribute>
  </mbean>
```

4. Finally we define the configuration properties:

```
  <mbean
    code="org.jboss.mail.MailService"
    name="jboss:service=Mail">
    ...
    <attribute name="Configuration">
      <configuration>
        <property name="mail.store.protocol"
                  value="pop3"/>
        <property name="mail.transport.protocol"
                  value="smtp"/>
```

147

```
            <property name="mail.user"
                      value="meeraj@heaven.com"/>
            <property name="mail.pop3.host"
                      value="myserver.pop3.com"/>
            <property name="mail.smtp.host"
                      value="myserver.exchg.com"/>
            <property name="mail.from"
                      value="meeraj@heaven.com"/>
            <property name="mail.debug"
                      value="false"/>
        </configuration>
      </attribute>
    </mbean>

  </server>
```

The mail session configured above can be looked up by the `java:/mail` JNDI name. However, in your EJBs and web applications, you will be using resource references to map the coded JNDI name of the mail sessions to the actual JNDI name (see *Section 18.3.2: Name Mapping*).

JBoss 3.0

Administration and Deployment

Handbook

11

11

Configuring Jetty

The core JBoss server doesn't come with a built-in web container. However, JBoss does provide an MBean that can be used for embedding a web container within the JBoss process. You can download the JBoss installation with either an embedded Tomcat or Jetty web server. In fact, Jetty is included as the default web container with the JBoss standard installation bundle. In this chapter, we will look at configuring Jetty with JBoss. We will also look at how to run the JBoss-Jetty combination with IIS and Apache front-end web servers. In fact, Jetty has a fully optimized web server suitable for the production environment. Hence, unless you have compelling reasons, you don't need to use a front-end web server with Jetty.

Integrating a web container involves the following three main steps:

❑ Handling WAR deployment

❑ Mapping the web **Environment Naming Context (ENC)** JNDI namespace to the JBoss JNDI namespace

❑ Delegating authentication and authorization in the web tier to the JBoss security service

Using an embedded web container with JBoss provides numerous advantages over running an out-of-process web container with JBoss server:

❑ Optimized invocations for in-VM EJB calls

❑ Integration with the JBoss JNDI naming context

❑ Integration with the JBoss security framework

❑ Administration by the JBoss JMX console

❑ Support for distributed sessions when running JBoss in a cluster

❑ Sharing classes across web and EJB modules using EAR deployment

To achieve the aforementioned purposes and to provide seamless integration with the JBoss core server, JBoss provides an abstract plug-in that the web container MBean services should extend. This plug-in is represented by the `org.jboss.web.AbstractWebContainer` class. The JBoss 3.0 default installation bundle comes with the `org.jboss.jetty.JettyService` class for embedding Jetty.

11.1 AbstractWebContainer

The `AbstractWebContainer` class provides consolidated JNDI and security contexts for the web applications that are deployed. Web containers embedded in JBoss are required to provide an MBean service that extends this class. This class uses the JBoss-specific web deployment descriptor, `jboss-web.xml`, for mapping the following properties defined within the standard deployment descriptor:

❑ Environment entries

❑ Resource references for datasources, JMS connection factories, URL factories, mail sessions, etc.

❑ Resource environment references for JMS destinations

❑ EJB references

❑ EJB local references

❑ Security constraints

The subclasses of the `AbstractWebContainer` class, provided by the web containers, are expected to perform the following tasks:

❑ Handle the deploying and un-deploying of web applications

❑ Use the JBoss authentication manager and realm mapping classes to integrate with the JBossSX security framework

The `AbstractWebContainer` instance will parse the standard and JBoss-specific web deployment descriptors to create the necessary deployment information that is passed to the concrete subclass to perform the deployment of the web application. During this process, it will create lists of environment entries, resource references, resource environment references, and EJB local and remote references. These can be accessed by the concrete subclasses for creating the `java:comp/env` naming context for the web applications that are deployed.

This class also provides methods for linking environment entries, resource references, resource environment references, and EJB local and remote references in the `java:comp/env` context to the JBoss JNDI naming context, and the security constraints to the JBoss security domain.

*In Section 16.1: The JBoss Web Deployment Descriptor, we will have a
closer look at the JBoss-specific web deployment descriptor. The main
purposes of the JBoss-specific web deployment descriptor include defining
the security domain for authentication and authorization, mapping the
java:comp/env naming context to the JBoss JNDI naming context, and
defining context paths and virtual hosts.*

11.2 Configuring Jetty

In this section, we will have a closer look at the various attributes that you can
configure for the JBoss Jetty embedded web container services.

Jetty is a Java web server and container compliant with the Servlet 2.3 and JSP 1.2
specifications. However, when you run Jetty as an embedded web container with
JBoss, the only way you can serve static or dynamic web pages is to make them part of
a J2EE web application and deploy the web application. More information about the
Jetty web container is available at http://jetty.mortbay.com. When you install the standard
JBoss 3.x bundle, it comes configured with an embedded Jetty service. The
org.jboss.jetty.JettyService Jetty web container service extends the
AbstractWebContainer class.

The Jetty service comes as a JBoss SAR component with the standard distribution. The
SAR component is available in exploded format in the \jbossweb.sar directory in the
\deploy directory under the default configuration set. The SAR deployment
descriptor, jboss-service.xml, which contains the MBean definition and the various
configurable attributes for the MBean, is available in the \META-INF directory.

*We will be covering the embedded Jetty configuration to enable distributed
sessions in detail in Section 13.3.6.2: Configuring Jetty for HTTP
Session Clustering.*

The definition of the Jetty service MBean is:

```
<mbean
    code="org.jboss.jetty.JettyService"
    name="jboss.web:service=JBossWeb">
```

11.2.1 Unpacking WAR Files

Jetty normally unpacks WAR files for deploying. This is mostly necessary for compiling
JSP files. You can turn off this default behavior by setting the UnpackWars attribute in
the jboss-service.xml file for the Jetty service MBean:

```
<mbean
    code="org.jboss.jetty.JettyService"
    name="jboss.web:service=JBossWeb">
```

```
   ...
   <attribute name="UnpackWars">true</attribute>
   ...
</mbean>
```

11.2.2 Java 2 Classloading Behavior

Jetty normally uses the parent classloader to load classes before resorting to the WAR classloader. This is the standard Java 2 classloading behavior. However, the Servlet 2.3 specification requires the WAR classloader to first try loading the classes by looking into the\WEB-INF\classes and \WEB-INF\lib directories. To enable Servlet 2.3 classloading, you need to set the Java2ClassLoadingCompliance attribute in the jboss-service.xml file for the Jetty service MBean:

```
<mbean
   code="org.jboss.jetty.JettyService"
   name="jboss.web:service=JBossWeb">
   ...
   <attribute name="Java2ClassLoadingCompliance">true</attribute>
   ...
</mbean>
```

The default value is true.

11.2.3 Custom Jetty Service Configuration

You can provide custom configuration to the embedded Jetty service using the ConfigurationElement attribute for the Jetty service MBean. This MBean attribute accepts an XML element as its content. This element can be used to configure a variety of services for the embedded Jetty web container. The diagram shown below depicts the structure of the XML fragment passed to the ConfigurationElement MBean attribute for the Jetty service MBean:

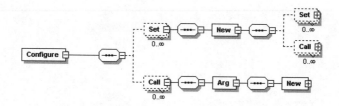

The Configure element may contain zero or more Call and/or Set elements. The Call element will call the method specified by the name attribute on the instance of the class specified by the class attribute of the Configure element. You can specify the arguments for the method using nested Arg elements to the Call element. The Arg elements can use the New element to create a new object that is passed as the argument. For argument types of primitives and strings, you can use the content of the Arg element. Call elements can be nested under New elements to call methods on newly created objects.

The Set element will call the JavaBean style mutator for the property specified by the name attribute on the instance of the class specified by the class attribute of the Configure element. You can specify the argument for the mutator using a nested New element to the Set element or specifying it as the text content of the Set element. Set elements can be nested within Arg, New, and other Set elements. When a Set element is nested, it will try to set the property on the instance of the class specified the class attribute of its immediate parent element.

The snippet below shows an example of Jetty service custom configuration using the ConfigurationElement MBean attribute:

```
<attribute name="ConfigurationElement">

  <Configure class="org.mortbay.jetty.Server">
    <Call name="addListener">
      <Arg>
        <New class="org.mortbay.http.SocketListener">
          <Set name="Port">8080</Set>
          <Set name="MinThreads">5</Set>
          <Set name="MaxThreads">255</Set>
          <Set name="MaxIdleTimeMs">30000</Set>
          <Set name="MaxReadTimeMs">10000</Set>
          <Set name="MaxStopTimeMs">5000</Set>
          <Set name="LowResourcePersistTimeMs">5000</Set>
        </New>
      </Arg>
    </Call>

    <Set name="DistributableHttpSessionStoreClass">
      org.jboss.jetty.session.ClusterStore
    </Set>

    <Set name="DistributableHttpSessionInterceptorClasses">
      <New class="java.util.ArrayList">
        <Call name="add">
          <Arg>org.mortbay.j2ee.session.TypeCheckingInterceptor</Arg>
        </Call>
        <Call name="add">
          <Arg>org.mortbay.j2ee.session.BindingInterceptor</Arg>
        </Call>
        <Call name="add">
          <Arg>org.mortbay.j2ee.session.MarshallingInterceptor</Arg>
        </Call>
      </New>
    </Set>

  </Configure>

</attribute>
```

> **If your configuration gets too complex, it is recommended to use jetty-web.xml, which has the same content model as the element structure for the Configure element, rather than specifying all the configuration information in the SAR deployment descriptor.**

Let's now look at the various properties that can be controlled using this extended configuration functionality.

11.2.3.1 HTTP Listener

Jetty uses the HTTP listener for accepting connections on the HTTP listen port. Jetty uses the XML element shown below to configure the HTTP listener:

```
<attribute name="ConfigurationElement">
  <Configure class="org.mortbay.jetty.Server">

    <Call name="addListener">
      <Arg>
        <New class="org.mortbay.http.SocketListener">
          <Set name="Port">
            <SystemProperty name="jetty.port" default="8080"/>
          </Set>
          <Set name="MinThreads">5</Set>
          <Set name="MaxThreads">255</Set>
          <Set name="MaxIdleTimeMs">30000</Set>
          <Set name="MaxReadTimeMs">10000</Set>
          <Set name="MaxStopTimeMs">5000</Set>
          <Set name="LowResourcePersistTimeMs">5000</Set>
        </New>
      </Arg>
    </Call>
    ...
  </Configure>
</attribute>
```

The configuration element shown above allows you to define the following properties:

Property	Description
HTTP Port	The default port on which Jetty listens for HTTP requests is 8080. This means that when accessing Jetty from the web browser, you need to specify the port address. You can change this to the default HTTP port number 80 if you don't want your clients to explicitly have to specify the port number.
	On a UNIX system, however, the user running the process must have root privileges to listen on any port number less than 1024. This can also be specified as the system property jetty.port.
MinThreads	Specifies the minimum number of concurrent threads that are used for serving the requests. The default value is 5.
MaxThreads	Specifies the maximum number of threads that are used for serving the requests. The default value is 255.

Property	Description
MaxIdleTimeMS	Specifies the maximum time, in milliseconds, that a thread can remain idle before expiring. The default value is 30000 (30 seconds).
MaxReadTimeMS	Specifies the maximum amount of time a thread can remain idle, in milliseconds, on serving a request. The default value is 10000 (10 seconds).
MaxStopTimeMS	Specifies the maximum time a thread is allowed to run, in milliseconds, before the Jetty service thread pool stops it. The default value is 5000 (5 seconds).
LowResourcePersist TimeMS	Specifies the time in milliseconds that idle threads are allowed to run when low on resources. The default value is 5000 (5 seconds).
ConfidentialPort	Specifies the port to which requests are redirected when a requested resource is configured in the web deployment descriptor to use confidential transport.
ConfidentialScheme	The protocol used for confidential transport. The default protocol is SSL.
IntegralPort	Specifies the port to which requests are redirected when a requested resource is configured in the web deployment descriptor to use integral transport.
IntegralScheme	The protocol used for integral transport. The default protocol is SSL.
DefaultScheme	The protocol used for default transport. The default protocol is HTTP.

If you change the listen port to 80, you will be able to access the Jetty web server without specifying a port number in the URL as shown below:

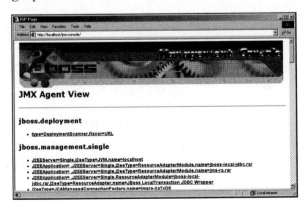

11.2.3.2 HTTP Request Logs

The Jetty web cvontainer service normally writes the HTTP request log to the \log directory of the configuration set that is used. The log files are rolled daily and are stored in the format yyyy_mm_dd.request.log. You can configure the request logs using the following configuration element:

```
<attribute name="ConfigurationElement">
  <Configure class="org.mortbay.jetty.Server">
    ...
    <Set name="RequestLog">
      <New class="org.mortbay.http.NCSARequestLog">
        <Arg>
          <SystemProperty name="jboss.server.home.dir"/>
          <SystemProperty name="jetty.log" default="/log"/>
          /yyyy_mm_dd.request.log
        </Arg>
        <Set name="retainDays">90</Set>
        <Set name="append">true</Set>
        <Set name="extended">true</Set>
        <Set name="LogTimeZone">GMT</Set>
      </New>
    </Set>
    ...
  </Configure>
</attribute>
```

You can change the name and location of the request log by changing the arguments that are passed to the NCSARequestLog class as highlighted below:

```
<attribute name="ConfigurationElement">
  <Configure class="org.mortbay.jetty.Server">
    ...
    <Set name="RequestLog">
      <New class="org.mortbay.http.NCSARequestLog">
        <Arg>
          <SystemProperty name="jboss.server.home.dir"/>
          <SystemProperty name="jetty.log" default="/log"/>
          /yyyy_mm_dd.request.log
        </Arg>
        ...
      </New>
    </Set>
    ...
  </Configure>
</attribute>
```

You can also set the following properties:

❑ retainDays
   The number of days the log file should be retained. The default value is 31.

❑ append
   If set to true, the log messages are appended to the existing file.
   Otherwise, new log files are created. The default value is true.

❑ extended
Stores the log messages in extended format. The default value for is this is true. In the extended mode, the logger writes the HTTP header information as well.

❑ LogTimeZone
This is used to define the time zone to use. If not specified, this will use the default time zone on the server.

11.2.3.3 Enabling SSL on Jetty

You can configure Jetty to use HTTPS instead of HTTP to enable secure transport.

To enable HTTPS, first you need to uncomment the following configuration element in the jboss-service.xml Jetty SAR deployment descriptor:

```
<Call name="addListener">
  <Arg>
    <New class="org.mortbay.http.SunJsseListener">
      <Set name="Port">443</Set>
      <Set name="MinThreads">5</Set>
      <Set name="MaxThreads">255</Set>
      <Set name="MaxIdleTimeMs">30000</Set>
      <Set name="MaxReadTimeMs">10000</Set>
      <Set name="MaxStopTimeMs">5000</Set>
      <Set name="LowResourcePersistTimeMs">2000</Set>
      <Set name="Keystore">
        <SystemProperty name="jetty.home" default="."/>
        /ssl/ssl.keystore
      </Set>
      <Set name="Password">password</Set>
      <Set name="KeyPassword">password</Set>
    </New>
  </Arg>
</Call>
```

In addition to the attributes supported by the standard HTTP listener, the SSL listener requires the following extra attributes:

Attribute	Function
Keystore	Defines the location of the keystore that contains the key pair to use. In the example above, it defaults to the ssl.keystore file in the \ssl directory under the current directory. The keystore location can also be set relative to the directory specified by the system property jetty.home.
Password	Defines the keystore password.
KeyPassword	Defines the key password. The keystore is protected by a password and each private key within the keystore is protected further by passwords.

Table continued on following page

159

Attribute	Function
Port	Defines the port on which the SSL listener listens. The default SSL port is 443. If you specify any other value, the clients will have to explicitly specify the port number in the browser.

Again, on UNIX systems, you need root privileges to listen to a port number less than 1024. |

In keystores, key pairs are keyed against unique alias names. Each keystore has a default key. Jetty uses the default key of the specified keystore. Next thing you need to do, is install **Java Secure Socket Extension (JSSE)**. If you are using JDK 1.4, you don't need to do this as JSSE bundles with JDK. If you are using an earlier version, refer to *Section 7.5: Enabling SSL* for instructions.

Now we need to generate the key pair. Again refer to *Section 7.5: Enabling SSL* for instructions.

Start JBoss and access the JMX console using the URL https://localhost/jmx-console. You will get the following warning window saying the certificate is not trusted. This is because your certificate is self-signed and not signed by a root CA:

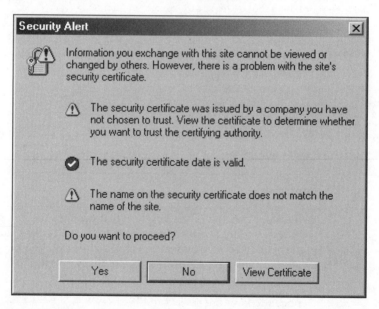

If you click Yes, the browser will display the JMX console. Please note that the protocol used is HTTPS and not HTTP:

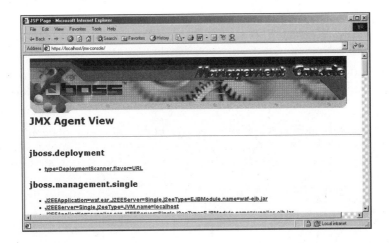

11.2.4 Running Jetty with Other Web Servers

In this section, we will have a look at how to configure Jetty with other web servers. We will cover Apache and Microsoft's Internet Information Server (IIS). Jetty provides a listener that implements the Jakarta **Apache JServ Protocol (AJP)** for integrating with both Apache and IIS.

> **The AJP v1.3 module implementation from Jakarta and the Apache Web Server version compatibility is currently in total chaos to say the least. You will find different versions of mod_jk and their compatibility with Apache varies with the different versions of Apache. The version of the DLLs used in this example will be made available from the Wrox web site and we will specify the exact build version of the Apache web server we use.**

Using the AJP protocol to connect to external web servers normally involve the following steps:

1. Register the web server plug-in. This plug-in will handle the communication from the web server to the web container. The plug-ins required for IIS and Apache can be downloaded from http://jakarta.apache.org/builds/jakarta-tomcat-connectors/:

   ❑ For IIS, you can download the ISAPI filter called `isapi_redirector2.dll`.

   ❑ For Apache, you need to download the platform-specific `mod_jk` module that is available on the Jakarta connector web site. There are two versions; `mod_jk`, and `mod_jk2`. It is safer to go for `mod_jk`, as `mod_jk2` is relatively new and hence not as stable as `mod_jk`.

2. Configure the web server with information required for connecting to the web container. This information is normally specified in a configuration file available to the web server.

3. Configure the web server to provide information regarding the URI patterns that should be handled by the web container. This information is also normally specified in a configuration file available to the web server.

To enable the AJP listener on Jetty, you need to add the following configuration element in your SAR deployment descriptor, `%JBOSS_HOME%\server\<config set>\deploy\jbossweb.sar\META-INF\jboss-service.xml`, as shown below:

```
<attribute name="ConfigurationElement">
  <Configure class="org.mortbay.jetty.Server">
    <Call name="addListener">
      <Arg>
        <New class="org.mortbay.http.ajp.AJP13Listener">
          <Set name="port">8009</Set>
        </New>
      </Arg>
    </Call>
    ...
  </Configure>
</attribute>
```

The AJP listener supports the following attributes:

Attribute	Function
bufferSize	Size of the AJP data buffers (default 8192).
ConfidentialPort	The port to redirect to in case a servlet security constraint of CONFIDENTIAL is not met. The default value of 0 means forbidden response.
ConfidentialScheme	The scheme to use for confidential redirections. The default is https.
host	The host or IP interface to listen on. The default value of 0.0.0.0 means no interfaces.
identifyListener	Set the listener name as a request attribute. The default is false.
lingerTimeSecs	The socket linger time for closing sockets in seconds. The default is 30 seconds.
maxIdleTimeMs	Milliseconds that a thread can be idle before the thread pool shrinks. The default value is 10000.

Attribute	Function
maxReadTimeMs	Milliseconds that a read will block on a connection. The default value of 0 means connections don't timeout.
maxStopTimeMs	Milliseconds to wait before gently shutting down listener. The default value of −1 means the thread pool stops the thread without giving any time to the thread.
MaxThreads	Maximum threads in thread pool for listener. The default value is 256.
MinThreads	Minimum threads in thread pool for listener. The default value is 2.
name	Name of the listener.
port	Port to listen on. The default is 8009.
threadClass	The class to be used for threads in the thread pool.

11.2.4.1 Configuring Apache

To configure Apache to use the AJP protocol to connect to the AJP listener, you need to perform the following steps. Please refer to *Professional Apache 2 (1-86100-722-1)* from Wrox Press for an in-depth coverage of Apache configuration. We will be using Apache 2 in this example:

1. Download the latest version of the Apache web server from http://www.apache.org for your platform. The version we have used is 2.0.43.

2. Download the Apache AJP module from the Jakarta web site and copy it to the \modules directory of your Apache installation. Please note that even though these pages are available under Tomcat on the Jakarta web site, you can use the AJP module for integrating any web container with Apache using AJP.

3. Create the configuration files required for Apache for connecting to Jetty. Store the contents shown below towards the end of the httpd.conf file in Apache \conf directory:

```
LoadModule jk_module modules/mod_jk.dll
JKWorkersFile "%JBOSS_HOME%/server/default/conf/workers.properties"
JKLogFile "%JBOSS_HOME%/server/default/log/jk.log"
JKLogLevel warn
JKMount /jmx-console/* ajp13
```

The above file defines the location of the workers file that contains host and port of the AJP worker thread, and asks Apache to delegate all requests with the URI pattern /jmx-console/* to the AJP worker thread. It also specifies the log file and log level for log messages produced by mod_jk. %JBOSS_HOME% should expand to the directory where you have installed the JBoss-Jetty bundle.

4. Now, you need to store the contents shown below to a file called workers.properties in the \conf directory of your JBoss default configuration set. This file specifies the details about the AJP worker process, such as host, port number, etc. You can also specify a variety of other properties to enable load balancing, use multiple versions of AJP, etc.:

```
ps=\
worker.list=ajp13
worker.ajp13.port=8009
worker.ajp13.host=localhost
worker.ajp13.type=ajp13
```

5. Make sure that Apache, and not a JBoss process, is listening on port 80. Start JBoss and then start Apache. You should now be able to access the JMX console from the browser without explicitly specifying the port number.

11.2.4.2 Configuring IIS

Configuring Jetty to run with IIS is the same as that for Apache on the Jetty side. The only thing we need to do is set up the AJP listener. Even though the configuration we need on the IIS side serves the same purpose as that for Apache, the actual task of configuration is significantly different. Please make sure that you have IIS installed and running before you proceed with the configuration. The steps involved in configuring IIS (we've used version 5) are explained below:

1. Create the configuration file used by the IIS web server plug-in to communicate with the AJP listener. This can be the same workers.properties file used for Apache.

2. Create a configuration file called uriworkermap.properties that defines the URI patterns that will be handled by the AJP listener. The contents of this file are shown below:

```
/jmx-console/*=ajp13
```

3. Store both the aforementioned files under the conf directory of your default configuration set within JBoss.

4. Create the following registry entries so that the IIS web server plug-in can locate the worker properties and URI mapping files. The best way to do it is to store the contents shown below, in a file with .reg extension, and double-click on it from Windows explorer:

```
REGEDIT4
[HKEY_LOCAL_MACHINE\SOFTWARE\Apache Software Foundation\Jakarta Isapi
Redirector\1.0]
"extension_uri"="/jakarta/isapi_redirect.dll"
"log_file"="%JBOSS_HOME%\\server\\default\\log\\iis_redirect.log"
"log_level"="info"
"worker_file"="%JBOSS_HOME%\\server\\default\\conf\\
                workers.properties"
"worker_mount_file"="%JBOSS_HOME%\\server\\default\\conf\\
                uriworkermap.properties"
```

Replace %JBOSS_HOME% in the above snippet with the JBoss installation directory. The registry entries will also point to the log file to which the messages are to be written along with the log level.

5. Install the ISAPI filter that handles communication between IIS and the AJP listener. For Apache, we used the Apache mod_jk module. We will use the ISAPI filter isapi_redirect.dll available from the Jakarta web site for IIS. Copy this file to the \bin directory of your JBoss installation. Run Control Panel | Administrative Tools | Internet Services Manager on your computer:

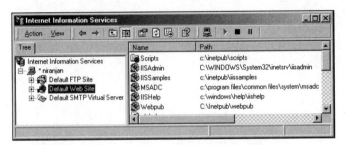

6. Right-click on the Default Web Site and click on Properties from the pop-up menu. In the Properties window, switch to the ISAPI Filters tab and click on the Add button. In the pop-up window, enter the filter name as jakarta, and for the filter path, select the ISAPI redirector DLL stored in the JBoss \bin directory:

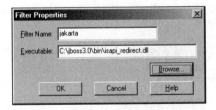

7. Restart IIS by right-clicking on the Default Web Site and selecting Stop and then Start. Now, if you go back to the Properties window and the ISAP Filters tab, you should see that the newly added filter has been loaded. The green arrow seen against it, as depicted in the picture below, indicates this:

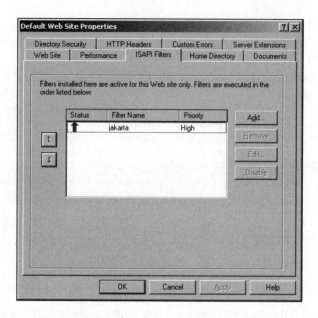

Now we need to create a virtual directory in the default web site by the name
jakarta. For this, right-click on the Default Web Site and select on New | Virtual Directory
from the pop-up menu. In the wizard for creating the virtual directory, enter the name
as jakarta. In the next window, select the path as the path to the JBoss \bin
directory that contains the ISAPI redirector DLL. In the next window, assign all
permissions apart from Write:

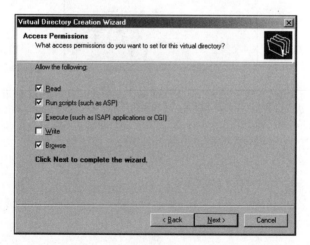

8. Complete the wizard and stop IIS. Start JBoss, making sure that none of the JBoss
    threads are listening on port 80, and then start IIS. You should now be able to
    access the JMX console from your browser without specifying the port number.

JBoss 3.0

Administration and Deployment

Handbook

12

12.1 Configuring Tomcat

12

Configuring Tomcat

In the last chapter, we had a look at configuring the embedded Jetty web container with JBoss to deploy and run J2EE web applications. JBoss also comes with an embedded Tomcat web container. In this chapter, we will look at configuring Tomcat with JBoss. We will also look at how to run the JBoss-Tomcat combination with IIS and Apache front-end web servers.

12.1 Configuring Tomcat

To run JBoss with Tomcat, you need to download the Jboss-3.*-Tomcat-4.* bundle from the JBoss or Sourceforge web site. The Tomcat bundle provides org.jboss.web.catalina.EmbeddedCatalinaServiceSX implementation of the AbstractWebContainer class. Refer to *Section 11.1: AbstractWebContainer* for more details on the AbstractWebContainer class. The installation will contain a Tomcat-4.1.x directory, which will contain all the required Tomcat libraries. The Tomcat embedded web container is made available as an MBean service. The MBean service descriptor is called tomcat4-service.xml, and is available in the \deploy directory of the default server configuration set. The MBean used for enabling embedded catalina service is shown below:

```
<mbean
  code="org.jboss.web.catalina.EmbeddedCatalinaServiceSX"
  name="jboss.web:service=EmbeddedCatalinaSX">
  ...
</mbean>
```

> *The embedded catalina configuration to enable distributed sessions will be covered in detail in Section 13.3.6.1: Configuring Tomcat for HTTP Clustering.*

Now, we look at the main attributes that can be configured for the embedded catalina service.

12.1.1 Deleting Work Directories

Tomcat normally does not delete work directories when the web applications are un-deployed. This can cause JSP compilation problems in some cases during re-deployment. You can use the `DeleteWorkDirs` attribute of the embedded catalina service MBean to get Tomcat to delete the work directories during un-deployment:

```
<mbean
   code="org.jboss.web.catalina.EmbeddedCatalinaServiceSX"
   name="jboss.web:service=EmbeddedCatalinaSX">
   <attribute name="DeleteWorkDirs">false</attribute>
   ...
</mbean>
```

12.1.2 Java 2 Classloading Behavior

Tomcat normally uses the parent classloader to load classes before resorting to the WAR classloader. This is the standard Java 2 classloading behavior. However, the Servlet 2.3 specification requires WAR classloader to first try loading the classes by looking into the `\WEB-INF\classes` and `\WEB-INF\lib` directories. To enable Servlet 2.3 classloading, you need to set the `Java2ClassLoadingCompliance` attribute to `true` for the embedded catalina service MBean:

```
<mbean
   code="org.jboss.web.catalina.EmbeddedCatalinaServiceSX"
   name="jboss.web:service=EmbeddedCatalinaSX">
   <attribute name="Java2ClassLoadingCompliance">true</attribute>
   ...
</mbean>
```

12.1.3 Custom Catalina Service Configuration

You can provide custom configuration to the embedded catalina service in the same manner as for the Jetty configuration. This is achieved by using the `Config` attribute for the embedded catalina service MBean. This MBean attribute accepts an XML fragment as its content. The content model of this element is the same as the standard Tomcat server configuration file (`server.xml`) structure.

The snippet below shows how this element is used:

```
<attribute name="Config">
   <Server>
     <Service>
        ...
     </Service>
   </Server>
</attribute>
```

The structure of the content model is shown below:

The Server element is the root element, and contains the following elements:

❑ The Service element represents the embedded catalina service

❑ The Connector element represents the various transport protocols supported by embedded catalina service, such as HTTP, SSL, AJP, etc.

❑ The Engine element handles the requests from the configured connector

❑ The Host element represents a virtual host configuration

❑ The Alias element is used to specify an alternative DNS name to the host

❑ The DefaultContext element is used to define a template web application context

❑ The Manager element is used to define session managers

❑ The Logger element is used to specify logging configuration

❑ The Valve element is used to specify additional components similar to JBoss interceptors for processing the request

❑ The Listener element is used to configure component lifecycle events

The structure explained above reflects the structure of the server.xml file used within Tomcat when it runs standalone. You will find the server.xml file in the \conf directory under Tomcat-4.1.x directory under the installation with JBoss-Tomcat bundle. However, the changes made to server.xml won't be reflected in embedded Tomcat service. Instead, you should change the tomcat41-service.xml file in the \deploy directory of the default configuration set.

Please refer to Professional Apache Tomcat (1-86100-773-6) *from Wrox Press for an in-depth coverage of the custom configuration elements.*

Here's the configuration for Tomcat that comes with the default configuration set:

```
<Server>
  <Service name = "JBoss-Tomcat">
    <Engine name="MainEngine" defaultHost="localhost">
      <Logger className = "org.jboss.web.catalina.Log4jLogger"
              verbosityLevel = "trace"
              category = "org.jboss.web.localhost.Engine"/>
      <Host name="localhost">
        <Valve className = "org.apache.catalina.valves.
                           AccessLogValve"
               prefix = "localhost_access" suffix = ".log"
               pattern = "common" directory = "../server/default/log"
        />
        <DefaultContext cookies = "true" crossContext = "true"
                        override = "true" />
      </Host>
    </Engine>

    <!-- A HTTP Connector on port 8080 -->
    <Connector className = "org.apache.catalina.connector.http.
                          HttpConnector"
               port = "8080" minProcessors = "3" maxProcessors = "10"
               enableLookups = "true" acceptCount = "10" debug = "0"
               connectionTimeout = "60000"/>
  </Service>

</Server>
```

Now we will look at how to use this extended configuration functionality to configure the various aspects of embedded catalina web container.

12.1.3.1 HTTP Listener

Tomcat uses the following connector for accepting HTTP connections:

```
<Connector
  className="org.apache.catalina.connector.http.HttpConnector"
  port="8080"
  minProcessors="3"
  maxProcessors="10"
  enableLookups="true"
  acceptCount="10"
  debug="0"
  connectionTimeout="60000"/>
```

These are some of the main attributes supported by the HTTP connector:

Attribute	Function
className	Java class name of the implementation to be used. This class must implement the org.apache.catalina.Connector interface.

Attribute	Function
enableLookups	Set to true if you want calls to request.getRemoteHost() to perform DNS lookups to return the actual host name of the remote client. Set to false to skip the DNS lookup and return the IP address in string form instead (thereby improving performance). By default, DNS lookups are enabled.
port	The TCP port number on which the HTTP connector will create a server socket and await incoming connections. Your operating system will allow only one server application to listen to a particular port number on a particular IP address.
address	For servers with more than one IP address, this attribute specifies which address will be used for listening on the specified port. By default, this port will be used on all IP addresses associated with the server.
minProcessors	The number of request processing threads that will be created when this connector is first started. This attribute should be set to a value smaller than that set for maxProcessors. The default value is 5.
maxProcessors	This is used to specify the maximum number of request-processing threads to be created by this connector. The value defined by default is 75.
acceptCount	The maximum queue length for incoming connection requests when all possible request-processing threads are in use. Any requests received when the queue is full will be refused. The default value is 10.
debug	The debugging detail level of log messages generated by this component, with higher numbers creating more detailed output. If not specified, this attribute is set to 0 (zero).
connectionTimeout	This property specifies the time in seconds the server will wait before disconnecting an inactive connection. The default value is 300 seconds.
scheme	Set this attribute to the name of the protocol you wish to have returned by calls to request.getScheme(). For example, you would set this attribute to https for an SSL Connector. The default value is http.
secure	Set this attribute to true if you wish to have calls to request.isSecure() to return true for requests received by this connector (you would want this on an SSL connector). The default value is false.

12.1.3.2 Enabling SSL

You can configure the embedded Tomcat service to use HTTPS instead of HTTP. To do this you need to perform the three main steps:

1. Install JSSE if not using JDK 1.4.

2. Create the keystore that contains the key pair.

3. Configure the JAAS security domain. As we have seen in *Section 7.3.6: JAAS Security Domain*, JAAS security domain extends JAAS security manager to provide cryptographic functionalities.

4. Set the SSL connection factory for embedded catalina service connector to use the keystore.

The first two steps are covered in *Section 7.5: Enabling SSL*.

12.1.3.2.1 Configure the JAAS Security Domain

Next you need to configure the JAAS security domain MBean. You can either do this in `jboss-service.xml` file in the `\conf` directory of your configuration set, or in the `tomcat41-service.xml` file in the `\deploy` directory of the `default` configuration set, that contains the embedded catalina service MBean. Use the snippet below to define the JAAS security domain MBean:

```
<mbean
    code="org.jboss.security.plugins.JaasSecurityDomain"
    name="jboss.security:service=JaasSecurityDomain,domain=RMI+SSL">
    <constructor>
      <arg type="java.lang.String" value="RMI+SSL"/>
    </constructor>
    <attribute name="KeyStoreURL">ssl/ssl.keystore</attribute>
    <attribute name="KeyStorePass">password</attribute>
</mbean>
```

The MBean listed above uses the keystore `ssl.keystore` in the `ssl` directory under the `bin` directory of JBoss and defines the keystore password as `password`.

12.1.3.2.2 Set the SSL Connection Factory

Next, you need to configure the SSL connection factory for the Tomcat HTTP connector. The embedded catalina service MBean uses the custom XML configuration `Connector` element for setting up protocol-specific listeners. This element can take an embedded `Factory` element to specify the factory class for creating the sockets. To use SSL, you can specify the SSL connection factory provided by JBoss. This factory expects the JNDI name of the JAAS security domain that it uses to obtain the keystore information. An example is shown below:

```
<Connector
    className="org.apache.catalina.connector.http.HttpConnector"
    port="443"
    scheme="https"
    secure="true">
```

```
<Factory
    className="org.jboss.web.catalina.security.SSLServerSocketFactory"
    securityDomainName="java:/jaas/RMI+SSL"
    clientAuth="false"
    protocol="TLS"/>
</Connector>
```

Start JBoss and access the JMX console using the URL https://localhost/jmx-console. You will get the following warning window saying the certificate is not trusted. This is because your certificate is self-signed and not signed by a root CA:

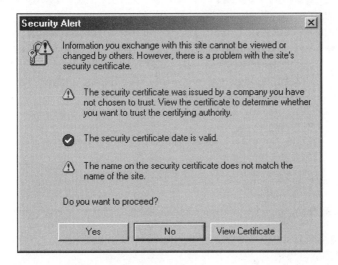

If you click Yes, the browser will display the JMX console. Please note that the protocol used is HTTPS and not HTTP:

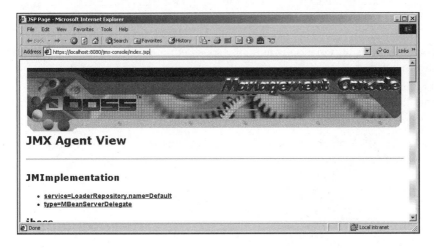

175

12.1.3.3 Running Tomcat with Other Web Servers

In this section, we will look at how to configure Tomcat with other web servers. We will cover Apache and Microsoft's Internet Information Server (IIS). Tomcat provides a listener that implements the Jakarta **Apache JServ Protocol (AJP)** for integrating with both Apache and IIS.

> **The AJP version 1.3 module implementation from Jakarta and the Apache Web Server version compatibility are currently in total chaos to say the least. You will find different versions of mod_jk, and their compatibility with Apache varies with the versions of Apache. The version of the DLLs used in this example will be made available from the Wrox website and we will specify the exact build version of the Apache web server we use.**

Using the AJP protocol to connect to external web servers normally involve the following steps:

1. Register a web server plug-in. This plug-in will handle the communication from the web server to the web container. The plug-ins required for IIS and Apache can be downloaded from http://jakarta.apache.org/builds/jakarta-tomcat-connectors/.

   ❑ For IIS, you can download the ISAPI filter called `isapi_redirector2.dll`.

   ❑ For Apache, you need to download the platform-specific `mod_jk` module available on the Jakarta connector website. There are two versions: `mod_jk`, and `mod_jk2`. It is safer to go for `mod_jk`, as `mod_jk2` is relatively new and hence not as stable as `mod_jk`.

2. Configure the web server with information required for connecting to the web container. This information is normally specified in a configuration file available to the web server.

3. Configure the web server to provide information regarding the URI patterns that should be handled by the web container. This information is also normally specified in a configuration file available to the web server.

To enable the AJP listener on Tomcat, you need to specify the following AJP connector in the custom configuration for the embedded Tomcat service MBean:

```
<Connector
  className="org.apache.ajp.tomcat4.Ajp13Connector"
  port="8009"
  minProcessors="5"
  maxProcessors="75"
  acceptCount="10"
  debug="0"
  tomcatAuthentication="true"/>
```

One of the important attributes that can be specified here is tomcatAuthentication. This flag indicates whether Tomcat or IIS/Apache will handle the authentication. If the attribute value is true, which is the default value, any principal authenticated by the native web server will be ignored, and Tomcat will take care of the authentication. If the attribute value is false, Tomcat will not attempt to authenticate a principal if the native web server has already authenticated one.

12.1.3.3.1 Configuring Apache

To configure Apache to use the AJP protocol to connect to the AJP listener, you need to perform the following steps (please refer to *Professional Apache 2 (ISBN: 1-86100-722-1)* from Wrox Press for an in-depth coverage of Apache configuration). We will be using Apache 2 in this example:

1. Download the latest version of the Apache web server from http://www.apache.org for your platform. The version we have used is 2.0.43.

2. Download the Apache AJP module from the Jakarta web site and copy it to the modules directory of your Apache installation. Please note that even though these pages are available under Tomcat on the Jakarta web site, you can use the AJP module for integrating any web container with Apache using AJP.

3. Create the configuration files required for Apache for connecting to Tomcat: store the contents shown below, towards the end of the httpd.conf file in Apache \conf directory:

```
LoadModule jk_module modules/mod_jk.dll
JKWorkersFile "%JBOSS_HOME%/server/default/conf/workers.properties"
JKLogFile "%JBOSS_HOME%/server/default/log/jk.log"
JKLogLevel warn
JKMount /jmx-console/* ajp13
```

The above file defines the location of the workers file that contains host and port of the AJP worker thread, and asks Apache to delegate all requests with the URI pattern /jmx-console/* to the AJP worker thread. It also specifies the log file and log level for log messages produced by mod_jk. %JBOSS_HOME% should expand to the directory where you have installed the JBoss-Tomcat bundle.

4. Now you need to store the contents shown below to a file called workers.properties in the \conf directory of your configuration set. This file specifies the details about the AJP worker process, such as host, port number, etc. You can also specify a variety of other properties to enable load balancing, use multiple versions of AJP, etc:

```
ps=\
worker.list=ajp13
worker.ajp13.port=8009
worker.ajp13.host=localhost
worker.ajp13.type=ajp13
```

5. Make sure that Apache, and not a JBoss process, is listening on port 80. Start JBoss and then start Apache. You should now be able to access the JMX console from the browser without explicitly specifying the port number.

12.1.3.3.12 Configuring IIS

Configuring Tomcat to run with IIS is similar to that for Apache. The only thing we need to do is setup the AJP listener. Even though the configuration we need on the IIS side serves the same purpose as that for Apache, the actual task of configuration is significantly different. Please make sure that you have IIS installed and running before you proceed with the configuration. The steps involved in configuring IIS (we've used version 5) are explained below:

1. Create the configuration file used by the IIS web server plug-in to communicate with the AJP listener. This can be the same `workers.properties` file used for Apache.

2. Create a configuration file called `uriworkermap.properties` that defines the URI patterns that will be handled by the AJP listener. The contents of this file are shown below:

```
/jmx-console/*=ajp13
```

3. Store both the aforementioned files under the `\conf` directory of your default configuration set within JBoss.

4. Create the following registry entries so that the IIS web server plug-in can locate the worker properties and URI mapping files. The best way to do it is to store the contents shown below, in a file with `.reg` extension, and double-click on it from Windows Explorer:

```
REGEDIT4
[HKEY_LOCAL_MACHINE\SOFTWARE\Apache Software Foundation\Jakarta Isapi
Redirector\1.0]
"extension_uri"="/jakarta/isapi_redirect.dll"
"log_file"="%JBOSS_HOME%\\server\\default\\log\\iis_redirect.log"
"log_level"="info"
"worker_file"="%JBOSS_HOME%\\server\\default\\conf\\
               workers.properties"
"worker_mount_file"="%JBOSS_HOME%\\server\\default\\conf\\
               uriworkermap.properties"
```

Replace %JBOSS_HOME% in the above snippet with the JBoss installation directory. The registry entries will also point to the log file to which the messages are to be written along with the log level.

5. Install the ISAPI filter that handles communication between IIS and the AJP listener. For Apache, we used the Apache `mod_jk` module. We will use the ISAPI filter `isapi_redirect.dll` available from the Jakarta website for IIS. Copy this file to the `\bin` directory of your JBoss installation. Run Control Panel | Administrative Tools | Internet Services Manager on your computer:

178

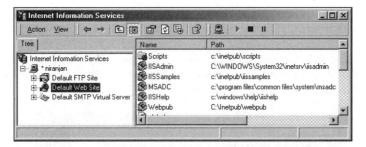

6. Right-click on the Default Web Site and click on Properties from the pop-up menu. In the Properties window, switch to the ISAPI Filters tab and click on the Add button. In the pop-up window, enter the filter name as `jakarta`, and for the filter path, select the ISAPI redirector DLL stored in the JBoss `\bin` directory:

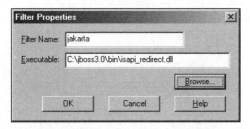

7. Restart IIS by right-clicking on the Default Web Site and selecting Stop and then Start. Now, if you go back to the Properties window and the ISAP Filters tab, you should see that the newly added filter has been loaded. The green arrow seen against it, as depicted in the picture below, indicates this:

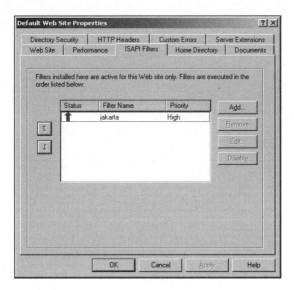

8. Now we need to create a virtual directory in the default web site by the name jakarta. For this, right-click on the **Default Web Site** and select on **New | Virtual Directory** from the pop-up menu. In the wizard for creating the virtual directory, enter the name as jakarta. In the next window, select the path as the path to the JBoss \bin directory that contains the ISAPI redirector DLL. In the next window, assign all permissions apart from **Write**:

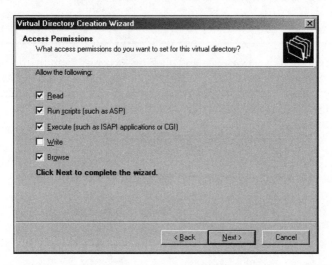

Complete the wizard and stop IIS. Start JBoss, making sure that none of the JBoss threads are listening on port 80, and then start IIS. You should now be able to access the JMX console from your browser without specifying the port number.

JBoss 3.0

Administration and Deployment

Handbook

13

13

Configuring Clusters

JBoss 3.0 provides clustering functionality to enhance the availability and scalability of your J2EE applications. In this chapter, we will cover the configuration of JBoss clusters in detail.

13.1 An Overview of Clustering

A cluster is a group of server instances that work as a single entity to achieve some common goals for the applications they host:

- ❑ High Availability
- ❑ Fault Tolerance
- ❑ Performance and Scalability
- ❑ Load Balancing

The server instances may run on separate physical machines or on the same machine. The diagram below depicts a typical cluster topology:

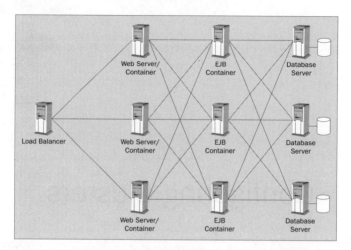

All the requests from the client normally come to a single point often called a load balancer or dispatcher. Normally, this load balancer will send the request to a web server/container node, based on some configured algorithm. The web container will use the clustering functionality provided by the EJB container to connect to an appropriate EJB container. The EJB containers may connect to cluster of replicated database servers.

13.1.1 Load Balancers

Load balancers can be implemented using a wide variety of techniques:

❑   DNS Round Robin

❑   Hardware Load Balancers

❑   Web Server Proxies

13.1.1.1 DNS Round Robin

In load balancing using a DNS round robin, the DNS server that resolves the domain names to IP addresses will have multiple IP addresses mapped to the same domain. As clients ask the DNS server for the IP address for a domain name, it will serve the first IP address in the queue. This IP address is then pushed to the back of the queue. This solution is very cost-effective.

However, even if one of the servers mapped in the domain lookup table goes down, the DNS server will forward the request to that server. This is because the DNS server doesn't know the status of the servers to which the domain name is mapped. This means that even though DNS round robin method provides load balancing, it doesn't guarantee availability, although there are some advanced DNS servers that can keep track of the status of the servers stored in the DNS lookup table.

Another significant handicap with DNS round robin is that it doesn't guarantee server affinity. In J2EE distributed web applications, it is required that once the load balancer pins down a server in the cluster for a user request, all the subsequent requests in that session should be sent to the same server. However, DNS round robin doesn't have any way of tracking cookies or URL rewriting to keep track of sessions.

13.1.1.2 Hardware Load Balancers

Hardware load balancers provide a more sophisticated approach for balancing the load. Hardware load balancers normally use virtual IP addresses that show a single IP address (which maps to multiple addresses in a cluster) to the outside world. An example of a hardware load balancer is Cisco CSS 11150 Content Services Switch.

When a request comes to a hardware load balancer, it amends the request header to point to one of the machines in the cluster. Hardware load balancers address many of the disadvantages associated with DNS round robin, by providing high availability, transparent fail-over, server affinity, etc. Most of the hardware load balancers provide a variety of matrix information including number of requests per second, active sessions, active sessions per server instance, etc.

However, hardware load balancers are quite expensive and relatively complex to set up. Another disadvantage is that the load balancer itself is a single point of failure.

13.1.1.3 Web Server Proxies

Web server proxies use a front-end web server to accept all the requests. This web server will perform tasks such as accepting HTTP requests, decrypting SSL requests, etc. Then, based on the nature of the request, the web server will pass it on to the appropriate web container for processing. A web server may be configured with multiple instances of web containers.

An example of this is an Apache or IIS instance connecting to multiple instances of Tomcat or Jetty, using the AJP protocol. Here, the mod_jk module or the AJP ISAPI filter will perform the task of balancing load. This is explained in detail in *Section 13.3.5: EJBs in a Cluster.*

13.2 Clustering Requirements

In this section, we look at the application behaviors that should be addressed by clustering from a J2EE perspective:

❏ **Transparent HTTP session fail-over**
Even if the web server/container to which the user is connected goes down, the next request from the client should be forwarded to another server in the cluster.

❏ **Replication of HTTP session data**
If the web server/container to which a client is connected goes down, it is not just required to forward the request to a new server in the cluster. It should also replicate the session data held by the old server to the new server.

❏ **Transparent fail-over for EJB home and remote objects**
If an EJB server that hosts the home or remote object owned by a client goes down, the cluster mechanism should forward the next invocation to another EJB container in the cluster.

❏ **State replication for stateful session beans**
If an EJB container that hosts a stateful session bean goes down, the state should be transferred to the new EJB container that will be servicing the invocations on the stateful session bean.

❏ **Cluster-side JMS destinations**
JMS destinations should be available cluster-wide as the failure of one server in the cluster wouldn't affect the JMS clients that send and receive messages.

❏ **Cluster-wide JNDI namespace**
JNDI is the heart of most of the J2EE applications. Clients will bind and/or look up objects such as EJB home objects, JMS connection factories, and destinations, mail sessions, datasources, etc. from the JNDI namespace. One important thing about JNDI in a clustered environment is that the location of the namespace to which an object is bound should be transparent to the client.

❏ **Cluster-wide hot deployment**
Application servers that support clustering, should provide a way of deploying applications cluster-wide. One solution is to share the code between all the nodes in the cluster. This means that the physical device that hosts the code is a single point of failure. Another alternative is to deploy the applications on all the nodes in the cluster.

13.3 JBoss Clustering

JBoss 3.0 clustering functionality provides the following features:

❏ The ability of nodes in a cluster to discover each other automatically

❏ High availability and load balancing for JNDI, entity beans and session beans

❏ State replication for stateful session beans

❏ HTTP session state replication with both Jetty and Tomcat

❏ Shared JNDI tree in the cluster

❑　Ability for clients to automatically discover JNDI servers

❑　Ability for cluster-wide hot deployment by deploying on one node in the cluster

❑　Customizable load balancing policies

❑　Ability to cluster custom objects using clustered RMI

13.3.1 Clustering Architecture

In JBoss, a **partition** identifies a group of server instances that work together as a cluster. Each server instance expresses its desire to participate in a partition by configuring an org.jboss.ha.framework.server.ClusterPartition MBean, which lets you specify a name for the partition in which the server should participate.

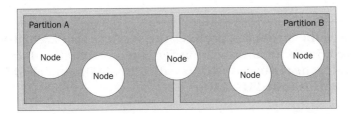

A server instance can be part of multiple partitions. Server instances in a partition can run on a single physical machine, multiple machines, or across subnets. However, when they run on the same machine, you need to make sure that they don't try to listen on conflicting port numbers for the various services such as HTTP, RMI, JNDI, or IIOP.

JBoss provides an abstract communication layer that can be used by the servers in a partition to discover each other. The structure of a cluster at any given time is termed as its **view**. The view of the cluster is updated each time a node enters or leaves the partition. You can plug in any communication framework to the JBoss abstract communication layer to allow the nodes in a partition to communicate with each other. JBoss currently uses the highly configurable **Javagroups Framework** (http://www.javagroups.com) for enabling communication between the nodes in a partition.

13.3.2 JBoss Proxies

JBoss uses a set of server instances as a partition to provide a clustered environment. However, there should be some scheme by which the client invocations are routed to an appropriate server instance in the partition, to provide transparent load balancing and fail-over. JBoss provides a solution that utilizes the most appropriate location to host this dispatcher logic. The dispatcher logic is implemented in the RMI stub proxies that are downloaded into the client process space during runtime.

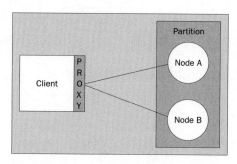

These proxies have enough information about all the nodes that participate in the partition. Hence, if an invocation to a particular node in the partition fails, the proxy can fall back to another node in the partition. In addition, each time that the client makes an invocation, JBoss updates the client proxies with the latest partition view.

> **In JBoss, the String HA- prefixes the services that are cluster-enabled. HA is an abbreviation for High Availability. For example, cluster-based JNDI is called HA-JNDI, and cluster-based RMI is called HA-RMI.**

13.3.3 Configuring Clusters

The `all` configuration set that comes with JBoss comes pre-configured to enable clustering. In addition to the required JAR files, one important file is `cluster-service.xml`, present in the `\deploy` directory. This file contains the core MBean definitions for enabling the cluster service. The most important among these is the `ClusterPartition` MBean. This MBean is used by a server instance to be part of a named partition or start one if it doesn't already exist. The MBean definition is:

```
<mbean
  code="org.jboss.ha.framework.server.ClusterPartition"
  name="jboss:service=MyPartition">
```

The MBean supports the following attributes:

Attribute	Function
PartitionName	An optional attribute used for specifying the name of the partition in which the node wishes to participate. As mentioned earlier, the node can be part of more than one partition. The default value of this attribute is `DefaultPartition`.

Attribute	Function
DeadlockDetection	An optional attribute used for setting a flag to run message deadlock detection. The default value is false.
PartitionProperties	An optional attribute used for specifying the properties required by the underlying communication framework. Currently, JBoss uses the Javagroups communication framework, which by default uses a UDP-based multicast protocol. However, Javagroups is highly configurable, and you can use other protocols if you wish.

The snippet below shows the default partition property that is used when the PartitionProperties attribute is not specified:

```
UDP(mcast_addr=228.1.2.3;mcast_port=45566;ip_ttl=64;mcast_send_buf
_size=150000;mcast_recv_buf_size=80000):
PING(timeout=2000;num_initial_members=3):
MERGE2(min_interval=5000;max_interval=10000):
FD:
VERIFY_SUSPECT(timeout=1500):
pbcast.STABLE(desired_avg_gossip=20000):
pbcast.NAKACK(gc_lag=50;retransmit_timeout=300,600,1200,2400,4800)
:
UNICAST(timeout=5000):
FRAG(down_thread=false;up_thread=false):
pbcast.GMS(join_timeout=5000;join_retry_timeout=2000;shun=false;pr
int_local_addr=true):
pbcast.STATE_TRANSFER
```

Please refer to documentation from http://www.javagroups.com for more information on partition properties.

An example of the MBean configuration is shown below:

```
<mbean
   code="org.jboss.ha.framework.server.ClusterPartition"
   name="jboss:service=MyPartition">
   <attribute name="PartitionName">MyPartition</attribute>
</mbean>
```

The MBean shown above starts a new partition called MyPartition if it is not already started, and makes the server in which the MBean is deployed a member of that partition.

189

13.3.4 Configuring HA-JNDI

In clustered configuration, JBoss supports a cluster-wide JNDI namespace (HA-JNDI) as well as local JNDI namespace for each server in the cluster. Clients can use either the local JNDI service or the HA-JNDI service to look up objects. If they use the local JNDI service, the object is looked for only in the local JNDI namespace. However, if the HA-JNDI service is used, JBoss first looks in the HA-JNDI namespace. If the object is not found, the HA-JNDI service delegates the lookup to the local JNDI service of the server to which the client is connected. If it still can't find the object, it will ask the local JNDI of all the nodes in the partition until it finds the looked-up object:

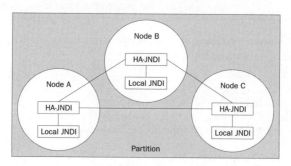

> **Please note that EJB home objects are always bound to the local JNDI context of the server on which the particular EJB is deployed.**

HA-JNDI is also normally configured in the `cluster-service.xml` file in the `\deploy` directory of every server participating in the partition using the HA-JNDI MBean explained below. The MBean definition is:

```
<mbean
  code="org.jboss.ha.jndi.HANamingService"
  name="jboss:service=HAJNDI">
```

The MBean supports the following attributes:

Attribute	Function
PartitionName	The name of the partition to which the HA-JNDI context is available. The default value is `DefaultPartition`.
BindAddress	The address to which the HA-JNDI server will bind, if you are using a machine that supports multiple IPs.

Attribute	Function
Port	The port on which the HA-JNDI server listens. The default value is 1100.
BackLog	Serves the same purpose as that for the local JNDI service MBean. Please refer to *Section 6.1: The JBoss Naming Service* for further details.
RmiPort	Serves the same purpose as that for the local JNDI service MBean. Please refer to *Section 6.1: The JBoss Naming* for further details.

The example below shows an example HA-JNDI MBean configuration:

```
<mbean
    code="org.jboss.ha.jndi.HANamingService"
    name="jboss:service=HAJNDI">
    <depends>jboss:service=MyPartition</depends>
    <attribute name="PartitionName">MyPartition</attribute>
    <attribute name="Port">2000</attribute>
</mbean>
```

The example above defines the HA JNDI service listening on port 2000 for the partition MyPartition.

> **Please note that it is always better to deploy your EJBs on all the nodes in the cluster, since it will speed up the lookup process through HA-JNDI.**

13.3.4.1 Configuring Clients for Automatic Discovery

In a non-clustered environment, clients normally use the Context.PROVIDER_URL property to specify the JNDI server to which they wish to connect. In JBoss, the default port is 1099, and the protocol is JNP. In a clustered environment, however, there are multiple servers and each server will be listening on two different ports: one for local JNDI, and the other for HA-JNDI. In this scenario, how will the client specify the provider URL?

One solution is for the client to specify the HA-JNDI port of one of the servers in the partition as shown below:

```
prop.put(Context.PROVIDER_URL, "jnp://poseidon:1100");

Context ctx = new InitialContext(prop);
```

Once the client gets the remote stub, the stub will have information regarding the partition view. Thus, even if the original server goes down, the client can connect to another server in the partition. However, if the server that the client is initially trying to connect to is down, the client won't be able to connect at all. To circumvent this problem, JBoss allows the clients to specify a comma-separated list of JNDI servers as shown below:

```
prop.put(Context.PROVIDER_URL,
    "jnp://poseidon:1100,jnp://pegasus:1100,jnp://hercules:1100");

Context ctx = new InitialContext(prop);
```

In the aforementioned scenario, the client will try establishing a connection with the servers in the list starting from the first one until it is successful or fails connecting to any of the servers in the list. However, this can at times be cumbersome if there are a lot of servers in the partition. Hence JBoss provides a third method where you don't specify any provider URL and if any of the servers in the list is reachable, the clients will try to connect to a HA-JNDI server through a multicast call on the address 230.0.0.4:1102.

13.3.5 EJBs in a Cluster

JBoss allows you to cluster both session (stateful and stateless) as well as entity EJBs. The behavior of EJBs in a cluster is configured using the <clustered> element of the JBoss-specific EJB deployment descriptor (jboss.xml). This is covered in detail in *Section 18.3.6: Clusters*.

However, to get clustered stateful session EJBs working, you need to configure one key MBean service. This is the HASessionState service, which is used for in-memory state replication of stateful session EJBs. This MBean is available in the cluster-service.xml file, and its definition is:

```
<mbean
    code="org.jboss.ha.hasessionstate.server.HASessionStateService"
    name="jboss:service=HASessionState">
```

The MBean supports the following attributes:

Attribute	Function
JndiName	An optional attribute to specify the JNDI name under which the service is bound. The default value is /HAPartition/Default.
PartitionName	To specify the name of the partition in which the session state service is used. The default value is DefaultPartition.

Attribute	Function
BeanCleaningDelay	To specify an optional time interval in which the session state service can clean up the state of a session bean that has not been modified. The default value is 30 minutes.

The snippet below shows an example of the session state MBean configuration:

```
<mbean
    code="org.jboss.ha.hasessionstate.server.HASessionStateService"
    name="jboss:service=HASessionState">
    <depends>jboss:service=MyPartition</depends>
    <JndiName>/HAPartition/MyService</JndiName>
    <PartitionName>MyPartition</PartitionName>
</mbean>
```

The example above defines the MBean definition for replicating stateful session beans deployed on servers participating in the cluster partition MyPartition.

13.3.5.1 Load Balancing Policy

JBoss provides two load balancing policies that you can configure your EJBs with:

❏ **Round robin**
   Always favors the next available target when an invocation is made.

❏ **First available**
   Always favors the first available target. This does not mean that fail-over will not occur if the first member in the list dies. In this case, fail-over will occur, and a new target will become the first member and invocation will continuously be invoked on the same new target until its death.

You specify your load balancing policy in the JBoss-specific EJB deployment descriptor, jboss.xml. EJB clustering is covered in detail in *Section 18.3.6: Clusters*. You can write your own load balancing policy by implementing the JBoss org.jboss.ha.framework.interfaces.LoadBalancePolicy interface.

13.3.6 HTTP Session Clustering

JBoss allows HTTP session replication for both the Tomcat and Jetty flavors. However, transparent session fail-over should be implemented at the load balancer level, which pins the JBoss server instance to a user session. This can be done using hardware load balancers or web server proxies. When using AJP, you can configure IIS or Apache in the workers properties file to work with multiple instances of JBoss-Tomcat/Jetty instances, and AJP will take care of load balancing. One thing you need to make sure is that whatever load balancing strategy you use, it should accommodate server affinity for user sessions.

At JBoss level, you need to have the clustering MBean, explained in *Section 13.3.3: Configuring Clusters*, and the `jbossha-httpsession.sar` SAR component deployed. This MBean provides support for clustered HTTP sessions.

13.3.6.1 Configuring Tomcat for HTTP Session Clustering

The embedded Tomcat service MBean, discussed in *Section 12.1: Configuring Tomcat* for configuring embedded Tomcat service defined in `tomcat4-service.xml`, provides two attributes for configuring clustered HTTP sessions:

Attribute	Function
SnapshotMode	To specify the mode for replicating session state across nodes in a partition. If set to `instant`, the state is replicated whenever it is changed. If the state is set to `interval`, it is replicated at regular intervals specified by the `SnapShotInterval` attribute.
SnapShotInterval	To specify the interval at which the state should be replicated when the snapshot mode is set to `interval`. The default value is 1000 milliseconds.

13.3.6.2 Configuring Jetty for HTTP Session Clustering

The embedded Jetty service MBean discussed in *Section 11.2: Configuring Jetty* provides powerful options for HTTP session replication. This MBean provides the following attributes to configure clustered sessions:

Attribute	Function
HttpSessionStorageStrategy	To specify the strategy for storing distributable sessions. This should specify a fully qualified class name that implements `org.mortbay.j2ee.session.Store`. JBoss provides two such classes: ❑ `org.mortbay.j2ee.session.CMPStore`: For Jetty-specific CMP-based session migration. ❑ `org.jboss.jetty.session.ClusterStore`: Will use the JBoss in-memory session replication. It is recommended to use the JBoss in-memory session replication.

Attribute	Function
HttpSessionSnapshot Frequency	To specify the interval at which session state is replicated. The possible values are never, idle, request, or the number of seconds.
HttpSessionSnapshot NotificationPolicy	To specify when to call the callback methods on session attributes that implement the session activation listener interface. The possible values are never, activate, passivate, or both.

13.3.6.3 Configuring AJP for HTTP Session Clustering

To achieve load balancing using AJP, you need multiple instances of JBoss-Tomcat/Jetty running. The AJP module on the Apache/IIS web server should be made aware of the multiple instances of the JBoss instances using the workers properties file (discussed in *Section 11.2.4: Running Jetty with Other Web Servers* and *Section 12.3.4: Running Tomcat with Other Web Servers*) as shown below:

```
ps=\
```

Define the worker list:

```
worker.list=JBoss1, JBoss2, loadbalancer
```

Define the second JBoss worker:

```
worker.JBoss1.port=1009
worker.JBoss1.host=poseidon
worker.JBoss1.type=ajp13
worker.JBoss1.lbfactor=100
```

Define the second JBoss worker:

```
worker.JBoss2.port=1009
worker.JBoss2.host=pegasus
worker.JBoss2.type=ajp13
worker.JBoss2.lbfactor=100
```

The load balancer (type lb) worker performs weighted round-robin load balancing with sticky sessions. If a worker dies, the load balancer will check its state once in a while. Until then all work is redirected to a peer worker:

```
worker.loadbalancer.type=lb
worker.loadbalancer.balanced_workers=JBoss1, JBoss2
```

195

13.3.7 Clustered Deployment

JBoss also supports farming, which enables the components that are deployed one server to be made available on all the other servers in the partition. This is not enabled by default. You can enable it by configuring the `FarmMemberService` MBean. The MBean definition is:

```
<mbean
    code="org.jboss.ha.framework,server.FarmMemberService"
    name="jboss:service=FarmMember,partition=MyPartition">
```

It supports the following attributes:

Attribute	Function
PartitionName	The partition for which farming is enabled. The default value is `DefaultPartition`.
FarmDeployDirectory	The directory that the JBoss deployment scanner component watches for deployment archives.
ScannerName	The object name of the deployment scanner MBean that is used. Deployment scanner MBean is covered in detail in *Section 15.1: Deployers*.

The snippet below shows an example of this MBean service:

```
<mbean
  code="org.jboss.ha.framework,server.FarmMemberService"
  name="jboss:service=FarmMember,partition=MyPartition">
  <depends>jboss:service=MyPartition</depends>
  <attribute name="PartitionName">MyPartition</attribute>
  <attribute name="FarmDeployDirectory">./deploy</attribute>
  <attribute name="ScannerName">
     jboss.deployment:type=DeploymentScanner,flavor=URL
  </attribute>
</mbean>
```

The snippet above defines the MBean service responsible for distributed deployment. This MBean will deploy a J2EE component across all the servers in the `MyPartition` partition. Please note that this MBean itself should be deployed on all the servers in the partition.

JBoss 3.0

Administration and Deployment

Handbook

14

14

Configuring Logging

Logging is one of the key aspects of enterprise application development, used extensively for diagnostic and bug tracking purposes. In this chapter we will have a look at how to configure logging within JBoss. JBoss uses **Log4J** as its sole logging API and version 3.0 comes with JAR files required for Log4J 1.2.x.

> **Please note that an in-depth coverage of Log4J is beyond the scope of this book. You can find more information on Log4J at http://jakarta.apache.org/log4j/**

14.1 The Logging MBean

JBoss provides an MBean that can be used for configuring logging options. This MBean is normally defined in the root configuration file `jboss-service.xml` available in the \conf directory of the server configuration set you are running. The MBean definition is:

```
<mbean
   code="org.jboss.logging.Log4jService"
   name="jboss.system:type=Log4jService,service=Logging">
```

This MBean supports the following attributes:

Attribute	Function
ConfigurationURL	Used to specify the location of the Log4J configuration file used for defining appenders, patterns, categories, and priorities. JBoss supports both properties file format as well as an XML format for configuring Log4J.
RefreshPeriod	Used to specify the refresh period in seconds for reloading the configuration information. The default value is 60.

The listing below shows an example for the Log4J MBean definition:

```
<mbean
    code="org.jboss.logging.Log4jService"
    name="jboss.system:type=Log4jService,service=Logging">
    <attribute name="ConfigurationURL">resource:log4j.xml</attribute>
</mbean>
```

This will load the logging configuration from the file log4j.xml, present in the \conf directory of the server home.

14.2 Log4J Overview

In this section we will have a brief overview of the Log4J API.

The three main components of Log4J are **loggers**, **appenders**, and **layouts**. Loggers decide what is logged, appenders decide where it is logged, and layouts decide in what format it is logged.

14.2.1 Category/Logger

Log4J allows you to disable certain log statements while allowing others to print unhindered. To do this Log4J uses a logging space, where all logging statements are categorized according to some developer-chosen criteria. Prior to v1.2, the class Category was used to represent an entity for which logging statements were enabled or disabled based on a severity level. However, since v1.2, the Logger class has replaced the Category class. The Logger class extends the Category class.

Loggers are named entities that follow a hierarchical naming rule. A logger is said to be an ancestor of another logger if its name followed by a dot is a prefix of the descendant logger name. A logger is said to be a parent of a child logger if there are no ancestors between it and the descendant logger. For example, the logger named "com.foo" is a parent of the logger named "com.foo.Bar". Similarly, "java" is a parent of "java.util" and an ancestor of "java.util.Vector".

The root logger resides at the top of the logger hierarchy. It always exists and it cannot be retrieved by name. Invoking the class static `Logger.getRootLogger()` method retrieves it. All other loggers are instantiated and retrieved with the class static `Logger.getLogger()` method. This method takes the name of the desired logger as a parameter. Some of the basic methods in the `Logger` class are listed below.

Methods for creating and retrieving loggers:

```
public static Logger getRootLogger();
public static Logger getLogger(String name);
```

Methods for logging messages with varying levels of priority:

```
public void debug(Object message);
public void info(Object message);
public void warn(Object message);
public void error(Object message);
public void fatal(Object message);
```

A generic logging method where you can specify a severity level:

```
public void log(Level l, Object message);
```

Loggers may be assigned levels. The set of possible levels, that is DEBUG, INFO, WARN, ERROR, and FATAL, is defined in the `org.apache.log4j.Level` class. If a given logger is not assigned a level, then it inherits one from its closest ancestor with an assigned level. The inherited level for a given logger is equal to the first non-null level in the logger hierarchy, starting at that logger and proceeding upwards in the hierarchy towards the root logger.

Logging requests are made by invoking one of the printing methods of a logger instance. These printing methods are debug(), info(), warn(), error(), fatal(), and log(). By definition, the printing method determines the level of a logging request. For example, if logger is a logger instance, then the statement `logger.info("..")` is a logging request of level INFO. A logging request is said to be enabled if its level is higher than or equal to the level of its logger. Otherwise, the request is said to be disabled. A logger without an assigned level will inherit one from the hierarchy. For the standard levels, the order is DEBUG < INFO < WARN < ERROR < FATAL.

Calling the getLogger() method with the same name will always return a reference to the exact same logger object. For example, in:

```
Logger x = Logger.getLogger("wombat");
Logger y = Logger.getLogger("wombat");
```

x and y refer to exactly the same Logger object.

Thus, it is possible to configure a logger and then to retrieve the same instance somewhere else in the code without passing around references.

Configuration of the Log4J environment is typically done at application initialization. The preferred way is by reading a configuration file.

Log4J makes it easy to name loggers by software component. This can be accomplished by statically instantiating a logger in each class, with the logger name equal to the fully qualified name of the class. This is a useful and straightforward method of defining loggers. As the log output bears the name of the generating logger, this naming strategy makes it easy to identify the origin of a log message.

14.2.2 Appenders

The ability to selectively enable or disable logging requests based on their logger is only part of the picture. Log4J allows logging requests to print to multiple destinations. In Log4J an output destination is called an **appender**. Currently, appenders exist for the console, files, GUI components, remote socket servers, JMS, NT Event Loggers, and remote UNIX Syslog daemons. It is also possible to log asynchronously. See *Section 14.3.1.1: Pre-build Appenders* for more details on these existing appenders and how to use them.

More than one appender can be attached to a logger. The addAppender() method adds an appender to a given logger. Each enabled logging request for a given logger will be forwarded to all the appenders in that logger as well as the appenders higher in the hierarchy. In other words, appenders are inherited additively from the logger hierarchy. For example, if a console appender is added to the root logger, then all enabled logging requests will at least print on the console. If in addition a file appender is added to a logger, say logger, then enabled logging requests for logger and logger's children will print on a file and on the console. It is possible to override this default behavior so that appender accumulation is no longer additive by setting the additivity flag to false.

14.2.3 Layout

More often than not, users wish to customize not only the output destination but also the output format. This is accomplished by associating a layout with an appender. The layout is responsible for formatting the logging request according to the user's wishes, whereas an appender takes care of sending the formatted output to its destination. The PatternLayout, part of the standard Log4J distribution, lets the user specify the output format according to conversion.

For example, the PatternLayout with the conversion pattern "%r [%t] %-5p %c - %m%n" will output something akin to:

```
176 [main] INFO  org.foo.Bar - Located nearest gas station.
```

The first field is the number of milliseconds elapsed since the start of the program. The second field is the thread making the log request. The third field is the level of the log statement. The fourth field is the name of the logger associated with the log request. The text after the '-' is the message of the statement.

14.2.4 Renderers

Log4J allows you to specify custom renderers for objects that are logged frequently. Please note that the print functions on the logger accept any type of Java objects and not just strings. Object rendering follows the class hierarchy. For example, assuming oranges are fruits, if you register a `FruitRenderer`, all fruits including oranges will be rendered by the `FruitRenderer`, unless of course you registered an orange-specific `OrangeRenderer`.

Object renderers have to implement the `ObjectRenderer` interface.

14.3 Configuring Logging

The Log4J configuration MBean discussed in the last section uses XML-based configuration. The configuration file as specified by the default JBoss installation is `log4j.xml` located in the `\conf` directory of the default configuration set. It has the following structure:

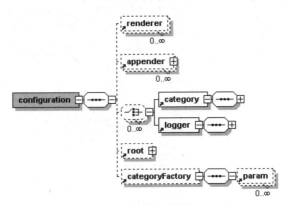

The root element for XML-based configuration is called `configuration`. The `configuration` element takes two attributes, `threshold` and `debug`:

❑ The `threshold` attribute takes a level value such that all logging statements with a level equal or below this value are disabled. The available levels are DEBUG, INFO, WARN, ERROR, and FATAL in increasing order of severity. However, the threshold defined here can be overridden at appender and filter/category levels.

❏ Setting the debug attribute to true enables the printing of internal Log4J logging statements. By default, the debug attribute is set to false, meaning that we not do touch internal Log4J logging settings.

In the next few sections we will have a closer look at the appender, root, category, and logger elements in detail.

For a more thorough coverage of configuring Log4J refer to its documentation at:
http://jakarta.apache.org/log4j/docs/documentation.html.

14.3.1 Appender

The configuration element can contain zero or more appender elements to configure Log4J appenders. Appenders in Log4J decide where the messages are logged. The appender element has the following structure:

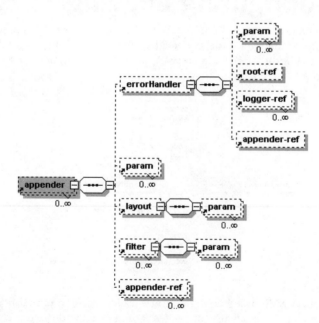

The appender element has two mandatory attributes, name and class. The name attribute assigns a unique name to the appender, and the class attribute defines the class name of the appender that implements the Log4J Appender interface. The appender element can have the following child elements:

Element	Description
errorHandler	An optional errorHandler element is used to set an error handler for the appender. This element has a class attribute to specify the fully qualified name of the class that implements the Log4J ErrorHandler interface. This element can also have zero or more param elements to set options specific to the error handler being used. Log4J defines a set of predefined filters. If an error handler is not specified, there won't be any error handling done.
param	Zero or more param elements to set options specific to the appender. The param element supports the attributes name and value used to specify the name and value of the option. All the appenders that extend the Log4J AppendorSkeleton class support the option Threshold to specify the level of the log messages that can be logged.
layout	An optional layout element to specify the class that will be responsible for formatting the log messages. This element has a class attribute to specify the fully qualified name of the class that extends the Log4J Layout class. This element can also have zero or more param elements to set options specific to the layout being used. If a layout is not specified, the appender will use a layout specific to the appender. Different appenders have different default layouts.
filter	Zero or more filter elements to define custom filtering of log messages. This element has a class attribute to specify the fully qualified name of the class that extends the Log4J Filter class. This element can also have zero or more param elements to set options specific to the filter being used. Log4J defines a set of pre-defined filters. If a filter is not specified, the all messages sent to the appender will be logged.
appender-ref	Zero or more appender-ref elements, for chaining appenders. When you chain appenders the messages sent to the referring appender are sent to the referred appenders. This element takes a ref attribute that will refer to the name attribute of the referred appender.

14.3.1.1 Pre-built Appenders

Log4J provides quite a few pre-built appenders, which you can find in the JBoss log4j.xml configuration file.

14.3.1.1.1 ConsoleAppender

This appender sends the messages to the console and supports the following parameters:

❑ Target
Specifies whether the messages should be sent to System.out or System.err

The snippet below shows an example ConsoleAppender configuration:

```
<appender name="CONSOLE" class="org.apache.log4j.ConsoleAppender">
  <param name="Threshold" value="INFO"/>
  <param name="Target" value="System.out"/>

  <layout class="org.apache.log4j.PatternLayout">
    <param name="ConversionPattern"
      value="%d{ABSOLUTE} %-5p [%c{1}] %m%n"/>
  </layout>

</appender>
```

The snippet above defines an appender called CONSOLE that uses the Log4J console appender and uses the Log4J pattern layout. The threshold is set to INFO and the log messages are sent to System.out.

14.3.1.1.2 FileAppender

This appender sends the messages to a file and supports the following parameters:

❑ Append
Specifies whether the messages should be appended to an existing file or if a new file should be created

❑ BufferedIO
A Boolean flag to specify whether buffering should be enabled

❑ BufferSize
The buffer size if buffering is enabled

❑ File
The file to which the messages are written

This appender has subclasses called DailyRollingFileAppender, which rolls the log file every day, and RollingFileAppender which can roll the log file based on date and/or size. The RollingFileAppender supports two additional parameters:

❑ MaxFileSize
The maximum size the logging file can grow to before being rolled over into a new file

❑ MaxBackupIndex
The number of backup log files that should be held at any time

The snippet below shows an example FileAppender configuration:

```
<appender
  name="FILE"
  class="org.jboss.logging.appender.RollingFileAppender">
```

```
<param name="Threshold" value="DEBUG"/>
<param name="File" value="${jboss.server.home.dir}/log/server.log"/>
<param name="Append" value="false"/>
<param name="MaxFileSize" value="500KB"/>
<param name="MaxBackupIndex" value="1"/>

<layout class="org.apache.log4j.PatternLayout">
  <param name="ConversionPattern" value="%d %-5p [%c] %m%n"/>
</layout>
</appender>
```

The snippet above defines an appender called FILE that uses the Log4J rolling file appender and the Log4J pattern layout. The threshold is set to DEBUG and the log messages are sent to the server.log file under the \log directory of the configuration set you use. The file is rolled every 500 KB and the last file that was rolled is archived.

14.3.1.1.3 JMSAppender

A simple appender that publishes events to a JMS topic. The events are serialized and transmitted as a JMS object message. JMS appenders are useful for logging from EJBs where file I/O is not allowed according to the specification. This appender supports the following parameters:

❑ InitialContextFactoryName
  Specifies the initial context factory to use when creating a JNDI initial context to look up the JMS connection factory and topic

❑ ProviderURL
  Specifies the provider URL to use when creating a JNDI initial context to look up the JMS connection factory and topic

❑ URLPkgPrefixes
  Specifies the URL package prefixes to use when creating a JNDI initial context to look up the JMS connection factory and topic

❑ SecurityCredentials
  Specifies the security credentials to use when creating a JNDI initial context to look up the JMS connection factory and topic

❑ SecurityPrincipalName
  Specifies the security principal to use when creating a JNDI initial context to look up the JMS connection factory and topic

❑ TopicName
  Specifies the JNDI name of the topic connection that is used

❑ TopicConnectionFactoryName
  Specifies the JNDI name of the JMS topic connection factory

❑ UserName
  Specifies the user name used for creating topic sessions

❑ Password
  Specifies the password used for creating topic sessions

The snippet below shows an example `JMSAppender` configuration:

```
<appender name="JMS" class="org.apache.log4j.net.JMSAppender">
  <param name="Threshold" value="DEBUG"/>
  <param name="TopicConnectionFactoryBindingName"
    value="java:/ConnectionFactory"/>
  <param name="TopicBindingName" value="topic/MyErrorsTopic"/>
</appender>
```

If the initial context properties are not specified (as in the code above), the appender will create the initial context without specifying any properties.

The snippet above defines an appender called `JMS` that logs messages to the topic `MyErrorsTopic` with a threshold set to `DEBUG`.

14.3.1.1.4 SMTPAppender

This appender sends an e-mail when a specific logging event occurs, typically on errors or fatal errors. This appender supports the following parameters:

- ❑ From
  A string value which should be the e-mail address of the sender.

- ❑ SMTPHost
  A string value which should be the host name of the SMTP server that will send the e-mail message.

- ❑ To
  A string value which should be a comma-separated list of the e-mail addresses of the recipients.

- ❑ Subject
  Specifies the security credentials to use when creating a JNDI initial context to look up the JMS connection factory and topic.

- ❑ BufferSize
  A positive integer representing the maximum number of logging events to collect in a cyclic buffer. When the buffer size is reached, the oldest events are deleted as new events are added to the buffer. By default the size of the cyclic buffer is 512 events.

- ❑ LocationInfo
  A Boolean value. By default, it is set to `false` which means there will be no effort to extract the location information related to the event. As a result, the layout that formats the events as they are sent out in an e-mail is likely to place the wrong location information (if present in the format). Location information extraction is comparatively very slow and should be avoided unless performance is not a concern.

The snippet below shows an example `SMTPAppender` configuration:

```
<appender name="SMTP" class="org.apache.log4j.net.AMTPAppender">
  <param name="Threshold" value="ERROR"/>
  <param name="From" value="fred@flintstone.com"/>
```

```
<param name="To" value="barney@rubble.com"/>
<param name="Subject" value="Error"/>
<param name="SMTPHost" value="mail.exchb01.com"/>
</appender>
```

The snippet above defines an appender called SMTP that sends an e-mail message for messages with severity as ERROR.

14.3.1.1.5 AsyncAppender

The AsyncAppender lets users log events asynchronously. It uses a bounded buffer to store logging events. The AsyncAppender will collect the events sent to it and then dispatch them to all the appenders that are attached to it. You can attach multiple appenders to an AsyncAppender. The AsyncAppender uses a separate thread to serve the events in its bounded buffer. It supports the following single option:

❑ BufferSize
  Specifies the buffer size for the asynchronous appender. By default this appender can buffer 128 logging events.

The snippet below shows an example AsyncAppender configuration:

```
<appender name="ASYNC" class="org.apache.log4j.AsyncAppender">
  <appender-ref ref="FILE"/>
  <appender-ref ref="CONSOLE"/>
  <appender-ref ref="SMTP"/>
</appender>
```

The snippet above defines an appender called ASYNC that uses the Log4J asynchronous appender. The appender buffers messages sent to it and later sends it to the named appenders defined using the appender-ref elements. You can use asynchronous appenders for improving performance.

14.3.1.1.6 Other Appenders

Other appenders provided by Log4J include (please refer to the Log4J API documentation for the configurable attributes of the appenders listed below):

❑ JDBCAppender
  For logging to a database.

❑ LF5Appender
  Logs events to a Swing-based logging console. The swing console supports turning categories on and off and multiple detail level views, as well as full text searching and many other capabilities.

❑ NTEventLogAppender
  Logs to the NT event log system. This appender can only be installed and used on a Windows system.

❑   SocketAppender
    Sends the log messages to a remote log server.

❑   SyslogAppender
    Sends log messages to the UNIX syslog daemon.

14.3.2 Renderer

The renderer element is used to define classes that will provide custom conversion of message objects to string patterns as explained in *Section 14.2.4: Renderers*. This element takes two attributes, renderingClass and renderedClass. The rendered class is the class for which the renderer is defined and the rendering class is a class that implements the Log4J object renderer interface.

```
<renderer
   renderingClass="com.MyRenderer"
   renderedClass="com.MyClass"/>
```

In the above scenario, whenever a print method on a logger is called with an object of type com.MyClass, Log4J will ask an instance of com.MyRenderer to render the object. com.MyRenderer needs to implement the Log4J ObjectRenderer interface.

14.3.3 Root

The root element is used to define the logging properties for the root category/logger. Category is a class provided by Log4J for logging messages. The Log4J Logger class extends Category and Category has been now deprecated. Previously, to log messages from a class, you had to call:

```
Category cat = Category.getInstance(getClass());
cat.info("My message");
```

or:

```
Category cat = Category.getInstance(getClass().getName());
cat.info("My message");
```

The argument that is passed to these methods is used to define a named category. It is a common practice to use the fully qualified class name of the class from where the messages are logged as the category name. You can associate appenders and priorities/levels with categories. The Log4J class Level extends the Priority class and the Priority class has been deprecated now. These classes are used to set a threshold for the severity of the messages that are logged.

However, the recommended approach now is to use the Logger class as shown below:

```
Logger log = Logger.getLogger(getClass());
log.info("My message");
```

or:

```
Logger log = Logger.getLogger(getClass().getName());
log.info("My message");
```

The `root` element is used to define appenders and threshold for the root category/logger. The threshold defined here can be overridden at individual category/logger level. Log4J also allows you to have a hierarchy of loggers/categories similar to the Java package structure. For example, a named logger `com.foo` is considered as the parent of `com.foo.bar`. If you don't specify an explicit threshold for `com.foo.bar`, it will inherit the priority of `com.foo`. If there is no threshold defined anywhere in the hierarchy, Log4J will use the threshold defined for the root category. If the `root` category hasn't got a threshold, Log4J will set the threshold at DEBUG. Similarly categories/loggers also inherit the appenders set for parent categories/loggers.

The structure of the `root` element is shown below:

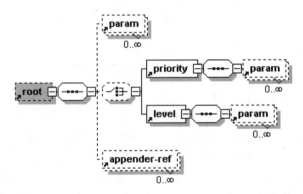

❑ The `param` element is used to set options specific to the root.

❑ The `priority` or `level` element is used to set a threshold for the root category or logger. Prior to version 1.2 the `Priority` class was used to represent message severity. The `Level` class in v1.2 has replaced this.

❑ The `appender-ref` elements are used to set one or more appenders to the root category/logger. See *Section 14.2.1.1: Pre-built Appenders* for a list of appenders.

The snippet below shows an example of the `root` category/logger configuration:

```
<root>
    <level value="INFO"/>
    <appender-ref ref="CONSOLE"/>
    <appender-ref ref="FILE"/>
</root>
```

The example above sets the threshold for the root category/logger at `INFO` and sets the two named appenders `CONSOLE` and `FILE`. This means for any named category/logger for which the threshold is not explicitly defined, it will use the `INFO` level and all the categories/loggers within the system will send messages to the `CONSOLE` and `FILE` appenders.

14.3.4 Category/Logger

The `configuration` element can have zero or more `category` or `logger` elements to define thresholds and appenders for named categories or loggers. The structure of these elements is:

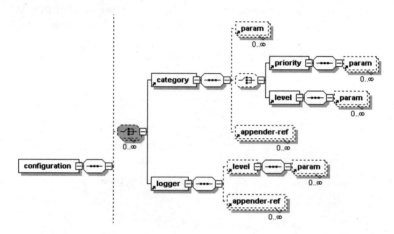

Both `category` and `logger` elements have a name attribute to define the name of the category/logger. Both of them can define their own list of appenders in addition to the appenders defined for their parent categories/loggers using the `appender-ref` elements. The `category` element can use the `priority` or `level` element to override the threshold set for its parent category whereas the `logger` element can use the `level` element to do the same.

In the snippet below, category `foo.bar` overrides the threshold set by its parent category to define that `foo.bar` and its sub-categories will log all messages with a priority greater than `DEBUG` and will use a named appender `SOCKET` *in addition to* the appenders defined for its parent category:

```
<category name="foo.bar">
   <priority value="DEBUG"/>
   <appender-ref ref="SOCKET"/>
</category>
```

Log4J also allows you to define custom priorities and levels. This is explained in detail in *Section 14.5: TRACE Priority.*

14.3.5 JBoss Default Logging Configuration

The default configuration that comes out-of-the-box with JBoss is shown below:

```
<?xml version="1.0" encoding="UTF-8"?>
<!DOCTYPE log4j:configuration SYSTEM "log4j.dtd">

<log4j:configuration xmlns:log4j="http://jakarta.apache.org/log4j/"
                     debug="false">

  <!-- A time/date based rolling appender -->
  <appender name="FILE"
    class="org.jboss.logging.appender.DailyRollingFileAppender">
    <param name="File"
      value="${jboss.server.home.dir}/log/server.log"/>
    <param name="Append" value="false"/>

    <!-- Rollover at midnight each day -->
    <param name="DatePattern" value="'.'yyyy-MM-dd"/>

    <layout class="org.apache.log4j.PatternLayout">
      <!-- The default pattern: Date Priority [Category] Message\n -->
      <param name="ConversionPattern" value="%d %-5p [%c] %m%n"/>
    </layout>
  </appender>

  <!-- Console appender -->
  <appender name="CONSOLE" class="org.apache.log4j.ConsoleAppender">
    <param name="Threshold" value="INFO"/>
    <param name="Target" value="System.out"/>

    <layout class="org.apache.log4j.PatternLayout">
      <!-- The default pattern: Date Priority [Category] Message\n -->
      <param name="ConversionPattern"
        value="%d{ABSOLUTE} %-5p [%c{1}] %m%n"/>
    </layout>
  </appender>

  <!-- Setup the Root category -->
  <root>
    <appender-ref ref="CONSOLE"/>
    <appender-ref ref="FILE"/>
  </root>

</log4j:configuration>
```

The configuration above defines two appenders; one a date/time based rolling file appender that is rolled every day, and a console appender. The file appender writes to the file server.log under the \logs directory of your configuration set. The console appender has a threshold of INFO and the file appender has a threshold of DEBUG. The root category is configured to use both the appenders.

14.4 Administering Logging

As with any other MBean, the Log4J MBean can also be administered using the JMX console. Using the JMX console you can modify the values for the configuration URL and refresh period MBean attributes. In addition to this, you can invoke the following operations to control the behavior of the logging service:

```
public void setLoggerPriority(String logger, String priority)
public String getLoggerPriority(String loggerName)
```

The above methods are used to get and set priorities for a named logger in the Log4J configuration file:

```
public void reconfigure(String configurationURL)
public String reconfigure ()
```

The above methods are used to reconfigure the logging behavior. The first method accepts a URL pointing to the Log4J configuration file and the second method uses the configuration URL already in use.

Alternatively we can administer the MBean using the JMX console:

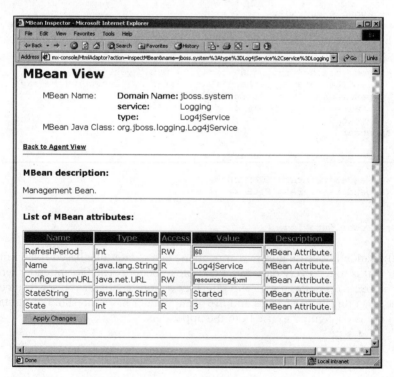

14.5 TRACE Priority

JBoss also introduces a custom priority level called TRACE. This is below the level of the standard Log4J DEBUG priority. This lower priority is useful for logging events that should only be displayed when deep debugging is required. The class org.jboss.logging.Logger that acts as a wrapper around the Log4J Category class provides the utility method isTraceEnabled(). You can use this method before sending a log message with TRACE priority.

The snippet below shows how to use this priority for a named category in the Log4J configuration file, log4j.xml available in the \conf directory of your configuration set.

```
<category
  name="org.jboss.ejb.plugins">
  <priority
    value="TRACE"
    class="org.jboss.logging.XLevel"/>
</category>
```

JBoss 3.0

Administration and Deployment

Handbook

15

15

The JBoss Deployment Architecture

One of the important issues addressed during deployment is the resolution of class dependencies across your components. Hence, it is important that you are well versed with the deployment architecture of the application server you use. In this chapter, we'll look at the deployment architecture that JBoss uses. You should also refer to *Section 5.1: JBoss Classloading* for a discussion on the JBoss classloading architecture.

15.1 Deployers

In this section, we will have a look at the various deployers that are available with JBoss and how they are organized. JBoss uses a main deployer to orchestrate all deployment processes. This main deployer delegates the actual deployment process of specific components to subdeployers. Hence, JBoss comes with six different subdeployers to handle the deployment of WAR, EAR, JAR, EJB, RAR, and SAR components as shown in the figure below:

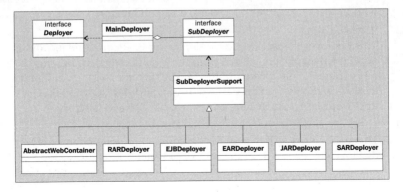

The main deployer is represented by the org.jboss.deployment.Deployer interface and JBoss provides the org.jboss.deployment.MainDeployer implementation class. An instance of this class is registered as an MBean during server startup. All the subdeployers implement the org.jboss.deployment.SubDeployer interface by extending the org.jboss.deployment.SubDeployerSupport adapter class.

The deployers are:

❑ MainDeployer
The main deployer is registered statically as an MBean during JBoss startup, and is responsible for initiating the deployment of the services specified in the root configuration file.

❑ AbstractWebContainer
This deployer MBean is responsible for deploying WAR components. It deploys files with a war extension and directories with web.xml available in a \META-INF subdirectory.

❑ JARDeployer
This deployer is again registered statically during startup and is responsible for deploying all JAR files that don't contain a \WEB-INF directory. Please note that JAR deployers are different from EJB deployers. The responsibility of the JAR deployer is to load the classes present in the JAR files and make them available in the unified classloader repository.

❑ SARDeployer
This deployer is also registered statically during server startup, and is responsible for SAR deployment. It deploys files with a sar extension and directories with jboss-service.xml available in a \META-INF subdirectory. It also deploys standalone XML files whose name ends with service.xml, as in jboss-service.xml.

❑ RARDeployer
This deployer is responsible for deploying JCA resource adapter components and is normally dynamically loaded from the SAR deployment descriptor jca-service.xml file located in the \deploy directory of the configuration set. This deploys files with a rar extension and directories with ra.xml available in a \META-INF subdirectory.

❑ EARDeployer
This deployer is responsible for deploying EAR components, and is normally dynamically loaded from the root deployment descriptor jboss-service.xml file located in the \conf directory of the configuration set. It deploys archives with an ear extension, and directories with application.xml available in a \META-INF subdirectory.

❑ EJBDeployer
This deployer is responsible for deploying EJB components and is normally dynamically loaded from the root deployment descriptor jboss-service.xml file located in the \conf directory of the configuration set. It deploys archives with a jar extension, and directories with ejb-jar.xml available in a \META-INF subdirectory.

Each deployer is capable of recursive deployment. For example, during the process of deployment, an EAR deployer will delegate the deployment of component EJB, WAR, RAR components, etc. to the relevant subdeployers through the main deployer. The subdeployers are also capable of reading the classpath manifest attribute to deploy the JAR files specified in the manifest through the JAR deployer. During the deployment of the components, the subdeployers create a unified classloader pointing to the URL of the component archive being deployed and registers it with loader repository. See *Section 5.1.3: UnifiedClassLoader* for a discussion on how classloading works for J2EE components.

15.2 Hot Deployment

Hot deployment is the process of adding new components (such as enterprise beans, servlets, and JSP) to a running server without having to stop the application server process and restart it. In JBoss, deployment scanners perform hot deployment. JBoss provides two deployment scanners, as MBean services, which are capable of performing hot deployment.

15.2.1 The URLDeploymentScanner MBean

This MBean is the scanner that is enabled out-of-the-box in JBoss, and its definition is:

```
<mbean
    code="org.jboss.deployment.scanner.URLDeploymentScanner"
    name="jboss.deployment:type=DeploymentScanner,flavor=URL">
```

The URL deployment scanner accepts the following attributes:

Attribute	Function
URLComparator	Used to check whether files have changed. JBoss provides the following comparators: org.jboss.deployment.DeploymentSorter Enabled by default and it sorts by file extension, as follows: sar, service.xml, rar, jar, war, wsr, ear, zip, * org.jboss.deployment.scanner.PrefixDeploymentSorter If the name portion of the URL begins with 1 or more digits, those digits are converted to an int (ignoring leading zeroes), and files are deployed in that order. Files that do not start with any digits will be deployed last, and they will be sorted by extension as above with the DeploymentSorter. You can use this comparator if you want more control on the order in which the various components are deployed.

Table continued on following page

Attribute	Function
Filter	A filter for files that don't require deployment. The filter `org.jboss.deployment.scanner.DeploymentFilter`, which comes with JBoss, provides a file filter that filters a variety of extensions, such as `*.old`, `*.orig`, `*.rej`, `*.bak`, etc.
URLs	URLs are comma-separated and are resolved relative to the server home (specific to the configuration set you use) unless the given path is absolute. Any referenced directories cannot be unpackaged archives; use the parent directory of the unpacked archive instead. A `file:` protocol will be assumed if not specified otherwise (for example `http:`).
ScanPeriod	The scanning interval period specified in milliseconds. This can be very useful when deploying across a network as the JBoss deployer can sometimes throw exceptions when trying to deploy components that are still being transmitted across the network. This happens because the write to the `\deploy` directory hasn't finished yet.

The listing below shows an example URL deployment scanner MBean service for handling hot deployment:

```
<mbean
  code="org.jboss.deployment.scanner.URLDeploymentScanner"
  name="jboss.deployment:type=DeploymentScanner,flavor=URL">
  <depends optional-attribute-name="Deployer">
    jboss.system:service=MainDeployer
  </depends>
  <attribute name="URLComparator">
    org.jboss.deployment.DeploymentSorter
  </attribute>
  <attribute name="Filter">
    org.jboss.deployment.scanner.DeploymentFilter
  </attribute>
  <attribute name="ScanPeriod">5000</attribute>
  <attribute name="URLs">./deploy</attribute>
</mbean>
```

15.2.2 The URLDirectoryScanner MBean

This MBean allows you to specify which URLs are directories to scan, and which are URLs to be deployed directly. `URLDeploymentScanner` assumes that all directories are to be scanned, which can cause problems if directory referred to in the deploy attribute is an exploded archive. The MBean definition is:

```
<mbean
  code="org.jboss.deployment.scanner.URLDirectoryScanner"
  name="jboss.deployment:type=DeploymentScanner,flavor=URL">
```

The URL directory scanner MBean supports the following attributes:

Attribute	Function
URLComparator	Has the same meaning as that for the URLDeploymentScanner. See *Section: 15.2.1: The URLDeploymentScanner MBean.*
Filter	Has the same meaning as that for the URLDeploymentScanner. See *Section: 15.2.1: The URLDeploymentScanner MBean.*
URLs	Each entry specifies either a dir (directory to be scanned), or url (URL to be deployed). Like the URLs for the URLDeploymentScanner above, a file: protocol will be assumed if not specified otherwise.
ScanPeriod	Has the same meaning as that for the URLDeploymentScanner. See *Section: 15.2.1: The URLDeploymentScanner MBean.*

The listing below shows an example URL directory scanner MBean service for handling hot deployment:

```
<mbean
    code="org.jboss.deployment.scanner.URLDirectoryScanner"
    name="jboss.deployment:type=DeploymentScanner,flavor=URL">

    <depends optional-attribute-name="Deployer">
        jboss.system:service=MainDeployer
    </depends>
    <attribute name="URLComparator">
        org.jboss.deployment.DeploymentSorter
    </attribute>
    <attribute name="Filter">
        org.jboss.deployment.scanner.DeploymentFilter
    </attribute>
    <attribute name="ScanPeriod">5000</attribute>
    <attribute name="URLs">
        <urls>
            <dir name="./deploy" />
            <url name="./deploy/examples/myapp.ear" />
            <dir name="./deploy/examples" />
            <url name="http://www.test.com/samples/myapp.ear" />
        </urls>
    </attribute>
</mbean>
```

15.3 The Deployment Process

In JBoss you can initiate a deployment process by simply copying the deployment unit to one of the locations scanned by the deployment scanner. The deployment scanner will then delegate the deployment process to the main deployer. The main deployer depending on the type of the deployment unit will delegate the deployment to one of the relevant subdeployers. Once the deployment is successful, you will be able to see a deployment completed message on the console as well as the log file:

If the deployment fails, JBoss writes appropriate error messages to the console and the log file:

The above error message was caused because the datasources were not configured on the server before deploying the CMP beans that referred to the datasource. You can also access the main deployer MBean through the JMX console to check the deployment status. The object name for this MBean is `jboss.system:service=MainDeployer`. This MBean can be found on the JMX console home page under the **jboss.system** domain as shown overleaf:

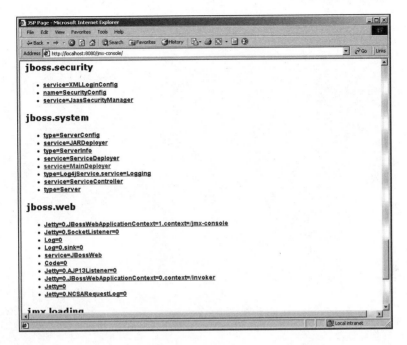

You can view the MBean page by clicking on its object name. The MBean provides a variety of operations to check the deployment status:

```
public Collection listDeployed()
```

This method returns a collection of currently deployed packages.

```
public Collection listIncompletelyDeployed()
```

This method returns a list of packages that have not deployed completely.

```
public void deploy(String urlspec)
public void deploy(URL url)
```

These methods deploy the package identified by the URL.

```
public void redeploy(String urlspec)
public void redeploy(URL url)
```

These methods redeploy the package identified by the URL.

```
public void undeploy(String urlspec)
public void undeploy(URL url)
```

Finally, these methods undeploy the package identified by the URL.

223

JBoss 3.0

Administration and Deployment

Handbook

16

16.1 The JBoss Web Deployment Descriptor

16

Configuring WAR Deployment

In this chapter, we look at deploying WAR components within JBoss/Jetty and JBoss/Tomcat. JBoss supports WAR deployment in both standalone WAR format and part of an EAR file. You can also deploy WAR files in exploded format by copying the directory containing the web application root, and its contents, to any location monitored by your deployment scanner. See *Section 15.3: The Deployment Process* for more info on how WARs are deployed.

16.1 The JBoss Web Deployment Descriptor

You can use a JBoss-specific web deployment descriptor for accomplishing the following tasks:

- ❏ Mapping resource references
- ❏ Mapping resource environment references
- ❏ Mapping EJB remote references
- ❏ Setting up security domains
- ❏ Setting virtual hosts
- ❏ Setting context paths

This file should be called `jboss-web.xml` and should be made available in the `\WEB-INF` directory of your web application. The descriptor uses the `jboss-web_3_0.dtd`, which describes the following XML structure:

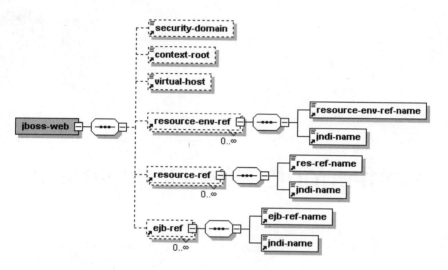

16.1.1 Security Domain

You can restrict access to your web application URIs methods by using the `security-role` and `security-constraint` elements in the standard web deployment descriptor. However, enforcement of this declarative security in an operational environment is performed in a web container-specific manner. In *Section 7.3.3: Login Configuration*, we looked at how to use JAAS within JBoss to define login modules in the `login-config.xml` file.

When a request comes in for a secure URI, JBoss tries to evaluate the credentials of the thread using the `security-domain` element in the JBoss web deployment descriptor. This element should refer to a login module configured within the system. The JBoss JAAS security manager will use the login module to resolve the caller's credentials and access rights. The snippet below shows how to define a security domain for performing authentication/authorization:

```
<jboss-web>
   <security-domain>java:jaas/MyLoginModule</security-domain>
   ...
</jboss-web>
```

Here, `MyLoginModule` is a login module configured within JBoss. For a detailed discussion on how to configure login modules, please refer to *Section 7.3.3.3: Login Configuration Data*.

16.1.2 JNDI References

It is good practice to refer to JNDI objects using a coded name within your web applications, instead of referring to the actual JNDI name. Coded names are defined in the java:comp/env/ namespace of the web application using web-ref, resource-env-ref, ejb-ref, and ejb-local-ref in the standard web deployment descriptor. These elements are used for defining coded names for:

❑ Resource factories such as datasources, mail sessions, JMS connection factories, URLs, etc.

❑ JMS destinations (queues and topics)

❑ EJB remote references

❑ EJB local references

The mapping of coded JNDI names to actual JNDI names is performed in a web container-specific way. In JBoss, this is performed in jboss-web.xml using the following elements:

❑ resource-ref for resource references such as data sources, mail sessions, URL connection factories, JMS connection factories, etc.

❑ resource-env-ref for resource environment references such as JMS queues and topics

❑ ejb-ref for remote EJB references

16.1.2.1 Mapping EJB References

Since local EJBs need to co-exist in the same VM as the web application, you don't need to use the JBoss web deployment descriptor for mapping the coded name to the actual EJB. This can be done using the ejb-local-ref/ejb-link element in the standard web deployment descriptor as shown below:

```
<web-app>

  <display-name>AdminWAR</display-name>
  <description>
    WebTier for the Admin Client for the PetStore
  </description>

  ...

  <ejb-local-ref>
    <ejb-ref-name>ejb/local/AsyncSender</ejb-ref-name>
    <ejb-ref-type>Session</ejb-ref-type>
    <local-home>
      com.sun.j2ee.blueprints.asyncsender.ejb.AsyncSenderLocalHome
    </local-home>
    <local>com.sun.j2ee.blueprints.asyncsender.ejb.AsyncSender</local>
    <ejb-link>AsyncSenderAdminEJB</ejb-link>
  </ejb-local-ref>

</web-app>

</ejb-jar>
```

Here, the `ejb-local-ref/ejb-link` element refers to the EJB name of the referred bean. However, you can't do this if the referred bean is remote. In such scenarios, you will have to use the JBoss EJB deployment descriptor, as shown below, for mapping the coded name of the EJB to the remote JNDI name:

```
<jboss-web>

  <ejb-ref>
    <ejb-ref-name>ejb/remote/OPCAdminFacade</ejb-ref-name>
    <jndi-name>ejb/remote/opc/opc/OPCAdminFacadeEJB</jndi-name>
  </ejb-ref>

</jboss-web>
```

Here, `ejb-ref/ejb-ref-name` refers to the coded name, and `ejb-ref/jndi-name` refers to the remote JNDI name.

16.1.2.2 Resource Environment References

Coded names for resource environment references are mapped to the actual JNDI names, using the `resource-env-ref` element as shown below:

```
<jboss-web>

  ...

  <resource-env-ref>
    <resource-env-ref-name>
      jms/topic/opc/InvoiceTopic
    </resource-env-ref-name>
    <jndi-name>topic/opc/InvoiceTopic</jndi-name>
  </resource-env-ref>

</jboss-web>
```

Here, the `resource-env-ref-name` is the coded name, and `jndi-name` is the actual name.

16.1.2.3 Resource References

In JBoss, the `resource-ref` element can be used for mapping coded names of resource factories to actual JNDI names or URLs. Non-URL resources are mapped as shown below:

```
<jboss-web>

  <resource-ref>
    <res-ref-name>jms/topic/TopicConnectionFactory</res-ref-name>
    <jndi-name>ConnectionFactory</jndi-name>
  </resource-ref>

</jboss-web>
```

Here the `res-ref-name` refers to the coded name of the resource, and `jndi-name` refers to the actual JNDI name. URL resources are mapped as shown below:

```
<jboss-web>

  <resource-ref>
    <res-ref-name>url/CatalogDAOSQLURL</res-ref-name>
    <res-url>
       http://localhost:8080/petstore/CatalogDAOSQL.xml
    </res-url>
  </resource-ref>

</jboss-web>
```

Here, the `res-ref-name` refers to the coded name of the resource, and `res-url` refers to the URL of the resource.

16.1.3 Context Path

If you deploy a WAR component by copying the unexploded WAR file to the \deploy directory, JBoss will use the name of the WAR file as the context path. Thus, if the file is called `petstore.war`, the context path will be /petstore. If you are deploying the WAR as an exploded directory, JBoss will use the name of the root folder as the context path.

> **If you are deploying the WAR as part of an EAR, the context URI is specified in `application.xml`.**

However, sometimes you may want to specify a context path other than the WAR file name in standalone EAR files. In JBoss, you can specify this using the `context-root` element in the JBoss web deployment descriptor as shown below:

```
<jboss-web>
  ...
  <context-root>
    /
  </context-root>
  ...
<jboss-web>
```

In the above example, you will be able to access the web application without specifying a context path.

> **With Tomcat, accessing the web application without specifying a context path is also possible by calling the `ROOT.war` WAR component. Please note that the name is case-sensitive.**

16.1.4 Virtual Host

You can use virtual hosts within JBoss to group your web applications into different DNS names. Although J2EE specifications don't mention anything about virtual hosts, you can specify them in JBoss using the `virtual-host` element in the JBoss web deployment descriptor, as shown below:

```
<jboss-web>
  ...
  <virtual-host>
     www.flintstone.com
  </virtual-host>
  ...
</jboss-web>
```

The virtual host you define should be available in the web container's operational environment.

JBoss 3.0

Administration and Deployment

Handbook

17

17

EJB Container Architecture

In this chapter, we look at the JBoss EJB container architecture in detail. This will be followed by detailed coverage of EJB deployment configuration in JBoss in the next chapter.

17.1 EJB Container Architecture

We will start our discussion with an in-depth look at the JBoss EJB container architecture. JBoss 3.0 provides a highly modular, configurable, and pluggable EJB container architecture that supports a high degree of customization. You can customize the behavior of the EJB container by writing your own modules and plugging them into the EJB container. The diagram below depicts a high-level overview of the JBoss EJB container architecture:

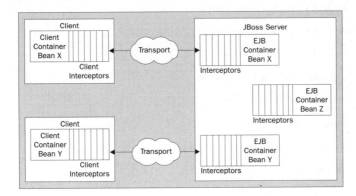

Unlike some of the other application servers, JBoss doesn't use generated classes for implementing EJB home and remote objects. Instead, JBoss relies heavily on dynamic proxies introduced in JDK 1.3 for implementing the EJB home and remote objects. Hence deploying EJBs on JBoss doesn't involve the additional EJB compilation step required with some other EJB containers for generating the home and remote object implementations.

As illustrated in the previous figure, for every EJB deployed on the server, JBoss creates an instance of an EJB container and a client container (only for the bean types that have a client view). The client container uses dynamic proxies to intercept a bean or home invocation, pass it through a series of interceptors, and finally send it to the JBoss server. The type of the EJB container depends on the type of the EJB that is deployed. The client container acts as the invocation handler implementation for the home and remote invocations on the client side. When the client and the bean are hosted within the same VM, JBoss will use local transport for propagating the invocation from the client to the bean. However, the invocation still passes through the client- and server-side containers that use various interceptors to implement functionalities such as security, transactions, etc.

Both the client and the EJB containers use an interceptor-based architecture. A strongly typed home or remote invocation on the client side will pass through a set of configured interceptors before it leaves the client container as an untyped invocation. Similarly, once the untyped invocation reaches the EJB container, it goes through a series of interceptors before it reaches the target bean instance.

These interceptors can be used for implementing a variety of functionality, such as transactions, security, call logging, etc. The interceptors that are configured on the client and server sides can be controlled using the JBoss-specific EJB deployment descriptor, jboss.xml. However, JBoss specifies a set of standard configurations for the following types of beans as they appear in the standardjboss.xml file available in the \conf directory:

- Standard CMP 2.x EntityBean
- Instance Per Transaction CMP 2.x EntityBean
- Standard CMP EntityBean (EJB 1.1)
- Clustered CMP 2.x EntityBean
- Clustered CMP EntityBean (EJB 1.1)
- Standard Stateless SessionBean
- Clustered Stateless SessionBean
- Standard Stateful SessionBean
- Standard BMP EntityBean
- Instance Per Transaction BMP EntityBean

- ❑ Clustered BMP EntityBean

- ❑ Standard Message Driven Bean

- ❑ IIOP CMP 2.x EntityBean

- ❑ IIOP CMP EntityBean

- ❑ IIOP Stateless SessionBean

- ❑ IIOP Stateful SessionBean

- ❑ IIOP BMP EntityBean

If the configuration for a bean is not explicitly overridden in the JBoss-specific EJB deployment descriptor (jboss.xml), JBoss will use the configurations specified in this standardjboss.xml file depending on the type of the bean. Depending on the type of the bean used, JBoss defines a specialized set of interceptors in the standardjboss.xml file. Instead of defining your own set of configuration from scratch, JBoss allows you to extend an existing configuration and lets you override or add required behavior (see *Section 18.2.1: Extending Container Configurations*). In addition to the interceptors, this file also contains other information that is used to control the behavior of the EJB that is deployed.

17.1.1 Container Classes

This section will provide a high-level overview of the core classes and interfaces that constitute the JBoss 3.0 EJB container architecture and their main purposes.

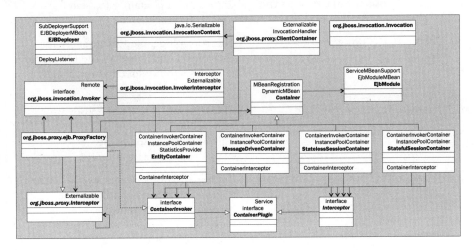

Class/Interface	Purpose
org.jboss.ejb.EJBDeployer	The core EJB deployer MBean responsible for deploying EJBs on JBoss.
org.jboss.proxy.ClientContainer	Implements the invocation handler interface for dynamic proxies, and is responsible for sitting in the client process space and translating and passing the various home and component invocations on to the server. The exact semantics of how the data is serialized depends on the wire protocol that is used. JBoss allows you to use a variety of protocols (including JRMP, IIOP, and HTTP) for EJB invocation.
org.jboss.ejb.Container	This abstract class acts as the superclass for all the various types of EJB containers.
org.jboss.ejb.EntityContainer	Represents a container for entity beans.
org.jboss.ejb.MessageDriven Container	Represents a container for message-driven beans.
org.jboss.ejb.StatelessSession Container	Represents a container for stateless session beans.
org.jboss.ejb.StatefulContainer	Represents a container for stateful session beans.
org.jboss.ejb.ContainerPlugin	The core pluggable functionality for JBoss EJB containers. All the pluggable modules should directly or indirectly implement this interface.
org.jboss.ejb.Interceptor	All the server-side interceptors are required to implement this interface. This interface extends the ContainerPlugin interface.
org.jboss.ejb.ContainerInvoker	Implementations of this interface are responsible for receiving remote invocations of EJBs and to forward these requests to the container it is being used with.
org.jboss.ejb.EJBModule	Encapsulates the EJB metadata for each EJB deployed in a deployment unit.

Class/Interface	Purpose
org.jboss.proxy.ejb.ProxyFactory	Responsible for creating the home and component proxy instances and binding the home dynamic proxy in the JNDI namespace.
org.jboss.invocation.Invoker	A generic interface for modeling an object that performs an untyped invocation. Depending on the transport protocol that is used, JBoss provides invoker implementations for in-VM for local EJB calls, JRMP for standard RMI calls, HTTP for EJB invocation through a firewall, IIOP for interoperable CORBA-compliant invocations, etc. This is the last point in the client container before an invocation leaves the client container to the server via the transport mechanism.
org.jboss.invocation.Invocation	Represents an untyped invocation.
org.jboss.invocation.Invocation Context	Describes the context in which this invocation is being executed in the interceptors.
org.jboss.invocation.Invoker Interceptor	Responsible for routing an invocation to the JBoss server from the client container.
org.jboss.proxy.Interceptor	All client-side interceptors are required to extend this interface.

17.2 EJB Deployment

This section covers the internals of deploying an EJB in JBoss server. Dropping your EJB JAR file in a location scanned by the JBoss deployment scanner triggers the deployment process in JBoss. For EJB JAR files, the main deployer delegates the actual deployment task to the EJB deployer.

17.2.1 The EJB Deployer

The EJB deployer is implemented using the org.jboss.ejb.EJBDeployer MBean, the definition of which is:

```
<mbean
   code="org.jboss.ejb.EJBDeployer"
   name="jboss.ejb:service=EJBDeployer">
```

This MBean supports the following attributes:

Attribute	Function
VerifyDeployments	A flag to indicate whether the beans should be verified during deployment for compliance with the specification.
ValidateDTDs	A flag to indicate whether the standard and JBoss-specific EJB deployment descriptors associated with the MBean should be validated during deployment. It is recommended to set this to true to make sure that all the deployment descriptors are validated against appropriate DTDs.
MetricsEnabled	If this flag is set to true, the deployer will add a server-side metrics-type interceptor for logging invocation information.

The snippet below shows an example of the EJB deployer MBean. This is MBean is normally defined in the root configuration file jboss-service.xml available in the \conf directory of the configuration:

```
<mbean
    code="org.jboss.ejb.EJBDeployer"
    name="jboss.ejb:service=EJBDeployer">
    <attribute name="VerifyDeployments">true</attribute>
    <attribute name="ValidateDTDs">true</attribute>
    <attribute name="MetricsEnabled">true</attribute>
</mbean>
```

17.2.2 The EJB Deployment Process

When the EJB deployer deploys an EJB module, the following tasks are performed:

❑ For each EJB in the deployment unit, the deployer creates an instance of the org.jboss.ejb.EJBModule class that encapsulates the deployment information present in the standard and JBoss-specific EJB deployment descriptors.

❑ An instance of the org.jboss.proxy.ejb.ProxyFactory class is created, which is responsible for creating the client-side dynamic proxy. The dynamic proxy consists of an instance of org.jboss.proxy.ClientContainer, the EJB home interface, and the client-side interceptors through which the invocation passes. These interceptors are defined in the standardjboss.xml file for various types of EJBs as listed in *Section 17.1: EJB Container Architecture*. However, you can customize the behavior by writing your own interceptors and defining them in the JBoss-specific EJB deployment descriptor (jboss.xml). These custom interceptors should extend the org.jboss.proxy.Interceptor class.

❏ The dynamic proxy is then bound to the JNDI namespace. This is the object that is transported to the client process space when the client performs an EJB home lookup.

❏ An instance of an appropriate subclass of `org.jboss.ejb.Container` is then created. This represents the server-side container. A unique classloader for loading local resources and handling the `java:comp` namespace is created and assigned to the container. This is an instance of `org.jboss.web.WebClassLoader`, which is a simple subclass of `URLClassLoader`. This is used in conjunction with the `WebService` MBean to allow dynamic loading of resources and classes from deployed EARs, EJB JARs, and WARs.

❏ The container is then configured with the various attributes specified in the `standardjboss.xml` and the JBoss-specific EJB deployment descriptor. This information includes server-side interceptors and other plug-ins for controlling various behaviors such as instance pooling, instance caching, etc.

17.3 EJB Invocation

This section will cover the EJB invocation process within JBoss, as depicted in the diagram below:

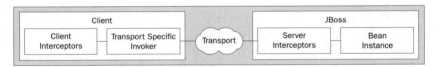

The client starts the EJB invocation process by looking up the home object. The home object is the dynamic proxy that contains client container as the invocation handler, EJB client view, and the various client-side interceptors.

17.3.1 Client-side Interceptors

The client-side interceptors extend the `org.jboss.proxy.Interceptor` class. When the client performs an operation on an EJB object, the dynamic proxy delegates the invocation to the client container that acts as the invocation handler. The client container creates an instance of the class `org.jboss.invocation.Invocation` that represents the client call. This object is passed through the list of configured client-side interceptors. Finally, it reaches the invoker interceptor which will use a transport-specific invoker for routing the invocation to a JBoss server.

17.3.2 EJB Invokers

The invoker, which is responsible for routing an invocation to a server-side container in a transport-specific manner, is represented by an instance of `org.jboss.invocation.Invoker` interface.

Some of the important invoker implementations provided by JBoss are listed below:

❑ `org.jboss.invocation.local.LocalInvoker`
Used for in-VM invocation

❑ `org.jboss.invocation.jrmp.server.JRMPInvoker`
Used for remote invocation using JRMP

❑ `org.jboss.invocation.http.server.HTTPInvoker`
Used for remote invocation using HTTP

❑ `org.jboss.invocation.jrmp.server.JRMPInvokerHA`
Used for remote invocation using JRMP in a clustered environment

All the above invokers are defined as MBean services and provide configurable MBean attributes. The JRMP invoker supports the following MBean attributes:

Attributes	Function
RMIObjectPort	The listen port for the RMI server socket. The default value is 4444.
RMIClientSocketFactory	The RMI client socket factory. If not specified, this will use the default RMI client socket factory.
RMIServerSocketFactory	The RMI server socket factory. If not specified, this will use the default RMI server socket factory.
ServerAddress	The server address for the RMI server socket in a multi-homed environment.
SecurityDomain	The JAAS security domain to use for invocation over SSL.

This MBean is normally specified in the root configuration file, `jboss-service.xml`, available in the `\conf` directory of the configuration set you use. The listing below shows an example:

```
<mbean
   code="org.jboss.invocation.jrmp.server.JRMPInvoker"
   name="jboss:service=invoker,type=jrmp">
     <attribute name="RMIObjectPort">4444</attribute>
</mbean>
```

The local invoker is also defined in the same file and the listing below shows an example:

```
<mbean
   code="org.jboss.invocation.local.LocalInvoker"
   name="jboss:service=invoker,type=local">
</mbean>
```

The clustered JRMP invoker supports all the attributes supported by the normal JRMP invoker and is by default found in the cluster-service.xml file in the \deploy directory of the all configuration set. The listing below shows an example:

```
<mbean
   code="org.jboss.invocation.jrmp.server.JRMPInvokerHA"
   name="jboss:service=invoker,type=jrmpha">
</mbean>
```

The HTTP invoker enables EJB invocation over HTTP. To use HTTP-based EJB invocation, you need to first define the HTTP invoker MBean. Then in the JBoss-specific EJB deployment descriptor, you need to set the bean and home invokers to the object name of the HTTP invoker MBean. Bean and home invokers are explained in *Section 18.3.5: Invokers*. The listing below shows an example of the HTTP invoker MBean:

```
<mbean
   code="org.jboss.invocation.http.server.HTTPInvoker"
   name="jboss:service=invoker,type=http">
      <attribute name="InvokerURL">${invokerServletPath}</attribute>
</mbean>
```

To use this you need to use the HTTP JNDI factory and HTTP provider URL explained in the *Section 6.6: HTTP-based JNDI*, to look up the EJB home object and set a system property called invoketServletPath to the initial context with the value set to http://<host:port>/invoker/JMXInvokerServlet. The MBean listed above will expand the system property specified by the system property invokerServletPath to set the InvokerURL attribute. The invokerServletPath system property specifies the public URL of the HTTP invoker servlet used by both JNDI/HTTP and RMI/HTTP. This must be set to the org.jboss.invocation.http.servlet.InvokerServlet servlet mapping defined in the \deploy\http-invoker.sar\invoker.war\WEB-INF\web.xml descriptor.

17.3.3 Server Interceptors

Server-side interceptors are similar to the client-side interceptors and they process the invocations in the server-side container before routing them to the EJB instance. Server-side interceptors are used for a variety of functionality including logging, transaction management, security, locking, caching, synchronization, etc. All the server-side interceptors are required to directly or indirectly implement the org.jboss.ejb.Interceptor interface. This interface in turn extends the org.jboss.ejb.ContainerPlugin interface.

The server-side interceptors for each type of EJB listed in *Section 17.1: Container Architecture* are configured in the `standardjboss.xml` file. However, you can override this for individual EJBs using the JBoss-specific EJB deployment descriptor (`jboss.xml`). JBoss provides a set of server-side interceptors specific to the different types of EJBs.

> **More often than not, you won't be changing the default server-side and client-side interceptor chain defined for the different types of EJBs in the `standardjboss.xml` file.**

Some of the standard server-side interceptors provided by JBoss are listed below:

- ❏   `org.jboss.ejb.plugins.LogInterceptor`
  Used to log all invocations. It also handles any unexpected exceptions.

- ❏   `org.jboss.ejb.plugins.SecurityInterceptor`
  This is where the EJB 2.0 declarative security model is enforced and where the caller identity propagation is controlled as well.

- ❏   `org.jboss.ejb.plugins.TxInterceptorCMT`
  Handles transactions for CMT beans.

- ❏   `org.jboss.ejb.plugins.MetricsInterceptor`
  Collects data from the bean invocation call and publishes it on a JMS topic.

- ❏   `org.jboss.ejb.plugins.TxInterceptorBMT`
  Handles transactions for BMT beans.

JBoss 3.0

Administration and Deployment

Handbook

18

18

Configuring EJBs

In this chapter, we look at configuring the EJBs that are deployed within JBoss. JBoss allows the customization of EJBs using an JBoss-specific deployment descriptor. This deployment descriptor should be called `jboss.xml` and should be available in the `\META-INF` directory of the deployment unit. This deployment descriptor is used to configure a variety of EJB behavior including:

- ❑ Local and remote JNDI names
- ❑ Client side interceptors
- ❑ Server side interceptors
- ❑ Instance pooling
- ❑ Instance caching
- ❑ Clustering
- ❑ Security

JBoss provides server-wide defaults for all the EJBs deployed in a server instance using the `standardjboss.xml` file available in the `\conf` directory of the configuration set you use. This file has the same structure as `jboss.xml`, and defines server-wide defaults for the various types of EJBs listed in *Section 17.1: EJB Container Architecture*.

18.1 Deployment Descriptor

In this section, we will have a high-level overview of the structure of `standardjboss.xml` and `jboss.xml` files. The diagram below shows the higher-level elements of these files:

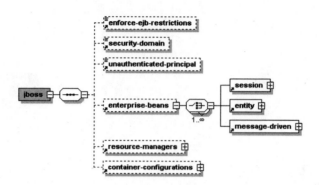

Both `standardjboss.xml` and `jboss.xml` share the same DTD (`jboss_3_0.dtd`) and can have any of the elements shown above. However, the `standardjboss.xml` file comes out-of-the-box with JBoss, and normally you won't modify it, whereas you define the `jboss.xml` file for each deployment unit you deploy, and you use it to override/extend the configuration specified in `standardjboss.xml`. The `standardjboss.xml` file uses the `container-configurations` element to define multiple container configurations for the different types of EJBs listed in *Section 17.1: EJB Container Architecture.*.

The root element is called `jboss` and this contains the following child elements:

Element	Description
`enforce-ejb-restrictions`	This is a Boolean flag to specify whether you want JBoss to enforce all the EJB restrictions specified in the specification. The `standardjboss.xml` file sets this to `false`. However, you can override this for individual deployment units in `jboss.xml`.
`security-domain`	This is used to specify a login module configured in `login-config.xml` to perform authentication/authorization when a secured EJB method is invoked. You would normally use this element at deployment unit level in `jboss.xml`.
`unauthenticated-principal`	You would normally use this at deployment unit level in the `jboss.xml` file to specify the caller principal that is returned from `getCallerPrincipal()` method on the enterprise context in unsecured methods.

Element	Description
enterprise-beans	This element would be normally used at deployment unit level in jboss.xml to define the properties of the EJBs that are deployed. This element can contain one or more session, entity, or message-driven elements corresponding the EJBs defined in ejb-jar.xml file. These elements are used to specify individual bean level properties such as local and/or remote JNDI names, bean and home invokers, mapping JNDI references for local and remote EJBs, resource and resource environment references, the behavior of the bean in a cluster, and the type of container configuration to use.
resource-managers	This element would be normally used at deployment unit level in jboss.xml to map coded names of resource manager connection factory references to their actual JNDI names.
container-configurations	This element is used within standardjboss.xml to define the container configurations for various types of EJBs. Container configurations cover functionalities such as client-side interceptors, server-side interceptors, instance pooling, instance caching, locking policies, etc. However, you can override/extend container configurations at deployment unit level in jboss.xml file.

18.2 Container Configuration

JBoss provides server-wide configuration for each type of EJB container specified in *Section 17.1: EJB Container Architecture* in the file standardjboss.xml file. This file uses the container-configurations element to define a set of container-configuration elements. Each container-configuration element defines the following properties for each type of EJB listed in section 17.1:

❑ Client-side interceptors

❑ Server-side interceptors

❑ Instance pool

❑ Instance cache

❑ Persistence manager

- ❏ Transaction manager
- ❏ Locking, etc.

The basic structure of the `container-configurations` element is shown below:

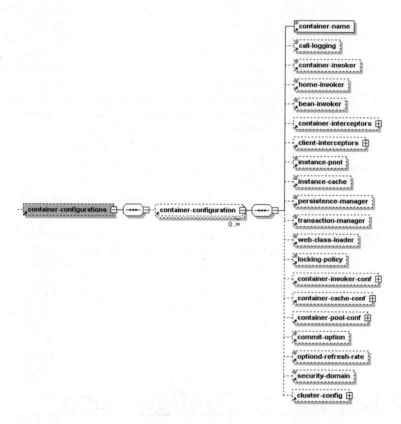

The `container-configurations` element can contain any number of `container-configuration` elements. Each `container-configuration` element defines the configuration for a specific type of container. Each container configuration is uniquely identified by a name specified as the content for the `container-name` element.

18.2.1 Extending Container Configuration

We have already mentioned that the `standardjboss.xml` file defines a standard set of container configurations. However, you can define new container configurations from scratch or extend one of the standard container configuration set at deployment unit level in `jboss.xml`. You would normally do this, if you want to override the default caching or pooling behavior set for a specific type of EJB in `standardjboss.xml` file. To define a container configuration from scratch, you would use the `container-configurations\container-configuration` element in `jboss.xml` file for the deployment unit. However, normally you would not do this. Instead, you would extend one of the existing container configurations and override the required properties.

To do this, the `container-configuration` element provides an `extends` attribute to specify the name of a container configuration that the current configuration is extending. Once you have defined your own container configuration, you can associate it with an EJB by specifying the container configuration name in the `configuration-name` element of that EJB. This element is available under the `session`, `entity`, and `message-driven` elements.

For example, if you want to extend the configuration of standard stateless session EJB to add some custom behavior. Suppose, the container configuration for standard stateless session bean doesn't do call logging. To define a container configuration for standard stateless session beans that does call logging, first you need to extend the container configuration for standard stateless session bean and enable call logging.

Call logging logs all the method calls to EJBs – see Section 18.2.2: Call Logging.

You can do this globally in `standardjboss.xml` or at deployment unit level in `jboss.xml`. Unless you have a compelling reason for defining a global configuration, you shouldn't be modifying `standardjboss.xml` file. The snippet below shows the relevant elements for extending container configuration:

```
<jboss>
   ...
   <container-configurations>
      <container-configuration extends="Standard Stateless SessionBean">
         <container-name>
            Call Logging Standard Stateless SessionBean
         <container-name>
         <call-logging>true</call-logging>
      </container-configuration>
</jboss>
```

Next, you need to associate the new container configuration with the stateless session bean for which you want call logging. You do this by specifying the new container name in the `configuration-name` element for the session bean in `jboss.xml` as shown below:

```
<jboss>
  ...
  <session>
    <ejb-name>MyCallLoggingEJB<ejb-name>
      <container-name>
      <configuration-name>
        Call Logging Standard Stateless SessionBean
      </configuration-name>
    </session>
</jboss>
```

If you don't specify a configuration name, JBoss will associate an appropriate container configuration from the standard set for the bean, depending on its type.

18.2.2 Call Logging

Call logging allows you to log every method call on the EJB instance. You can enable call logging for a container configuration for by using the `call-logging` element as shown below. Call logging can be useful for debugging purposes:

```
<container-configuration>
  ...
  <call-logging>true</call-logging>
  ...
</container-configuration>
```

18.2.3 Container Invoker

The `container-invoker` element gives the class name of the container invoker JBoss must use in this configuration. This class must implement the `org.jboss.ejb.ContainerInvoker` interface. The default is `org.jboss.proxy.ejb.ProxyFactory` for entity and session beans and `org.jboss.ejb.plugins.jms.JMSContainerInvoker` for message-driven beans. Containers supporting clustering use `org.jboss.proxy.ejb.ProxyFactoryHA`. Normally you won't be changing the container invoker when you extend a standard container configuration:

```
<container-configuration>
  <container-name>Standard Stateless SessionBean</container-name>
  ...
  <container-invoker>
    org.jboss.proxy.ejb.ProxyFactory
  </container-invoker>
  ...
<container-configuration>
```

18.2.4 Container Interceptors

The `container-interceptors` element gives the chain of interceptors (instances of `org.jboss.ejb.Interceptor`) that are associated with the container. The declared order of the interceptor elements corresponds to the order of the interceptor chain:

```
<container-configuration>
  <container-name>Standard Stateless SessionBean</container-name>

  <container-interceptors>
    <interceptor>
      org.jboss.ejb.plugins.LogInterceptor
    </interceptor>
    <interceptor>
      org.jboss.ejb.plugins.SecurityInterceptor
    </interceptor>
    <!-- CMT -->
    <interceptor transaction="Container">
      org.jboss.ejb.plugins.TxInterceptorCMT
    </interceptor>
    <interceptor transaction="Container" metricsEnabled="true">
      org.jboss.ejb.plugins.MetricsInterceptor</interceptor>
    <interceptor transaction = "Container">
      org.jboss.ejb.plugins.StatelessSessionInstanceInterceptor
    </interceptor>
    <!-- BMT -->
    <interceptor transaction="Bean">
      org.jboss.ejb.plugins.StatelessSessionInstanceInterceptor
    </interceptor>
    <interceptor transaction="Bean">
      org.jboss.ejb.plugins.TxInterceptorBMT
    </interceptor>
    <interceptor transaction="Bean" metricsEnabled="true">
      org.jboss.ejb.plugins.MetricsInterceptor
    </interceptor>
    <interceptor>
      org.jboss.resource.connectionmanager.CachedConnectionInterceptor
    </interceptor>
  </container-interceptors>

</container-configuration>
```

For example, if you want to have a standard stateless session bean configuration that doesn't need to do security checks, you would override the above configuration and redefine the container interceptor chain without specifying the security interceptor.

See *Section 17.3.3: Server Interceptors* for a list of container interceptors.

18.2.5 Client Interceptors

The `client-interceptors` element defines the home and bean client-side interceptor chain. The structure of this element is shown below:

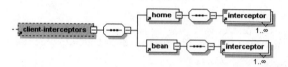

The bean element defines the chain of interceptors (instances of `org.jboss.proxy.Interceptor`) that are associated with the remote proxy and operate in the client VM. The declared order of the interceptor elements corresponds to the order of the interceptor chain.

The home element defines the chain of interceptors (instances of `org.jboss.proxy.Interceptor`) that are associated with the home proxy and operate in the client VM. The declared order of the `interceptor` elements corresponds to the order of the interceptor chain.

```
<container-configuration>
  <container-name>Standard Stateless SessionBean</container-name>
  ...
  <client-interceptors>
    <home>
      <interceptor>org.jboss.proxy.ejb.HomeInterceptor</interceptor>
      <interceptor>
        org.jboss.proxy.SecurityInterceptor
      </interceptor>
      <interceptor>
        org.jboss.proxy.TransactionInterceptor
      </interceptor>
      <interceptor>
        org.jboss.invocation.InvokerInterceptor
      </interceptor>
    </home>
    <bean>
      <interceptor>
        org.jboss.proxy.ejb.StatelessSessionInterceptor
      </interceptor>
      <interceptor>org.jboss.proxy.SecurityInterceptor</interceptor>
      <interceptor>
        org.jboss.proxy.TransactionInterceptor
      </interceptor>
      <interceptor>
        org.jboss.invocation.InvokerInterceptor
      </interceptor>
    </bean>
  </client-interceptors>
  ...
</container-configuration>
```

If you want to define a container configuration that doesn't check security, you would extend a standard container configuration and redefine the client interceptor chain without the security interceptor. Normally you won't be overriding the predefined client-side interceptor change when you extend one of the standard container configurations.

18.2.6 Instance Pools

JBoss manages instance pools for entity and stateless session EJBs for enhancing performance. The behavior of the pools can be configured at the container level. This is mainly done using the `instance-pool` and `container-pool-conf` elements.

The `instance-pool` element defines the fully qualified name of the class that implements the instance pooling functionality (implements `org.jboss.ejb.InstancePool`). JBoss provides the following instance pool implementations:

- ❏ `org.jboss.ejb.plugins.StatelessSessionInstancePool`
  This class implements the instance pooling functionality for stateless session EJBs.

- ❏ `org.jboss.ejb.plugins.EntityInstancePool`
  This class implements the instance pooling functionality for entity EJBs.

  The best way to write your own instance pool is to extend the adapter class provided by JBoss,
  `org.jboss.ejb.plugins.AbstractInstancePool`.

The `container-pool-conf` element provides the pool configuration information for the classes that implement instance pooling logic. You can use this element to configure the maximum size of the pool, if you are sub-classing `AbstractInstancePool`. The structure of the `container-pool-conf` element is shown below:

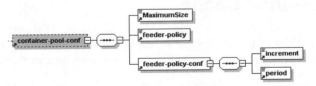

The `container-pool-conf` element holds configuration data for the instance pool. JBoss does not read directly the subtree for this element; instead, the XML fragment is passed to the instance pool instance for it to load its parameters. The default instance pools, `EntityInstancePool` and `StatelessSessionInstancePool`, both accept the element structure shown above. The `MaximumSize` element defines the capacity of the pool. The pool feeder will feed the pool with new instances, the pool size being limited by this value. This is not a hard limit; if instances are needed when the pool is at its `MaximumSize`, new instances will be created following the demand.

The `feeder-policy` element is only valid if the instance pool is a subclass of `AbstractInstancePool`. This element defines the class that implements `org.jboss.ejb.InstancePoolFeeder` and is responsible to feed the pool with new instances of bean. If not present, no feeder thread is started and the pool will have a size of 1. `org.jboss.ejb.plugins.TimedInstancePoolFeeder` is the first implementation available. The `feeder-policy-conf` element describes properties that the `InstancePoolFeeder` implementation will read to configure itself. The two attributes are used here for `TimedInstancePoolFeeder` are `increment` and `period`. The pool feeder will feed the pool with number of new instances specified by the `increment` element at a regular period specified by the `period` element.

If you want to define a container configuration that overrides the default pool configuration, you would extend a standard container configuration and redefine the container pool configuration element. Unlike the container configuration properties discussed so far, you will be overriding instance-pooling configuration to cater for your application's requirements:

```
<instance-pool>
  org.jboss.ejb.plugins.StatelessSessionInstancePool
</instance-pool>
...
<container-pool-conf>
  <MaximumSize>100</MaximumSize>
</container-pool-conf>
```

> **Please note that the container-wide pool configuration can be overridden for individual beans using `jboss.xml`.**

18.2.7 Instance Cache

JBoss allows you to cache EJB types such as entity and session EJBs that have client identities. The behavior of the caches can be configured at the container level. This is done using the `instance-cache` and `container-cache-conf` elements.

The `instance-cache` element defines the fully qualified name of the class that implements the instance caching functionality (implements `org.jboss.ejb.InstanceCache`). JBoss provides the following instance cache implementations:

❑ `org.jboss.ejb.plugins.StatefulSessionInstanceCache`
  This class implements the instance pooling functionality for stateful session EJBs.

❑ `org.jboss.ejb.plugins.EntityInstanceCache`
  This class implements the instance caching functionality for entity EJBs.

The best way to write your own instance cache is to extend the adapter class provided by JBoss,
`org.jboss.ejb.plugins.AbstractInstanceCache.`

The `container-cache-conf` element provides the cache configuration information for the classes that implement instance caching logic. The structure of this element is shown below:

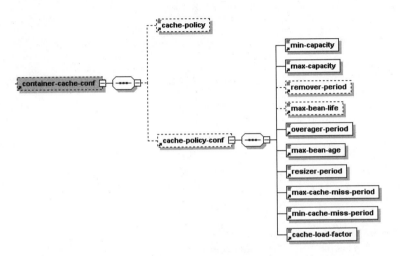

JBoss provides two subclasses, `StatefulSessionInstanceCache` and `EntityInstanceCache`, for the `AbstractInstanceCache` class. For these subclasses, you can specify the following properties:

❑ `cache-policy`
   This should specify the fully qualified class name that implements the
   `org.jboss.util.CachePolicy` interface. JBoss provides two
   implementations for this interface:

   • `org.jboss.ejb.plugins.`
     `LRUEnterpriseContextCachePolicy`
     This is used for entity bean caches.

   • `org.jboss.ejb.plugins.`
     `LRUStatefulContextCachePolicy`
     This is used for stateful session bean caches.

❑ `cache-policy-conf`
   This element is used to configure the cache policy instance and supports
   the following properties:

- `min-capacity`
  The minimum capacity of the cache.

- `max-capacity`
  The maximum capacity of the cache.

- `overager-period`
  Time, in seconds, in which to check whether there is any bean in the cache past the maximum bean age.

- `max-bean-age`
  The maximum time in seconds for inactive beans to stay in the cache.

- `resizer-period`
  Time in seconds the cache should be resized.

- `max-cache-miss-period`
  Time ins seconds in which a cache miss should trigger a decrease in cache resize.

- `min-cache-miss-period`
  Time in seconds in which a cache miss should trigger an increase in cache resize.

- `cache-load-factor`
  The factory by which the cache is resized.

The cache policy for stateful session beans support the following additional properties:

- `remover-period`
  Time in seconds in which a task is run to remove passivated beans that have not been accessed after the maximum bean life.

- `max-bean-life`
  Maximum time in seconds a passivated bean can stay inactive before it is removed.

The listing below shows an example cache configuration of an entity bean:

```
<instance-cache>
  org.jboss.ejb.plugins.EntityInstanceCache
</instance-cache>
...
<container-cache-conf>
  <cache-policy>
    org.jboss.ejb.plugins.LRUEnterpriseContextCachePolicy
  </cache-policy>
  <cache-policy-conf>
    <min-capacity>50</min-capacity>
    <max-capacity>1000000</max-capacity>
    <overager-period>300</overager-period>
    <max-bean-age>600</max-bean-age>
```

```
        <resizer-period>400</resizer-period>
        <max-cache-miss-period>60</max-cache-miss-period>
        <min-cache-miss-period>1</min-cache-miss-period>
        <cache-load-factor>0.75</cache-load-factor>
      </cache-policy-conf>
    </container-cache-conf>
```

Similar to container configuration properties for instance pooling, you will be overriding instance-caching configuration to cater for your application's requirements.

> **Please note that the container-wide cache configuration can be overridden for individual beans using jboss.xml.**

18.2.8 Persistence Manager

JBoss allows you to have pluggable persistence managers for CMP and BMP entity beans and stateful session EJBs. This is defined using the persistence-manager element. JBoss provides the following persistent manager interfaces:

❏ org.jboss.ejb.StatefulSessionPersistenceManager
The persistence manager for a stateful session bean should implement this interface.

❏ org.jboss.ejb.EntityPersistenceManager
Persistence managers for BMP and CMP 1.1 entity beans should implement this interface.

❏ org.jboss.ejb.EntityPersistenceStore
Persistence managers for BMP entity beans should implement this interface.

JBoss provides standard implementations for all the aforementioned interfaces to suit the different types of EJBs. The snippet below shows the persistence manager definition for a standard CMP 2.0 entity bean:

```
<container-configuration>
  ...
  <persistence-manager>
     org.jboss.ejb.plugins.cmp.jdbc.JDBCStoreManager
  </persistence-manager>
  ...
</container-configuration>
```

18.2.9 Commit Options

JBoss EJB container allows caching of entity beans with configurable commit options. The commit option is specified for a container configuration using the `commit-option` and `optiond-refresh-rate` elements. The `commit-option` value must be one of the following:

❏ A

JBoss assumes that the database is not shared with any other application, and it has the exclusive use of the database. Hence JBoss caches entity bean instances, and synchronizes the entity bean instances with the underlying persistent storage in a **lazy** manner.

❏ B

JBoss still caches the entity bean instance. However, it resynchronizes the bean data with that in the underlying storage at the beginning of the transaction. This means that a method executed in the context of a transaction can't make use of the functionality. However, methods that don't have a transaction context can make use of the cached data.

❏ C

Entity beans are never cached and instances are discarded at the end of the transaction.

❏ D

Similar to option A; however, bean instances are periodically resynchronized with the persistent storage at regular intervals specified by the `optiond-refresh-rate` element.

The "Standard CMP 2.x EntityBean" container configuration defined in `standardjboss.xml` uses commit option B. However, if you want to have an entity bean container configuration that uses a different commit option, you can extend the above container configuration in `jboss.xml` for your deployment unit to override the commit-option as shown below:

```
<jboss>
  ...
  <entity>
    <ejb-name>MyEntityEJB<ejb-name>
      <container-name>
        <configuration-name>
          Commit Option D CMP 2.x EntityBean
        </configuration-name>
      </container-name>
  </entity>
  ...
  <container-configurations>
    <container-configuration extends="Standard CMP 2.x EntityBean">
      <container-name>
        Commit Option D CMP 2.x EntityBean
      <container-name>
```

```
            <commit-option>D</commit-option>
            <optiond-refresh-rate>100</optiond-refresh-rate>
        </container-configuration>
    </jboss>
```

The above snippet extends the "Standard CMP 2.x EntityBean" container configuration and overrides the commit option to D, and associates the new container configuration with MyEntityEJB. The default value for the option D refresh rate is 30 seconds.

18.2.10 Locking

In traditional client-server database applications, the database server normally performs locking data across multiple transactions to achieve data integrity. However, J2EE application servers normally cache data using entity EJBs to enhance performance. In such scenarios, application servers may need to implement their own locking strategy to ensure transaction isolation. In this section, we will have a look at the JBoss locking policies for entity beans in transactions and how we can configure them.

18.2.10.1 Default Policy

By default JBoss uses a single instance of an entity bean identified by its home and primary key, across the transactions. As soon as a transaction accesses a bean instance, it is locked out and other transactions are forbidden from accessing the bean until the first transaction finishes (either committed or rolled back). The JBoss entity bean container ensures this using the following server-side container interceptors:

❏ org.jboss.ejb.plugins.EntityLockInterceptor
This interceptor is responsible for acquiring and releasing locks on entity bean instances.

❏ org.jboss.ejb.plugins.EntityInstanceInterceptor
This interceptor is responsible for creating or getting entity bean instances from the cache.

❏ org.jboss.ejb.plugins.EntitySynchronizationInterceptor
This interceptor is responsible for the synchronizing the entity bean instance with the underlying persistent store.

These are the interceptors defined in the "Standard CMP 2.x EntityBean", "Standard CMP EntityBean", and "Standard CMP EntityBean" container configurations.

18.2.10.2 Instance per Transaction

However, the default policy above can often cause deadlock when two transactions wait for locks on bean instances locked by each other. To circumvent this problem, JBoss provides container interceptors that can maintain multiple instances of entity beans with the same identity. This means that if bean A with home A and primary key A is accessed concurrently by two transactions, JBoss will maintain two instances of the bean.

This behavior is achieved using the two interceptors shown below:

❏ org.jboss.ejb.plugins.EntityMultiInstanceInterceptor

❏ org.jboss.ejb.plugins.EntityMultiInstanceSynchronization Interceptor

These additional interceptors are included in the "Instance Per Transaction CMP 2.x EntityBean", "Instance Per Transaction CMP EntityBean", and "Instance Per Transaction CMP EntityBean" container configurations.

> **The instance per transaction policy current limits you to commit option B and C only (see *Section 18.2.9: Commit Options*), and is also subject to repeatable reads (a transaction could have access to a stale copy of the bean).**

18.2.10.3 Defining Locking Policy

You can set the locking policy for a container using the locking-policy element under container-configuration. This should be the fully qualified name of the class that implements the org.jboss.ejb.BeanLock interface. JBoss provides the following implementations:

❏ org.jboss.ejb.plugins.lock.MethodOnlyEJBLock
This provides a non-pessimistic method-only lock on beans participating in transactions.

❏ org.jboss.ejb.plugins.lock.QueuedPessimisticEJBLock
This uses pessimistic locking implemented using a first-in-first-out based queue for maintaining the threads waiting for a lock. This is the default locking policy for non-instance per transaction containers.

❏ org.jboss.ejb.plugins.lock.SimplePessimisticEJBLock
This uses a pessimistic locking logic by locking all the threads and notifying them on lock release using the native Java threading mechanism.

❏ org.jboss.ejb.plugins.lock.NoLock
Defines no locking policy. Used by default by the instance per transaction containers.

Most of the entity container configurations defined in standardjboss.xml uses a QueuedPessimisticEJBLock, except those already configured for instance per transaction. However, if you want to have an entity bean container configuration that uses a different commit option, you can extend container configuration in jboss.xml for your deployment unit to override the locking-policy as shown below:

```
<jboss>
  ...
  <entity>
    <ejb-name>MyEntityEJB<ejb-name>
      <container-name>
      <configuration-name>
        Method Locking CMP 2.x EntityBean
      </configuration-name>
    </entity>
  ...
  <container-configurations>
    <container-configuration extends="Standard CMP 2.x EntityBean">
      <container-name>
        Method Locking CMP 2.x EntityBean
      <container-name>
      <locking-policy>
        org.jboss.ejb.plugins.lock.MethodOnlyEJBLock
      </locking-policy>
    </container-configuration>
</jboss>
```

18.2.11 Security Domain

You can set the security domain that should be used for performing authentication and authorization when secured EJB methods are invoked using the security-domain element. This element can be specified for a container configuration. However, you can override this at the deployment unit level by embedding the security-domain element directly within the JBoss element as shown below:

```
<jboss>

  <security-domain>java:/mySecureDomain</security-domain>

  <enterprise-beans>

    <session>
      <ejb-name>MySecureSessionBean</ejb-name>

      <configuration-name>
        Secured Stateless SessionBean
      </configuration-name>

    </session>

  </enterprise-beans>

  <container-configurations>
    <container-configuration extends="Standard Stateless SessionBean">
      <container-name>
```

```
        SecuredStateless SessionBean
      <container-name>
        <security-domain>java:/secureDomain</security-domain>
    </container-configuration>
  </container-configurations>

</jboss>
```

The example above defines a new container configuration called "Secured Stateless SessionBean" by extending the "Standard Stateless SessionBean" container configuration and defining the java:/secureDomain security domain. The MySecureSessionBean session bean declares to use the container configuration "Secured Stateless SessionBean". However, the container will use the java:/mySecureDomain security domain instead of java:/secureDomain, as the one specified at the deployment unit level overrides the one defined in container configuration. If we hadn't specified the java:/mySecureDomain security domain, JBoss would use the security domain java:/secureDomain.

The security domains are configured in the file login-config.xml file as explained in *Section 7.3.3.3: Login Configuration.*

18.3 Deployment Unit Level Configuration

As we have already discussed, both standardjboss.xml and jboss.xml files share the same DTD (jboss_3_0.dtd). The standardjboss.xml file comes out-of-the-box with a set of standard container configurations. Even though it is possible to edit the contents of this file, you would not normally do it. Instead, you would extend existing container configurations and override required behavior such as pooling, caching, locking, etc. at deployment unit level in the jboss.xml file.

The jboss.xml deployment descriptor can be used for:

❑   Setting a container configuration for the EJB

❑   Defining your own container configurations, either from scratch or extending the standard ones provided in standardjboss.xml

❑   Defining JNDI names for the home object

❑   Resolving JNDI resource, resource environment, and EJB remote and local references

❑   Defining security properties such as domains and proxies

❑   Marking your beans as read-only

❑   Configuring the behavior of EJBs in a cluster

❑ Defining invokers for home and EJB objects

❑ Defining various properties required for MDBs such as destination JNDI name, durable subscriptions, etc.

You would normally use the following elements in the `jboss.xml` file:

❑ `security-domain` for defining security domain JNDI names

❑ `enterprise-beans\session|entity|message-driven` elements for defining properties specific to each EJB in the deployment unit, such as JNDI name, resource references, etc.

❑ `resource-managers` element to map coded names of resource manager connection factory references to real JNDI names

❑ `container-configurations` element to extend and override the standard container configuration

In this section, we look at how to use the child elements of `enterprise-beans\session|entity|message-driven` elements to configure the behavior of EJBs. All the three aforementioned elements share some common child elements as shown below:

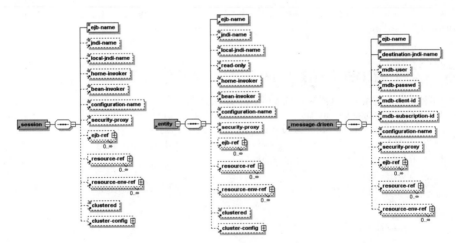

18.3.1 Defining JNDI Name

You can use the JBoss deployment EJB deployment descriptor (`jboss.xml`) for defining the JNDI names to which the EJB home objects are bound. If you don't specify a value, JBoss will use the EJB name defined in the standard EJB deployment descriptor, `ejb-jar.xml`, using the `ejb-name` element as the JNDI name. The listing below shows how a local JNDI name is defined for the local home object:

```
<jboss>
  <enterprise-beans>
    <session>
      <ejb-name>ShoppingControllerEJB</ejb-name>
      <local-jndi-name>
        ejb/local/petstore/petstore/ShoppingController
      </local-jndi-name>
    </session>
  </enterprise-beans>
</jboss>
```

The snippet below shows how a remote JNDI name is defined for the remote home object:

```
<jboss>
  <enterprise-beans>
    <session>
      <ejb-name>OPCAdminFacadeEJB</ejb-name>
      <jndi-name>ejb/remote/opc/opc/OPCAdminFacadeEJB</jndi-name>
    </session>
  </enterprise-beans>
</jboss>
```

If your bean has both remote and local client views, you can specify both local and remote JNDI names.

18.3.2 Name Mapping

It is a good practice to refer to JNDI objects using a coded name within your beans, instead of referring to the actual JNDI name. Coded names are defined in the `java:comp/env/` namespace of the beans using `resource-ref`, `resource-env-ref`, `ejb-ref`, and `ejb-local-ref` in the standard EJB deployment descriptor. These elements are used for defining coded names for:

❑ Resource factories such as datasources, mail sessions, JMS connection factories, URLs, etc.

❑ JMS destinations (queues and topics)

❑ EJB remote references

❑ EJB local references

The mapping of coded JNDI names to actual JNDI names is performed in an application server-specific way. In JBoss, this is performed in the JBoss EJB deployment descriptor using the following subelements of `entity|session|message-driven`:

❑ resource-ref
For resource references like data sources, mail sessions, etc.

❑ resource-env-ref
For resource environment references like JMS destinations

❑ ejb-ref
For remote EJB references

❑ ejb-local-ref
For EJB local references

18.3.2.1 Mapping EJB References

Since local EJBs need to co-exist in the same VM as the referring EJB, you don't need to use the JBoss EJB deployment descriptor for mapping the coded name to the actual EJB. This can be done using the ejb-local-ref and ejb-link elements in the standard EJB deployment descriptor as shown below:

```
<ejb-jar>
   <description>order process controller</description>
   <display-name>OrderProcessingCenterJAR</display-name>
   <enterprise-beans>

     <session>
       <description>The Admin OPC Facade</description>
       <display-name>OrderProcessingCenterAdminFacadeSB</display-name>
       <ejb-name>OPCAdminFacadeEJB</ejb-name>
       <home>
         com.sun.j2ee.blueprints.opc.admin.ejb.OPCAdminFacadeHome
       </home>
       <remote>
         com.sun.j2ee.blueprints.opc.admin.ejb.OPCAdminFacade
       </remote>
       <ejb-class>
         com.sun.j2ee.blueprints.opc.admin.ejb.OPCAdminFacadeEJB
       </ejb-class>
       <session-type>Stateless</session-type>
       <transaction-type>Container</transaction-type>

       <ejb-local-ref>
         <ejb-ref-name>ejb/local/ProcessManager</ejb-ref-name>
         <ejb-ref-type>Session</ejb-ref-type>
         <local-home>
           com.sun.j2ee.blueprints.processmanager.ejb.
           ProcessManagerLocalHome
         </local-home>
         <local>
           com.sun.j2ee.blueprints.processmanager.ejb.
           ProcessManagerLocal
         </local>
```

265

```
          <ejb-link>ProcessManagerEJB</ejb-link>
      </ejb-local-ref>


      ...

   </session>

 </enterprise-beans>

</ejb-jar>
```

Here the `ejb-local-ref`/`ejb-link` element refers to the EJB name of the referred bean. However, you can't do this if the referred bean is remote. In such scenarios, you will have to use the JBoss EJB deployment descriptor for mapping the coded name of the EJB to the remote JNDI name, as shown below:

```
<jboss>

  <enterprise-beans>
    <session>
      <ejb-name>ShoppingControllerEJB</ejb-name>
      ...
      <ejb-ref>
        <ejb-ref-name>ejb/remote/OPCAdminFacade</ejb-ref-name>
        <jndi-name>ejb/remote/opc/opc/OPCAdminFacadeEJB</jndi-name>
      </ejb-ref>
      ...
    </session>
  <enterprise-beans>

</jboss>
```

Here, `ejb-ref-name` refers to the coded name, and `jndi-name` refers to the remote JNDI name.

18.3.2.2 Resource Environment References

Coded names for resource environment references are mapped to the actual JNDI names using the `resource-env-ref` element as shown below:

```
<jboss>
  <enterprise-beans>
    <message-driven>
      <ejb-name>PurchaseOrderMDB</ejb-name>
      ...
      <resource-env-ref>
        <resource-env-ref-name>
          jms/queue/OrderApprovalQueue
        </resource-env-ref-name>
```

```
            <jndi-name>queue/opc/OrderApprovalQueue</jndi-name>
          </resource-env-ref>
        </message-driven>
      </enterprise-beans>
    </jboss>
```

Here, the `resource-env-ref-name` is the coded name, and `jndi-name` is the actual name.

18.3.2.3 Resource References

In JBoss, the `resource-ref` element can be used for mapping coded names of resource factories to actual JNDI names or URLs. Non-URL resources are mapped as shown below:

```
<jboss>
  <enterprise-beans>
    <message-driven>
      <ejb-name>PurchaseOrderMDB</ejb-name>
        . . .
      <resource-ref>
        <res-ref-name>jms/queue/QueueConnectionFactory</res-ref-name>
        <jndi-name>ConnectionFactory</jndi-name>
      </resource-ref>
    </message-driven>
  <enterprise-beans>
<jboss>
```

Here, the `res-ref-name` refers to the coded name of the resource, and `jndi-name` refers to the actual JNDI name.

URL resources are mapped as shown below:

```
<jboss>
  <enterprise-beans>
    <message-driven>
      <ejb-name>PurchaseOrderMDB</ejb-name>
        . . .
      <resource-ref>
        <res-ref-name>jms/queue/QueueConnectionFactory</res-ref-name>
        <jndi-name>ConnectionFactory</jndi-name>
      </resource-ref>
      <resource-ref>
        <res-ref-name>url/EntityCatalogURL</res-ref-name>
        <res-url>http://localhost:8080/opc/EntityCatalog.jsp</res-url>
      </resource-ref>
    </message-driven>
  <enterprise-beans>
<jboss>
```

Here, the `res-ref-name` refers to the coded name of the resource, and `res-url` refers to the URL of the resource.

There is an alternative way of mapping resource references. Instead of using the `jndi-name` or `res-url` elements, you use the `resource-name` element. The content of this element should map to a resource defined using the `resource-manager` element as shown below:

```
<jboss>
   <enterprise-beans>
      <message-driven>
         <ejb-name>PurchaseOrderMDB</ejb-name>
            ...
         <resource-ref>
            <res-ref-name>jms/queue/QueueConnectionFactory</res-ref-name>
            <resource-name>cf</resource-name>
         </resource-ref>
         <resource-ref>
            <res-ref-name>url/EntityCatalogURL</res-ref-name>
            <resource-name>catalogURL<resource-name>
         </resource-ref>
      </message-driven>
   <enterprise-beans>

   <resource-managers>

      <resource-manager>
         <res-name>cf<res-name>
         <res-jndi-name>ConnectionFactory</res-jndi-name>
      </resource-manager>

      <resource-manager>
         <res-name>catalogURL</res-name>
         <res-url>
            http://localhost:8080/opc/EntityCatalog.jsp
         </res-url>
      </resource-manager>

   </resource-managers>
<jboss>
```

18.3.3 Read-only

If you don't want your entity beans to participate in transactions, you can declare them as read-only as shown below:

```
<jboss>
   <enterprise-beans>
      <entity>
         <ejb-name>MyEntityEJB</ejb-name>
         <read-only>True</read-only>
      </ entity >
   </enterprise-beans>

</jboss>
```

Instead of declaring the whole bean as read-only you can declare individual methods as read-only. This will be useful if you want only the methods that are used in read-only transactions as read-only:

```
<jboss>
  <enterprise-beans>
    <entity>
      <ejb-name>MyEntityEJB</ejb-name>
      <method-attributes>
        <method>
          <method-name>myMethod</method-name>
          <read-only>True</read-only>
        <method>
      </method-attributes>
    </entity >
  </enterprise-beans>
</jboss>
```

The above deployment descriptor defines myMethod as read-only. You can also use wild cards to specify the method names.

18.3.4 Message-Driven Bean Configuration

In this section, we look at the configuration elements in the JBoss EJB deployment descriptor specific to message-driven beans (MDB). For message-driven beans, JBoss allows you to specify the following elements:

Element	Description
destination-jndi-name	This is the JNDI name of the JMS destination the MDB is monitoring.
mdb-user	This is the user name to access secured destinations.
mdb-passwd	This is the password to access secured destinations.
mdb-client-id	This is the client ID for JMS connections.
mdb-subscription-id	This is used for defining durable subscriptions.

An example MDB deployment descriptor is shown below:

```
<jboss>
  <enterprise-beans>
    <message-driven>
      <ejb-name>PurchaseOrderMDB</ejb-name>
      <destination-jndi-name>
```

```
            queue/opc/OrderQueue
          </destination-jndi-name>
          <mdb-user>blacksabath<mdb-user>
          <mdb-passwd>aliceinchains</mdb-passwd>
          <mdb-client-id>test#123</mdb-client-id>
       </message-driven>
     </enterprise-beans>
   </jboss>
```

18.3.5 Invokers

JBoss normally uses a local VM or JRMP invoker depending on whether the bean is local or remote. In *Section 17.3.2: EJB Invokers*, we saw that both these invokers were defined as MBeans. However, if you want to use a different invoker, you need to specify so explicitly in the JBoss deployment descriptor. Examples include EJB invocation over HTTP, and JRMP-based EJB invocation using SSL.

To use a different invoker, you set the `bean-invoker` and `home-invoker` elements as shown below:

```
<jboss>

  <enterprise-beans>
    <session>
      <ejb-name>ShoppingControllerEJB</ejb-name>
      ...
      <home-invoker>jboss:service=invoker,type=http</home-invoker>
      <bean-invoker>jboss:service=invoker,type=http</bean-invoker>
      ...
    </session>
  <enterprise-beans>

</jboss>
```

The element content should specify the object name of the invoker MBean. We will have a look at an elaborate example of using this in *Section 18.3.7.3: EJB SSL Invocation.*

18.3.6 Clustering EJBs·

In JBoss 3.0, entity beans and stateful/stateless session EJBs can operate in a cluster. However, for a bean to operate in a cluster you need to explicitly enable it using the `clustered` element as shown below:

```
<jboss>

  <enterprise-beans>
    <session>
      <ejb-name>ShoppingControllerEJB</ejb-name>
      ...
```

```
            <clustered>true</clustered>
        ...
      </session>
   <enterprise-beans>

</jboss>
```

In addition to this, you can use `cluster-config` element (subelement of `jboss\containerconfigurations\containerconfiguration`) for setting additional properties. The structure of this element is shown below:

The `cluster-config` element can be mainly used to specify load-balancing policies for home and bean proxies, and the partition in which the bean participates. The `cluster-config` element supports the following subelements:

Element	Description
partition-name	Defines the cluster (by the name of partition) in which the bean will run. See *Section 13.3.1 Clustering Architecture.*
home-load-balance-policy	Defines the fully qualified class that determines the load balancing policy used by the home proxy. The default is round robin.
bean-load-balance-policy	Defines the fully qualified class that determines the load balancing policy used by the remote proxy. The default is round robin.
session-state-manager-jndi-name	Stateful session bean cluster configuration accepts an extra element called `session-state-manager-jndi-name` to specify the JNDI name of a distributed service used for session replication. If not specified, it will use the default value `/HASessionState/Default`.

Please refer to the *Section 13.3.5.1: Load Balancing Policy* for a discussion on load balancing policies. You can write your own load balancing policy by implementing the JBoss `org.jboss.ha.framework.interfaces.LoadBalancePolicy` interface, but JBoss comes with two predefined policy classes:

❑ `org.jboss.ha.framework.interfaces.RoundRobin`
For a round robin-based load balancing policy.

❑ `org.jboss.ha.framework.interfaces.FirstAvailable`
For a first available-based load balancing policy.

> **Please note that for stateful session beans, EJB object invocations will not use load balancing because of the usage of server affinity, where invocations to a particular session bean will always be routed to the same server. However, it supports transparent fail over.**

An example is shown below:

```
<clustered>true</cluster>
<cluster-config>
  <partition-name>MyPartition</partition-name>
  <home-load-balance-policy>
    org.jboss.ha.framework.interfaces.RoundRobin
  </home-load-balance-policy>
  <bean-load-balance-policy>
    org.jboss.ha.framework.interfaces.FirstAvailable
  </bean-load-balance-policy>
</cluster-config>
```

> **Entity beans participating in a cluster don't support distributed locking or caching.**

18.3.7 EJB Security

In this section, we look at how to configure the various aspects of security using the JBoss EJB deployment descriptor.

18.3.7.1 Method Permissions

You can restrict access to your EJB methods by using the `security-role` and `method-permission` elements in the standard EJB deployment descriptor. However, enforcement of this declarative security in an operational environment is performed in an application server-specific manner. In *Section 7.3.3.3: Login Configuration Data*, we looked at how to use JAAS within JBoss to define login modules in the `login-config.xml` file.

When a thread tries to access a secure method, JBoss tries to evaluate the credentials of the thread using the `security-domain` element in the JBoss EJB deployment descriptor. This element should refer to a login module configured within the system. The JBoss JAAS security manager will use the login module to resolve the caller's credentials and access rights. The snippet below shows how to define a security domain for performing authentication/authorization:

```
<jboss>
   <security-domain>java:jaas/MyLoginModule</security-domain>
   <enterprise-beans>
     ...
   <enterprise-beans>

</jboss>
```

Here, `MyLoginModule` is a login module configured within JBoss. For a detailed discussion on how to configure login modules, please refer to *Section 7.3.3: Login Configuration.*

> **Method permissions are checked only for remote references. For local references, it is always assumed that the client has been authenticated and has been granted sufficient access rights.**

18.3.7.2 Unauthenticated Principal

You can use the element `unauthenticated-principal` to define a value that should be returned when `EJBContext.getCallerPrincipal()` is called in an unauthenticated thread:

```
<jboss>
   <unauthenticated-principal>
     Bob the Builder
   </unauthenticated-principal >
   <enterprise-beans>
     ...
   <enterprise-beans>

</jboss>
```

18.3.7.3 EJB SSL Invocation

JBoss allows you to perform JRMP-based EJB invocation over SSL, using the following steps:

1. Install JSSE
    You don't need to do this if you are using JDK 1.4. Please refer to *Section 7.5: Enabling SSL* on a discussion on how to install JSSE.

2. Create Keystore
    The keystore is used to store the key pair used for SSL. Please refer to *Section 7.5: Enabling SSL* for a discussion on how to create a keystore.

3. Setup the JAAS Security Domain
    The JAAS security domain is an MBean that extends JAAS security manager to provide cryptographic functionality. To configure the JAAS security domain, use the following MBean definition:

```
<mbean
    code="org.jboss.security.plugins.JaasSecurityDomain"
    name="jboss.security:service=JaasSecurityDomain,domain=RMI+SSL">
    <constructor>
      <arg type="java.lang.String" value="RMI+SSL"/>
    </constructor>
    <attribute name="KeyStoreURL">rmi.keystore</attribute>
    <attribute name="KeyStorePass">barkatthemoon</attribute>
</mbean>
```

The JAAS security domain is mainly used to set up the keystore as the database for the key pair and certificates that are used by the secure socket factories configured for the JRMP invoker. You can add this MBean to your root configuration file (`jboss-service.xml`) or any file that is visible to your SAR deployer.

4. Configure Secure JRMP Invoker
    Now we need to create a JRMP invoker, which will use secure sockets for communication. Remember that JBoss defines both the local in-VM and JRMP invokers as MBeans. In a similar way, we will define our secure version of the JRMP invoker:

```
<mbean
    code="org.jboss.invocation.jrmp.server.JRMPInvoker"
    name="jbpss:service=invoker,type=JRMP,socketType=SSL">
    <attribute name="RMIObjectPort">8888</attribute>
    <attribute name="RMIClientSocketFactory">
      org.jboss.security.ssl.RMISSLClientSocketFactory
    </attribute>
    <attribute name="RMIServerSocketFactory">
      org.jboss.security.ssl.RMISSLServerSocketFactory
    </attribute>
    <attribute name="SecurityDomain">
      jboss.security:service=JaasSecurityDomain,domain=RMI+SSL
    </attribute>
</mbean>
```

5. Configure the EJB

Now you need to use the JBoss EJB deployment descriptor to use the new JRMP invoker over SSL instead of the default invoker. The listing below shows an example:

```
<jboss>

  <enterprise-beans>
    <session>
      <ejb-name>ShoppingControllerEJB</ejb-name>
      ...
      <home-invoker>
        jboss:service=invoker,type=jrmp, socketType=SSL
      </home-invoker>
      <bean-invoker>
        jboss:service=invoker,type=jrmp, socketType=SSL
      </bean-invoker>
      ...
    </session>
  <enterprise-beans>

</jboss>
```

Now when we invoke the EJB, we will be doing so securely using SSL over JRMP.

> **If you are using self-signed certificates for testing, make sure that you set your keystore as a trust store on the client-side.**

18.3.7.4 Security Proxy

J2EE provides a declarative way of handling security for EJB and web applications, where user identities are mapped to roles. Even though this is a very powerful way of handling security, it falls short when your security policies are tightly coupled to your domain data. For example, if you want to make security decisions based on the argument values that are passed to bean methods, there is no way you can handle this using declarative security.

JBoss provides a non-intrusive way of handling this by decoupling the security logic from the bean code using the interceptor architecture. You can define security interceptors at the bean level in the JBoss-specific EJB deployment descriptor as shown below:

```
<jboss>

  <enterprise-beans>
    <session>
      <ejb-name>ShoppingControllerEJB</ejb-name>
      ...
      <security-proxy>
        com.acme.security.MySecurityInterceptor
      <security-proxy>
      ...
    </session>
  <enterprise-beans>

</jboss>
```

The `security-proxy` element should define the fully qualified name of the class that implements the interface `org.jboss.security.SecurityProxy`. If a security-proxy element is present, JBoss dynamically adds an interceptor of type `org.jboss.ejb.plugins.SecurityProxyInterceptor` during deployment. This interceptor will delegate the running of custom security logic to the proxy implementation. The proxy class needs to implement the following methods:

```
public void init(Class beanHome,
                 Class beanRemote,
                 Object securityMgr) throws InstantiationException;
```

This method is called after the instance is initialized.

```
public void setEJBContext(EJBContext ctx);
```

This method is called prior to any method invocation to set the current EJB context.

```
public void invokeHome(Method m,
                       Object[] args) throws SecurityException;
```

This method is called to allow the security proxy to perform any custom security checks required for the EJB home interface method.

```
public void invoke(Method m,
                   Object[] args, Object bean)
    throws SecurityException;
```

This method is called to allow the security proxy to perform any custom security checks required for the EJB remote interface method.

JBoss 3.0

Administration and Deployment

Handbook

19

Configuring CMP 2.0

Container-managed persistent EJBs are one of the most widely used J2EE components. The significance of CMP beans has become manifold in the J2EE world since the introduction of EJB 2.0 and the support for container-managed relations. JBoss 3.0 comes with a pluggable CMP engine that supports almost all features of CMP 2.0. In this chapter, we will have a close look at the JBoss CMP 2.0 implementation.

> *Throughout this chapter, we will be using examples from the Petstore implementation to illustrate the various CMP features that are available with JBoss 3.0. In particular, we will be using the purchase order component.*

19.1 CMP Configuration Files

The CMP features provided by JBoss are:

❑ Table creation during bean deployment, and removal during bean undeployment.

❑ Allowing different entities within a deployment unit to map to different datasources from different database vendors.

❑ Mapping of container managed persistence fields: Mapping of container managed relationship fields using both foreign keys and relationship tables.

❑ Extending EJB-QL.

❑ Mapping JavaBean-style persistent fields to multiple database columns.

❑ Tuning performance using eager/lazy loading.

❑ Customizing the CMP behavior by mapping database vendor-specific functionality to CMP operations.

To start with, we'll have a quick look at the main configuration files used within JBoss for configuring the CMP engine as well as CMP components:

❏ `standardjbosscmp-jdbc.xml`
This file is used for defining the global configuration for CMP 2.0 EJBs. This file is used for defining various default values when those values are not defined in bean-level CMP configuration files, as well as providing mapping information for some of the mainstream database vendors. This mapping information mainly includes the SQL specific for the database vendors for creating primary keys/foreign keys, SQL functions to EJB-QL functions, SQL to attain row locking, etc.

❏ `jbosscmp-jdbc.xml`
This file is used for defining bean-level configuration for CMP EJBs. This file can be used for defining type mapping, relation mapping, finder mapping, etc. This file should be present in the `\META-INF` directory of your EJB JAR file. This file will mainly contain the object-to-relational mapping information for all the entity EJBs as well as their relations specified in the `ejb-jar.xml` file.

Both the above files follow the DTD specified in the `jbosscmp-jdbc_3_0.dtd` file. The basic structure of the XML is shown below:

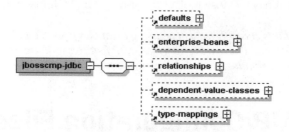

The above structure contains the following children for the `jboss-cmp-jdbc` root element:

❏ `defaults`
This element is used to define container-wide or deployment unit-wide defaults. The container-wide defaults are set in the `standardjbosscmp-jdbc.xml` file present in the `\conf` directory of the configuration set you use. The default set at deployment unit level will be defined in the `jbosscmp-jdbc.xml` file present in the `\META-INF` directory for the deployment unit. The diagram below shows the structure of this element. The various sub-elements of this element are discussed in detail in the subsequent sections:

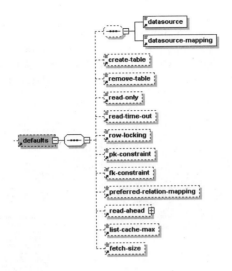

❑ enterprise-beans
This element is used mainly within the `jbosscmp-jdbc.xml` file of the deployment unit for mapping the entity EJBs defined in the `ejb-jar.xml` file to database tables. The entities defined within this element can use its various child elements to override the defaults set at container level or deployment unit level. The diagram below depicts the structure of this element. The various sub-elements of this element are discussed in detail in the subsequent sections:

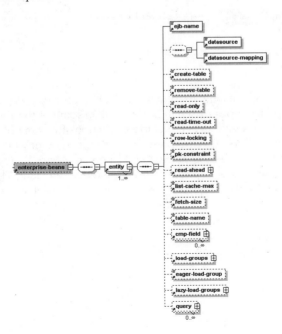

❏ relationships:
This element is used mainly within the jbosscmp-jdbc.xml file of the deployment unit for mapping the entity EJBs defined in the ejb-jar.xml file to database tables. The diagram below depicts the structure of this element. Its various sub-elements are discussed in detail in *Section 19.9: Mapping Relationships*:

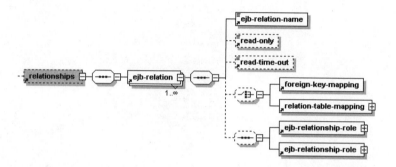

❏ dependent-value-classes
This element is used mainly within the jbosscmp-jdbc.xml file of the deployment unit for defining dependent value classes. The diagram below depicts the structure of this element. The various sub-elements of this element are discussed in detail in *Section 19.8: Mapping CMP Fields*:

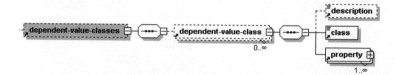

❏ type-mappings
This element is mainly used in standardjbosscmp-jdbc.xml file for mapping Java types to SQL types as well as some of the JBoss custom functions used in finders to database functions for some of the major database vendors. The database vendors that come preconfigured with JBoss include Sybase, Oracle, DB2, Hypersonic, MySQL, PostgreSQL, etc. The diagram below depicts the structure of this element. The various sub-elements of this element are discussed in detail in subsequent sections:

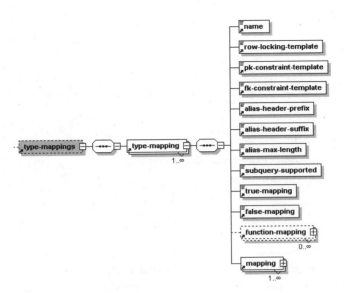

19.2 Mapping EJB Names

The content of the `ejb-name` elements defined in the `jbosscmp-jdbc.xml` file should match those defined in the standard `ejb-jar.xml` file for the deployment unit. The snippet below shows the excerpts from the `ejb-jar.xml` file for the purchase order component:

```
<?xml version="1.0" encoding="US-ASCII"?>

<!DOCTYPE ejb-jar
    PUBLIC "-//Sun Microsystems, Inc.//DTD Enterprise JavaBeans 2.0//EN"
    "http://java.sun.com/dtd/ejb-jar_2_0.dtd">

<ejb-jar>
    <description>PO</description>
    <display-name>PurchaseOrderJAR</display-name>
    <enterprise-beans>

        <entity>
            <description>PurchaseOrder CMP EJB</description>
            <display-name>PurchaseOrderEB</display-name>
            <ejb-name>PurchaseOrderEJB</ejb-name>
            ...
        </entity>
        ...
    </enterprise-beans>
    ...
</ejb-jar>
```

The snippet below shows excerpts from the corresponding `jbosscmp-jdbc.xml` file:

```xml
<?xml version="1.0" encoding="UTF-8"?>

<!DOCTYPE jbosscmp-jdbc PUBLIC
   "-//JBoss//DTD JBOSSCMP-JDBC 3.0//EN"
   "http://www.jboss.org/j2ee/dtd/jbosscmp-jdbc_3_0.dtd">

<jbosscmp-jdbc>
  ...
  <enterprise-beans>
    <entity>
      <ejb-name>PurchaseOrderEJB</ejb-name>
      ...
    </entity>
    ...
  </enterprise-beans>
  ...
</jbosscmp-jdbc>
```

> **Please note that JBoss currently requires the EJB names to be unique across multiple deployment units in a server instance.**

19.3 Datasource Mapping

JBoss uses datasource mapping to map the entity object model to a relational model specific to the target database system. When you deploy entity beans within JBoss, you need to specify the datasource mapping for the entity beans defined in the deployment unit. This specified mapping should be one of the predefined datasource mappings defined in the `standardjbosscmp-jdbc.xml` file, or one you define within your deployment unit in the `jbosscmp-jdbc.xml` file.

You can define this at the entity bean level, deployment level, or globally. Defining the datasource mapping for the individual entity bean is useful if you have different entity beans persisted to different database systems within the same deployment unit. An example is shown below:

```xml
<jbosscmp-jdbc>
  ...
  <enterprise-beans>
    ...
    <entity>
      ...
      <datasource-mapping>Sybase<datasource-mapping>
      ...
    <entity>
    <entity>
      ...
      <datasource-mapping>Oracle9i<datasource-mapping>
      ...
    <entity>
    ...
  <enterprise-beans>
  ...
</jbosscmp-jdbc>
```

If all the entity beans defined in a deployment unit are persisted to the same type of database system, you can define a default datasource mapping for all the entity EJBs in the `jbosscmp-jdbc.xml` for that deployment unit, as shown below:

```
<jbosscmp-jdbc>
  <defaults>
    ...
    <datasource-mapping>Sybase<datasource-mapping>
    ...
  <defaults>
  ...
</jbosscmp-jdbc>
```

If you don't specify EJB-level or deployment unit-wide default, JBoss will use the global default specified in `standardjbosscmp-jdbc.xml` file. The default global datasource mapping set for JBoss is Hypersonic SQL.

The global default is set in the same way as the deployment unit level default. The only difference is that for the deployment unit-level default, the `datasource-mapping` is specified in the `jbosscmp-jdbc.xml` file available in the `\META-INF` directory of the deployment unit, and for global defaults it is specified in the `standardjbosscmp-jdbc.xml` file available in the `\conf` directory of the configuration set you use. If you want, you can modify `standardjbosscmp-jdbc.xml` to change the global default.

19.3.1 Type Mappings

JBoss defines the named datasource mappings for various database management systems using the `type-mappings` element in the `standardjbosscmp-jdbc.xml` file. This element can contain zero or more `type-mapping` elements to specify type mapping information for each database vendors.

19.3.1.1 Type Mapping Name

The `type-mapping` element uses the `name` element to define a unique name for the datasource mapping. This is used to define the datasource mapping for entity EJBs as explained in the last section. JBoss supports the following database management systems:

- InterBase
- DB2
- Oracle 9i, 6, and 7
- Oracle 8
- Oracle 7
- Sybase
- PostgreSQL 7.2

❑ Hypersonic SQL

❑ PointBase

❑ SOLID

❑ mySQL

❑ MS SQL Server 7.0 and 2000

❑ DB2/400

❑ SapDB

❑ Cloudscape

❑ Informix

You can add new datasource mappings to this file, if your preferred database is not in the above list.

19.3.1.2 Row Locking Template

This is the template used to create a rowlock on the selected rows. The arguments supplied are as follows:

❑ SELECT clause

❑ FROM clause

❑ WHERE clause

If row locking is not supported in the SELECT statement, this element should be empty. The most common form of row locking is SELECT FOR UPDATE as in the example shown below:

```
<row-locking-template>
   SELECT ?1 FROM ?2 WHERE ?3 FOR UPDATE
</row-locking-template>
```

You can specify whether you require row locking at entity level in jbosscmp-jdbc.xml as shown below:

```
<jbosscmp-jdbc>
  ...
  <enterprise-beans>
    ...
    <entity>
      ...
      <row-locking>true</row-locking>
      ...
    <entity>
    ...
  <enterprise-beans>
  ...
</jbosscmp-jdbc>
```

If all the entity beans defined in a deployment unit need row locking, you can define a default row locking for all the entity EJBs in the `jbosscmp-jdbc.xml` for that deployment unit as shown below:

```
<jbosscmp-jdbc>
  <defaults>
    . . .
    <row-locking>true</row-locking>
    . . .
  <defaults>
  . . .
</jbosscmp-jdbc>
```

If you don't specify an EJB-level or a deployment unit-wide default, JBoss will use the global default specified in the `standardjbosscmp-jdbc.xml` file. The default row locking policy set for JBoss is `false`.

The global default is set in the same way as the deployment unit-level default. The only difference is, for the deployment unit level default, the `row-locking` option is specified in the `jbosscmp-jdbc.xml` file available in the `\META-INF` directory of the deployment unit, and for global defaults it is specified in the `standardjbosscmp-jdbc.xml` file available in the `\conf` directory of the configuration set you use. If you want, you can modify `standardjbosscmp-jdbc.xml` to change the global default.

19.3.1.3 Primary Keys

This is the template used to create a primary key constraint in the CREATE TABLE statement. The arguments supplied are as follows:

❑ Primary key constraint name, which is always `pk_{table-name}`

❑ Comma-separated list of primary key column names

If a primary key constraint clause is not supported in a CREATE TABLE statement, this element should be empty. An example is shown below:

```
<type-mapping>
  . . .
  <pk-constraint-template>
    CONSTRAINT ?1 PRIMARY KEY (?2)
  </pk-constraint-template>
  . . .
</type-mapping>
```

19.3.1.4 Foreign Keys

This is the template used to create a foreign key constraint in a separate statement. The arguments supplied are as follows:

❑ Table name

❑ Foreign key constraint name, which is always `fk_{table-name}_{cmr-field-name}`

❑ Comma-separated list of foreign key column names

❑   References table name

❑   Comma-separated list of the referenced primary key column names

If the datasource does not support foreign key constraints, this element should be empty. An example is shown below:

```
<type-mapping>
  ...
  <fk-constraint-template>
    ALTER TABLE ?1 ADD CONSTRAINT ?2 FOREIGN KEY (?3)
    REFERENCES ?4 (?5)
  </fk-constraint-template>
  ...
</type-mapping
```

19.3.1.5 Aliases

An alias header is prefixed to a generated table alias by the EJB-QL compiler to prevent name collisions. An alias header is composed of the contents of `alias-header-prefix`, `alias-header-suffix` and an incrementing value. An alias header is constructed as `alias-header-prefix` + `int_counter` + `alias-header-suffix`. The maximum length of aliases is limited by `alias-max-length`:

```
<type-mapping>
  ...
  <alias-header-prefix>t</alias-header-prefix>
  <alias-header-suffix>_</alias-header-suffix>
  <alias-max-length>32</alias-max-length>
  ...
<type-mapping>
```

For example, if your EJB-QL contains three tables, with the above example the aliases generated by JBoss in the generated SQL for the tables will be `t0_`, `t1_`, and `t2_`.

19.3.1.6 Sub-Query

This is used to specify whether the database system supports sub-queries. If `true`, the JBoss EJB-QL compiler will use sub-queries to generate the SQL for the target database, for certain EJB-QL queries. Otherwise, it will use a `LEFT JOIN` and the `isNull` function:

```
<sub-query>true</sub-query>
```

19.3.1.7 True and False

The `TRUE` and `FALSE` literals defined in EJB-QL are mapped to the values used in the target database system, as shown below:

```
<true-mapping>1</true-mapping>
<false-mapping>0</false-mapping>
```

19.3.1.8 Data Type Mapping

JBoss uses the mapping element to map the Java types of the persistent fields to the SQL types on the target database system. A type-mapping element may contain zero or more mapping elements. The content model of this element is:

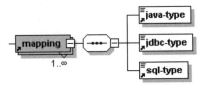

The java-type defines the Java type, the jdbc-type the type defined in the JDBC Types interface, and sql-type the type on the target database system. JBoss uses these types for getting and setting persistent data as well as generating DDLs when create tables on deployment are set to true. Creating tables during deployment is covered in detail in *Section 19.5: Create and Remove Table*. The snippet below shows an example:

```
<mapping>
  <java-type>java.lang.Byte</java-type>
  <jdbc-type>SMALLINT</jdbc-type>
  <sql-type>NUMBER(3)</sql-type>
</mapping>
```

If JBoss is to find a type mapping for a type in a given datasource mapping information, it will try to serialize and store that field.

19.3.1.9 Function Mapping

You can use the function-mapping element for mapping a function defined in EJB-QL or its extension JBoss-QL to an SQL function used in the target database system. A type-mapping element may contain zero or more function-mapping elements. The content model of this element is:

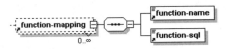

The function-name defines the name of the function in EJB-QL or JBoss-QL and function-sql the SQL to which the function is mapped. The SQL can contain parameters specified with a question mark followed by the base parameter number. The snippet below shows an example:

```
<function-mapping>
  <function-name>concat</function-name>
  <function-sql>(?1 || ?2)</function-sql>
</function-mapping>
```

289

19.4 Datasource

When you deploy an entity EJB, you need to specify the data store to which the state of the entity will be persisted. Most of the EJB containers allow you to do this by specifying the JNDI name of a datasource that points to the database to which the entity will be persisted. In JBoss you can specify this in three different ways.

The first is to define the datasource for the individual entity bean. This is useful if you have different entity beans persisted to different database systems within the same deployment unit. An example is shown below:

```
<jbosscmp-jdbc>
  ...
  <enterprise-beans>
    ...
    <entity>
      ...
      <datasource>java:/jdbc/opc/OPCDB</datasource>
      ...
    <entity>
    <entity>
      ...
      <datasource>java:/jdbc/opc/OPCDB</datasource>
      ...
    <entity>
    ...
  <enterprise-beans>
  ...
</jbosscmp-jdbc>
```

If all the entity beans defined in a deployment unit are persisted to the same data store, you can define a default datasource for all the entity EJBs in the `jbosscmp-jdbc.xml` for that deployment unit as shown below:

```
<jbosscmp-jdbc>
  <defaults>
    ...
    <datasource>java:/jdbc/opc/OPCDB</datasource>
    ...
  <defaults>
  ...
</jbosscmp-jdbc>
```

If you don't specify EJB-level or deployment unit-wide default, JBoss will use the global default specified in the `standardjbosscmp-jdbc.xml` file. The default global datasource set for JBoss is `java:/DefaultDS`.

The global default is set in the same way as the deployment unit level default. The only difference is for deployment unit-level default, the datasource is specified in `jbosscmp-jdbc.xml` file available in the `\META-INF` directory of the deployment unit, and for global defaults, it is specified in `standardjbosscmp-jdbc.xml` file available in the `\conf` directory of the configuration set you use. If you want, you can modify the `standardjbosscmp-jdbc.xml` file to change the global default.

19.5 Create and Remove Table

JBoss allows you to create tables (if they don't already exist) when you deploy the entity EJBs, and remove tables when you undeploy them. You can set this option at entity bean-level, deployment-level, or globally for all entity beans installed within a server instance. Along with the table creation and removal options, you can also specify whether you want the CMP engine to create primary keys and foreign keys at database level to reflect the entity bean primary keys and relationships.

> **Please note that you can't set the option to create foreign keys at entity bean level, as obviously foreign key creation involves two tables.**

The example below shows how to set these options on for individual entity beans:

```
<jbosscmp-jdbc>
  ...
  <enterprise-beans>
    ...
    <entity>
      ...
      <create-table>true</create-table>
      <remove-table>true</remove-table>
      <pk-constraint>true</pk-constraint>
      ...
    <entity>
    ...
  <enterprise-beans>
  ...
</jbosscmp-jdbc>
```

You can set these options globally for entity beans included in the deployment unit in the `jbosscmp-jdbc.xml`:

```
<jbosscmp-jdbc>
  <defaults>
    ...
    <create-table>true</create-table>
    <remove-table>true</remove-table>
    <pk-constraint>true</pk-constraint>
    <fk-constraint>true</fk-constraint>
    ...
  <defaults>
  ...
</jbosscmp-jdbc>
```

If you don't specify EJB-level or deployment unit-wide default, JBoss will use the global default specified in `standardjbosscmp-jdbc.xml` file. JBoss sets the `create-table` and `pk-constraint` options to `true`, and `remove-table` and `fk-constraint` options to `false`.

The global default is set in the same way as the deployment unit-level default. The only difference is for the deployment unit-level default, the table creation or removal defaults are specified in the `jbosscmp-jdbc.xml` file available in the `\META-INF` directory of the deployment unit, and for global defaults it is specified in the `standardjbosscmp-jdbc.xml` file available in the `\conf` directory of the configuration set you use. If you want, you can modify `standardjbosscmp-jdbc.xml` to change the global default.

19.6 Table Name

You can specify the database table to which the entity bean is mapped using the `table-name` element within the `entity` element, as shown below:

```
<jbosscmp-jdbc>
   ...
   <enterprise-beans>
     ...
     <entity>
        ...
        <table-name>CONTACT_INFO</table-name>
        ...
     <entity>
     ...
   <enterprise-beans>
   ...
</jbosscmp-jdbc>
```

If you don't specify the table name, the JBoss CMP engine will assume the contents of the `ejb-name` element as the table name.

19.7 Read-Only

You can set an entity bean as read-only with a read timeout value. The JBoss CMP engine wouldn't allow you to change the values of the fields of an entity bean declared as read-only. You can set the `read-only` option globally for all entity beans deployed within a server instance (normally you wouldn't be doing this), all entity beans included in a deployment unit, individual entity beans, or individual CMP fields.

The example below shows how to set the `read-only` option for individual entity beans in the `jbosscmp-jdbc.xml` file:

```
<jbosscmp-jdbc>
   ...
   <enterprise-beans>
     ...
     <entity>
        ...
        <read-only>true</read-only>
        <read-time-out>100</read-time-out>
```

```
      . . .
   <entity>
   . . .
 <enterprise-beans>
 . . .
</jbosscmp-jdbc>
```

The `read-time-out` value specifies the time in milliseconds before the values are refreshed. 0 means the values are refreshed at the beginning of each transaction and -1 means they are never refreshed.

You can set these options globally for entity beans included in the deployment unit in `jbosscmp-jdbc.xml`:

```
<jbosscmp-jdbc>
  <defaults>
    . . .
    <read-only>true</read-only>
    <read-time-out>100</read-time-out>
    . . .
  <defaults>
  . . .
</jbosscmp-jdbc>
```

If you don't specify an EJB-level or deployment unit-wide default, JBoss will use the global default specified in the `standardjbosscmp-jdbc.xml` file. JBoss sets `read-only` to `false` and `read-time-out` to 300 milliseconds for all the EJBs deployed within the server instance.

The global default is set in the same way as the deployment unit-level default. The only difference is for the deployment unit level default, the table `read-only` and `read-time-out` options are specified in the `jbosscmp-jdbc.xml` file available in the `\META-INF` directory of the deployment unit, and for global defaults, they are specified in the `standardjbosscmp-jdbc.xml` file available in the `\conf` directory of the configuration set you use. If you want, you can modify `standardjbosscmp-jdbc.xml` to change the global default.

19.8 Mapping CMP Fields

In this section, we look at how to map CMP fields to database columns. The CMP fields of an entity bean are mapped to database columns using zero or more `cmp-field` elements within the corresponding `entity` element in the `jbosscmp-jdbc.xml` file. The structure of the `cmp-field` element is shown below:

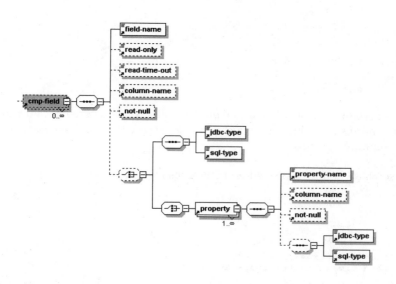

Element name	Description
field-name	Contains the name of the CMP field. This should match the corresponding cmp-field element in ejb-jar.xml file.
read-only	Sets the field as read-only – see *Section 19.7: Read-Only*.
read-time-out	Sets the timeout value, in milliseconds, before the field is refreshed – see *Section 19.7: Read-Only*.
column-name	Represents a database column to which the CMP field is mapped. If the column-name element is not present, JBoss will use the CMP name as the column name. The CMP engine will use these column names while creating the tables as well.
jdbc-type sql-type	Used for mapping the Java type of the CMP field to an SQL type on the target database system. If not specified, the CMP engine will resolve the mapping using the type mappings specified for the datasource mapping that is used.
not-null	If the empty not-null element is present, the CMP engine will add the NOT NULL clause of the column when creating the table. By default, the JBoss CMP engine will add NOT NULL for only primary key columns and columns with SQL types mapped to Java primitive data types.
property	Used for mapping custom JavaBean like CMP fields to multiple database columns. This is explained in detail in the next section.

The snippet below shows the CMP field mapping for the LineItemEJB in the order processing application of the petstore:

```
<jbosscmp-jdbc>
  ...
  <enterprise-beans>
    ...
    <entity>
      <entity>
        <ejb-name>O_LineItemEJB</ejb-name>
        <table-name>LineItemEJBTable</table-name>

        <cmp-field>
          <field-name>id</field-name>
          <column-name>id</column-name>
        </cmp-field>

        <cmp-field>
          <field-name>categoryId</field-name>
          <column-name>categoryId</column-name>
        </cmp-field>

        <cmp-field>
          <field-name>itemId</field-name>
          <column-name>itemId</column-name>
        </cmp-field>

        <cmp-field>
          <field-name>lineNumber</field-name>
          <column-name>lineNumber</column-name>
        </cmp-field>

        <cmp-field>
          <field-name>productId</field-name>
          <column-name>productId</column-name>
        </cmp-field>

        <cmp-field>
          <field-name>quantity</field-name>
          <column-name>quantity</column-name>
        </cmp-field>

        <cmp-field>
          <field-name>quantityShipped</field-name>
          <column-name>quantityShipped</column-name>
        </cmp-field>

        <cmp-field>
          <field-name>unitPrice</field-name>
          <column-name>unitPrice</column-name>
        </cmp-field>

      </entity>
      ...
  <enterprise-beans>
  ...
<jbosscmp-jdbc>
```

19.8.1 Dependent Value Classes

JBoss supports CMP fields of types other than the standard types such as primitives, strings and date types. By default, CMP fields of types other than the standard types are serialized and stored as a blob. However, if the type conforms to the standard JavaBean naming conventions for accessors and mutators for the fields, JBoss will allow you to map the properties of the CMP field to multiple database columns. These classes should be serializable and should have public no-argument constructors.

As an example, assume that in the purchase order example, you don't want the credit card to be a separate EJB as it is entirely dependent on the purchase order. Hence, you may define a class to model the credit card:

```
package com.sun.j3ee.blueprints.purchaseorder;

public class CreditCard implements java.io.Serializable {

    public CreditCard() {}

    private String number;
    public String getNumber() { return number; }
    public String setNumber(String val) { number = val; }

    private String type;
    public String getType() { return type; }
    public String setType(String val) { type = val; }

    private String expiryDate;
    public String getExpiryDate() { return expiryDate; }
    public String setExpiryDate(String val) { expiryDate = val; }

}
```

Now you need to define the CMP field accessor and mutator in the purchase order EJB for the credit card-dependent value class:

```
public abstract CreditCard getCreditCard();
public abstract void setCreditCard(CreditCard creditCard);
```

You also need to define the credit card CMP field in the `ejb-jar.xml` file:

```
<cmp-field>CreditCard</cmp-field>
```

On the JBoss side, the first thing you need to define the schema for the **Dependent Value Class (DVC)**. This can be done either in the `jbosscmp-jdbc.xml` or `standardjbosscmp-jdbc.xml` file. I prefer to do it in the `jbosscmp-jdbc.xml` file, if only one or more of the entity beans defined in that deployment unit only uses the DVC. This is done using the `dependent-value-classes` element:

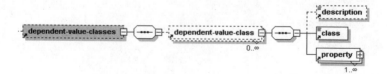

This element may contain zero or more dependent-value-class elements describing the schema of each DVC that is used.

The dependent-value-class element contains an optional description element, a mandatory class element that contains the fully qualified class name, and one or more property elements:

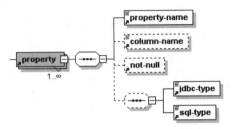

The property element contains a property-name element that contains the name of the property, an optional column-name element to which the property is mapped by default, an optional not-null element that has the same purpose as that in the cmp-field element, and an optional set of jdbc-type and sql-type elements that has the same purpose as that in the cmp-field element.

The type of the property can be either a simple type or a defined or undefined DVC. If it is a DVC and the column name is not specified, JBoss will create the column name by concatenating all the nested properties. For example, if the credit card DVC has a property called address, whose type is another DVC, and that DVC contains a simple property called country, and you don't specify the column name, JBoss will assume the column name as address_country.

The snippet below shows the DVC declaration for the credit card:

```
<jbosscmp-jdbc>
  <dependent-value-classes>
    <dependent-value-class>
      <description>Credit card DVC</description>
      <class>com.sun.j2ee.blueprints.purchaseorder.CreditCard</class>
      <property>
        <property-name>number</property-name>
        <column-name>cc_number</column-name>
      </property>
      <property>
        <property-name>type</property-name>
        <column-name>cc_type</column-name>
      </property>
      <property>
        <property-name>expiryDate</property-name>
        <column-name>cc_expiry_date</column-name>
      </property>
    <dependent-value-class>
  </dependent-value-class>
</jbosscmp-jdbc>
```

Now you need to map this CMP field in the purchase order entity bean:

```
<jbosscmp-jdbc>
  <enterprise-beans>

    <entity>
      <ejb-name>PurchaseOrderEJB</ejb-name>
      <table-name>PurchaseOrderEJBTable</table-name>

      <cmp-field>
        <field-name>creditCard</field-name>
      </cmp-field>

  </enterprise-beans>
</jbosscmp-jdbc>
```

Now, the properties of the credit card DVC will be persisted to the cc_number, cc_type, and cc_expiry_date columns of the PurchaseOrderEJBTable. You can override the property descriptions defined in the dependent-value class element using the cmp-field element as shown below:

```
<jbosscmp-jdbc>
  <enterprise-beans>

    <entity>
      <ejb-name>PurchaseOrderEJB</ejb-name>
      <table-name>PurchaseOrderEJBTable</table-name>

      <cmp-field>
        <field-name>creditCard</field-name>
        <property>
          <property-name>number</property-name>
          <column-name>cc_number</column-name>
        </property>
        <property>
          <property-name>type</property-name>
          <column-name>cc_type</column-name>
        </property>
        <property>
          <property-name>expiryDate</property-name>
          <column-name>cc_expiry_date</column-name>
        </property>
      </cmp-field>

  </enterprise-beans>
</jbosscmp-jdbc>
```

This is extremely important if you want to define small column names instead of the lengthy column names generated by the CMP engine in case of nested DVC properties. The example below shows how to define a simpler column name for a DVC containing another nested DVC property:

```
<jbosscmp-jdbc>
  <enterprise-beans>

    <entity>
      <ejb-name>PurchaseOrderEJB</ejb-name>
      <table-name>PurchaseOrderEJBTable</table-name>
```

```
        <cmp-field>
          <field-name>creditCard</field-name>
          <property>
            <property-name>address.country</property-name>
            <column-name>cc_country</column-name>
          </property>
        </cmp-field>

    </enterprise-beans>
</jbosscmp-jdbc>
```

In the above case, the CMP engine will use the column name as cc_country instead of address_country for the country property of the credit card's address property.

19.9 Mapping Relationships

In these sections, we look at how to map the EJB relationships defined in the ejb-jar.xml file to a target database within JBoss. JBoss supports one-to-many and many-to-many cardinalities in both unidirectional and bi-directional navigability. JBoss supports relationship mapping based on both foreign keys as well as relationship tables. Relationship tables are similar to the association classes in the OO world and are the only way to map to many-to-many relationships.

You can define your preferred relationship mapping style at a deployment unit level as shown below:

```
<jbosscmp-jdbc>
  <defaults>
    . . .
    <preferred-relation-mapping>
      foreign-key
    </preferred-relation-mapping>
    <!--
    <preferred-relation-mapping>
      relation-table
    </preferred-relation-mapping>
    -->
    . . .
  <defaults>
  . . .
</jbosscmp-jdbc>
```

You can also specify this for individual relations. If not specified in either way, the CMP engine will use foreign key-based relations, which is the global default set in the standardjbosscmp-jdbc.xml file.

The global default is set in the same way as the deployment unit-level default. The only difference is for the deployment unit-level default, the preferred relationship mapping is specified in the jbosscmp-jdbc.xml file available in the \META-INF directory of the deployment unit, and for the global default, it is specified in the standardjbosscmp-jdbc.xml file available in the \conf directory of the configuration set you use. If you want, you can modify standardjbosscmp-jdbc.xml to change the global default.

The relationships specified in `ejb-jar.xml` files are mapped to the target database system using the `relationships` element in the `jbosscmp-jdbc.xml` file. This element may contain one or more `ejb-relation` elements. Each of these elements should correspond to the `ejb-relation` element specified in the `ejb-jar.xml` file. The structure of this element is:

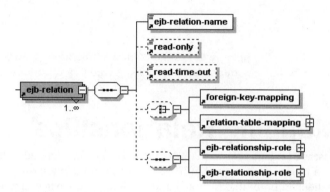

The `ejb-relation-name` element should map to the `ejb-relation-name` element in the file `ejb-jar.xml`. The optional `read-only` and `read-time-out` elements are used to define the relationship as read-only. This works in the same way as read-only CMP fields explained in *Section 19.7: Read-Only.*

If the `foreign-key-mapping` empty element is present, the CMP engine will use foreign keys to relate the two entities in relation. If you want to use relationship table based mapping, you can define the details using the `relation-table-mapping` element. This is explained in detail in the next section.

The two `ejb-relationship-role` elements should correspond to the same defined in the file `ejb-jar.xml`:

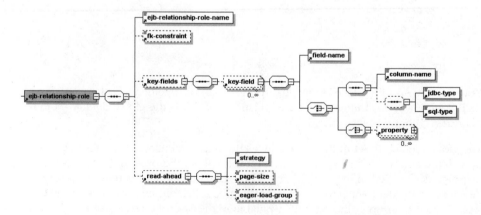

The `ejb-relationship-role-name` should to map to the same in the `ejb-jar.xml` file for that part of the relation. The `fk-constraint` element is used to specify whether the CMP engine should add a foreign key constraint while creating the tables. The `key-fields` element is used to map the primary key of EJB that is the source of the relation to the foreign key in the table that persists the other entity in the relation, in the case of foreign key-based mapping, and the relationship table in relation table-based mapping.

The `read-ahead` element is used for implementing optimized reading as explained in the last section.

The listing below shows the one-to-many unidirectional relationship between purchase order and line items in the standard `ejb-jar.xml` file:

```
<ejb-relation>
  <ejb-relation-name>PurchaseOrder-LineItem</ejb-relation-name>
  <ejb-relationship-role>
    <ejb-relationship-role-name>
      PurchaseOrderEJB
    </ejb-relationship-role-name>
    <multiplicity>One</multiplicity>
    <relationship-role-source>
      <ejb-name>PurchaseOrderEJB</ejb-name>
    </relationship-role-source>
    <cmr-field>
      <cmr-field-name>lineItems</cmr-field-name>
      <cmr-field-type>java.util.Collection</cmr-field-type>
    </cmr-field>
  </ejb-relationship-role>
  <ejb-relationship-role>
    <ejb-relationship-role-name>
      O_LineItemEJB
    </ejb-relationship-role-name>
    <multiplicity>Many</multiplicity>
    <cascade-delete />
    <relationship-role-source>
      <ejb-name>O_LineItemEJB</ejb-name>
    </relationship-role-source>
  </ejb-relationship-role>
</ejb-relation>
```

Here, the relationship role, with line item EJB as the source, doesn't contain any CMR fields as the navigability is only from purchase order to line item. The snippet below shows how this relation is mapped to a target database in the `jbosscmp-jdbc.xml` file. In the generated data model, the table that persist line items will have a foreign key column that stores the primary key of the purchase order to which each line item belongs:

```
<ejb-relation>
  <ejb-relation-name>PurchaseOrder-LineItem</ejb-relation-name>
  <foreign-key-mapping/>

  <ejb-relationship-role>
    <ejb-relationship-role-name>
      PurchaseOrderEJB
    </ejb-relationship-role-name>
    <key-fields>
      <key-field>
```

```
        <field-name>poId</field-name>
        <column-name>po_id</column-name>
      </key-field>
    </key-fields>
  </ejb-relationship-role>

  <ejb-relationship-role>
    <ejb-relationship-role-name>
      O_LineItemEJB
    </ejb-relationship-role-name>
    <key-fields/>
  </ejb-relationship-role>
</ejb-relation>
```

In the above example, the foreign key-style mapping is used and the table that persist line items will have a column called po_id to store the purchase order ID. JBoss will include this column in the DDL for the table if you have set the option to create the table on deployment to true.

Now we will have a look at a bi-directional relationship.

None of the Petstore entities involve bi-directional relationships. Hence for the sake of the example we will assume that the relationship between purchase order and credit card is bi-directional.

The listing below shows the one-to-one bi-directional relationship between purchase order and credit card in the standard ejb-jar.xml file:

```
<ejb-relation>
  <ejb-relation-name>PurchaseOrder-CreditCard</ejb-relation-name>
  <ejb-relationship-role>
    <ejb-relationship-role-name>
      PurchaseOrderEJB
    </ejb-relationship-role-name>
    <multiplicity>One</multiplicity>
    <relationship-role-source>
      <ejb-name>PurchaseOrderEJB</ejb-name>
    </relationship-role-source>
    <cmr-field>
      <cmr-field-name>creditCard</cmr-field-name>
    </cmr-field>
  </ejb-relationship-role>
  <ejb-relationship-role>
    <ejb-relationship-role-name>
      O_CreditCardEJB
    </ejb-relationship-role-name>
    <multiplicity>One</multiplicity>
    <relationship-role-source>
      <ejb-name>O_CreditCardEJB</ejb-name>
    </relationship-role-source>
    <cmr-field>
      <cmr-field-name>purchaseOrder</cmr-field-name>
    </cmr-field>
  </ejb-relationship-role>
</ejb-relation>
```

Here, the relationship is navigable in both directions. This means a purchase order can identify its credit card, and vice-versa. The snippet below shows how this relation is mapped to a target database in the jbosscmp-jdbc.xml file. In the generated data model, the table that persists credit card will have a foreign key column that stores the primary key of the purchase order to which the credit card belongs, and vice versa:

```xml
<ejb-relation>
    <ejb-relation-name>PurchaseOrder-CreditCard</ejb-relation-name>
    <foreign-key-mapping/>

    <ejb-relationship-role>
      <ejb-relationship-role-name>
        PurchaseOrderEJB
      </ejb-relationship-role-name>
      <key-fields>
        <key-field>
          <field-name>poId</field-name>
          <column-name>po_id</column-name>
        </key-field>
      </key-fields>
    </ejb-relationship-role>

    <ejb-relationship-role>
      <ejb-relationship-role-name>
        O_CreditCardEJB
      </ejb-relationship-role-name>
      <key-fields>
        <key-field>
          <field-name>id</field-name>
          <column-name>cc_id</column-name>
        </key-field>
      </key-fields>
    </ejb-relationship-role>
</ejb-relation>
```

As you can see from the snippet above, both sides of the relations now specify the foreign key for the table that persists the entity in the other side of the relation. The credit card table will have a column called po_id for storing the purchase order primary key and the purchase order table will have a column called cc_id for storing the credit card primary key.

> **Please note that it is not mandatory to define foreign keys in both the tables for bi-directional relations. Even if the foreign key is defined only for the table that persists the entity in one side of a bi-directional relation, the JBoss CMP engine will resolve the bi-directional navigability.**

19.9.1 Relationship Table Mapping

Sometimes it is difficult to map relationships in a database using foreign key mapping. A typical example is in many-to-many relations. In such cases, you may resort to using relationship tables. Relationship tables store primary keys from both tables in a relationship to implement many-to-many relations.

In JBoss, you can achieve this using `relation-table-mapping`, whose content model is shown below:

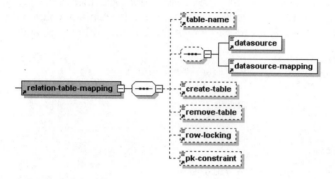

Element name	Description
table-name	Specifies the name of the relationship table. If not specified, JBoss will assume it as a concatenation of the two tables in relation separated by an underscore.
datasource	Identifies the datasource that will point to the database that contains this table. If not specified, JBoss will use the default specified either deployment unit wide or server-wide. The datasource-mapping element defines the mapping to use. If not specified, JBoss will use the default specified, either deployment unit-wide or server-wide.
create-table	See *Section 19.5: Create and Remove Table.*
remove-table	See *Section 19.5: Create and Remove Table.*
row-locking	See *Section 19.3.1.2: Row Locking Template.*
pk-constraint	See *Section 19.3.1.3: Primary Keys*

None of the Petstore entities involve many-to-many relationships. Hence, for the sake of the example, we will assume that the relationship between contact info and address is many-to-many.

The listing below shows the one-to-one bi-directional relationship between purchase order and credit card in the standard `ejb-jar.xml` file:

```
<ejb-relation>
  <ejb-relation-name>ContactInfo-Address</ejb-relation-name>
  <ejb-relationship-role>
    <ejb-relationship-role-name>
      ContactInfoEJB
    </ejb-relationship-role-name>
    <multiplicity>many</multiplicity>
    <relationship-role-source>
```

304

```
      <ejb-name>ContactInfoEJB</ejb-name>
    </relationship-role-source>
    <cmr-field>
      <cmr-field-name>contactInfos</cmr-field-name>
      <cmr-field-type>java.util.Collection</cmr-field-type>
    </cmr-field>
  </ejb-relationship-role>
  <ejb-relationship-role>
    <ejb-relationship-role-name>
      AddressEJB
    </ejb-relationship-role-name>
    <multiplicity>One</multiplicity>
    <relationship-role-source>
    <ejb-name>AddressEJB</ejb-name>
    </relationship-role-source>
    <cmr-field>
      <cmr-field-name>addresses</cmr-field-name>
      <cmr-field-type>java.util.Collection</cmr-field-type>
    </cmr-field>
  </ejb-relationship-role>
</ejb-relation>
```

The snippet below shows how this relation is mapped to a target database in the jbosscmp-jdbc.xml file:

```
<ejb-relation>
  <ejb-relation-name>ContactInfo-Address</ejb-relation-name>
  <relation-table-mapping>
    <table-name>
      contact_info_address
    </table-name>
  <relation-table-mapping>

  <ejb-relationship-role>
    <ejb-relationship-role-name>
      ContactInfoEJB
    </ejb-relationship-role-name>
    <key-fields>
      <key-field>
        <field-name>id</field-name>
        <column-name>ci_id</column-name>
      </key-field>
    </key-fields>
  </ejb-relationship-role>

  <ejb-relationship-role>
    <ejb-relationship-role-name>
      AddressEJB
    </ejb-relationship-role-name>
    <key-fields>
      <key-field>
        <field-name>id</field-name>
        <column-name>add_id</column-name>
      </key-field>
    </key-fields>
  </ejb-relationship-role>
</ejb-relation>
```

The data model will have a table called `contact_info_address` with a `ci_id` column for storing the contact information primary key, and `add_id` for storing address primary keys. If the `create-table` option is `true`, the CMP engine will create the necessary table and columns.

19.10 Mapping Queries

One of the major enhancements in EJB 2.0 was the introduction of EJB-QL as a means of defining vendor-neutral queries. Even though EJB-QL is a major step forward, it is still in its early stages and doesn't support important features such as ordering data. Most of the container vendors have continued to offer custom query languages despite the introduction of EJB-QL. This mainly extends EJB-QL to provide enhanced querying functionalities. The advantage of not using anything other than EJB-QL is that your EJBs will be portable across CMP vendors. JBoss provides the following functionalities to extend EJB-QL:

❑ **JBossQL**
Extends EJB-QL to provide added functionalities like more functions, clauses, and keywords

❑ **DynamicQL**
Allows you to generate JBossQL statements dynamically during run time

❑ **DeclaredSQL**
Allows you to compose a query statement by specifying SELECT, FROM, WHERE clauses, etc.

You can override EJB-QL for a finder or select method, using `query` elements nested within the relevant `entity` element in the `jbosscmp-jdbc.xml` file. When you do this, you should leave the `ejb-ql` element in the `ejb-jar.xml` file for the corresponding query as an empty element. The structure of the `query` element is:

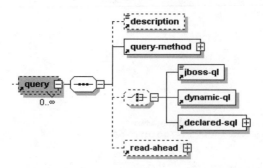

The `query-method` element has the same structure as the corresponding element in `ejb-jar.xml` file. This element is used to identify the finder or select method by specifying the method name and method parameters as shown below:

```
<query-method>
  <method-name>findPOBetweenDates</method-name>
  <method-params>
    <method-param>long</method-param>
    <method-param>long</method-param>
  </method-params>
</query-method>
```

The read-ahead element is used for implementing optimized reads. This is covered in detail in *Section 19.11.1: Read-Ahead Strategies.*

19.10.1 JBossQL

JBossQL extends EJB-QL to support the following features:

- ❏ ORDER BY clause
- ❏ Use of parameters in IN and LIKE clauses
- ❏ UCASE and LCASE functions

The example below shows how to use JBoss-QL to return a sorted list of purchase orders from the findPOBetweenDates finder method by purchase order date:

```
<query>
  <query-method>
    <method-name>findPOBetweenDates</method-name>
    <method-params>
      <method-param>long</method-param>
      <method-param>long</method-param>
    </method-params>
  </query-method>
  <jboss-ql>
    <![CDATA[
    SELECT OBJECT(a)
    FROM PurchaseOrder a
    WHERE a.poDate BETWEEN ?1 AND ?2
    ORDER BY a.poDate
    ]]>
  </jboss-ql>
</query>
```

The listing below shows how to use the like operator to return all the contact information with family names starting with the passed string:

```
<query>
  <query-method>
    <method-name>findByFamilyName</method-name>
    <method-params>
      <method-param>java.lang.String</method-param>
    </method-params>
  </query-method>
  <jboss-ql>
    <![CDATA[
    SELECT OBJECT(a)
```

```
        FROM ContactInfo a
        WHERE a.familyName like ?1
    ]]>
    </jboss-ql>
</query>
```

Please note that when you call the finder, you should pass the wild-card search character as part of the argument as shown below:

```
contactInfoHome.findByFamilyName("Ran%");
```

The listing below shows how to use the UCASE function to implement case-insensitive searches by family name:

```
<query>
    <query-method>
        <method-name>findByFamilyName</method-name>
        <method-params>
            <method-param>java.lang.String</method-param>
        </method-params>
    </query-method>
    <jboss-ql>
        <![CDATA[
        SELECT OBJECT(a)
        FROM ContactInfo a
        WHERE UCASE(a.familyName) = ?1
        ]]>
    </jboss-ql>
</query>
```

Please note that when you call the finder, you should convert the search string to upper case, and JBoss will match the passed argument against the family name column values converted to upper case:

```
contactInfoHome.findByFamilyName("Ranieri".toUpper());
```

The example above will return all contact information records with family names set to "Ranieri", regardless of the case.

19.10.2 DynamicQL

DynamicQL allows EJB select methods to take a dynamically compiled JBossQL statement and an array of parameters as arguments. Suppose you have an EJB home method that gives you a list of purchase order IDs falling between two dates ordered by purchase order date. You can dynamically generate the JBossQL and pass it an EJB select method to get back the required data. The only restriction is that the EJB select method should accept a string parameter representing the JBossQL that should be executed, and an object array representing the parameters that should be passed to the JBossQL. The example is shown below:

```
PurchaseOrderEJB {

   //Home method
   public Collection ejbHomePOIdBetweenDates(long fromDate,
       long toDate) {

     StringBuffer sb = new StringBuffer();
     sb.append("SELECT a.poId ");
     sb.append("FROM PurchaseOrder a ");
     sb.append("WHERE a.poDate BETWEEN ?1 AND ?2 ");
     sb.append("ORDER BY a.poDate");

     return ejbSelectPOIdBetweenDates(sb.toString(),
     new Object[] {new Long(fromDate), new Long(toDate)});
   }

   //EJB select method
   public abstract Collection ejbSelectPOIdBetweenDates(String jBossQL,
   Object[] args)
   throws FinderException;

   ...

}
```

The query description for the EJB select will look like:

```
<query>
  <query-method>
    <method-name>ejbSelectPOIdBetweenDates</method-name>
    <method-params>
      <method-param>long</method-param>
      <method-param>long</method-param>
    </method-params>
  </query-method>
  <dynamic-ql/>
</query>
```

19.10.3 DeclaredSQL

DeclaredSQL can be used if you have a query that is impossible to be expressed using EJB-QL or JBossQL, for example, if you want to utilize the full power of writing plain SQL. DeclaredSQL is composed of SELECT, FROM, WHERE, and ORDER BY clauses. The structure of the declared-sql element and its corresponding elements is shown below:

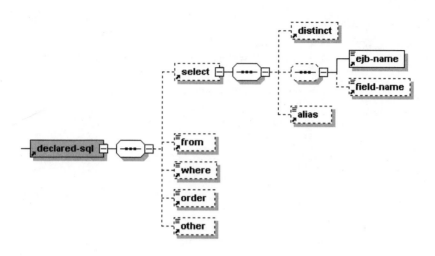

Element	Description
select	The optional select element can be used to list the columns that should be selected. By default, all columns are selected.
distinct	You can use the distinct empty element if you want to select distinct records. DymanicSQL for finder methods should have only the empty distinct element within the select element.
ejb-name field-name	The bean's name, and the name of a container-managed persistent field, respectively.
alias	Used for defining an alias name for the entity bean table in the generated FROM clause.
from	JBoss automatically includes the entity table in the FROM clause. Any extra tables you want in the FROM clause can be defined using the from element. Since the CMP engine automatically includes the entity bean table in the FROM clause, the contents of the from element should begin with a comma.
where	Used for defining the query criteria.
order	Used for specifying sort order.
other	Used for specifying any database-specific clause that is appended to the end of the query.
alias	Used for specifying table aliases.

The snippet below shows the declared SQL to select all the line items that belongs to the purchase order with maximum value sorted by the line item ID:

```
<declared-sql>
  <select>
    <distinct/>
    <ejb-name>O_LineItemEJB</ejb-name>
    <alias>l</alias>
  </select>
  <from>
    <![CDATA[
      , purchase_order p
    ]]>
  </from>
  <where>
    <![CDATA[
      l.po_id = p.po_id
      and p.poValue = (select max(po_value) from purchase_order)
    ]]>
  </where>
  <order>l.id</order>
</declared-sql>
```

This will generate the following SQL:

```
SELECT l.*
FROM line_item l, purchase_order p
WHERE l.po_id = p.po_id
AND p.po_value = (SELECT max(p.po_value) FROM purchase_order)
ORDER by l.po_id
```

19.11 Tuning CMP Performance

One of the main complaints that have been heard about EJBs (especially entity EJBs) since their inception is performance. This was mainly caused by the impedance mismatch between the object and relational technologies. However, container vendors have strived hard in the last two or three years to enhance entity bean performance. The EJB 2.0 specification aided these efforts tremendously by giving container vendors more control on how the CMP fields are persisted by abstract accessor and mutator methods. For example, since the CMP fields are mutated using abstract mutators, the containers know whether there is a field that is modified or not in a transaction. This means that the container vendors can transparently implement optimized writes depending on whether the fields are modified in a transaction or not.

However, EJB reads are still a problem, and container vendors provide custom solutions to implement optimized reads. JBoss provides a variety of methods to improve performance during entity EJB reads. Before we cover the JBoss features for optimized reads, we will have a quick look at some of the performance problems associated with entity EJB reads.

One of the biggest performance bottlenecks in entity EJB reads is in reading a list of entity beans. Normally when you invoke a finder to get a list of entities, the container would issue a SQL query to get the list of primary keys matching the query criteria. After that, the first time each entity in the list is accessed in a transaction, the container issues a SQL query to get the data for that entity by specifying the primary key. This means to read 100 records, the container issues 101 queries; this is called the n + 1 read problem in EJBs.

Another performance issue is that when the container loads an entity at the beginning of a transaction, it loads all the fields regardless of whether or not they are being used within that transaction. This results in loading of data that is never being used in a transaction.

JBoss solves the above problems with the following solutions:

❑ Read-ahead strategies

❑ Load Groups/Optimized loads

19.11.1 Read-Ahead Strategies

JBoss provides two read-ahead strategies for loading data into entity bean instances.

❑ On-find

❑ On-load

19.11.1.1 The On-find Strategy

In the on-find strategy, when a finder is issued, JBoss selects all the data expected for that finder from the database instead of loading just the primary keys. For example, if you issue a finder on the purchase order EJB to get all the purchase orders; so, instead of issuing this SQL:

```
SELECT poId FROM purchase_order
```

JBoss issues the following SQL:

```
SELECT poId, poDate, poStatus FROM purchase_order
```

The selected data is not immediately associated with entity bean instances. Instead, it's kept in a cache and associated with entity bean instances, as and when the beans are accessed. For finder and select methods, the read-ahead strategy is defined in the query element for the method in `jbosscmp-jdbc.xml` file:

```
<query>
  <query-method>
    <method-name<findAll</method-name>
    <method-params/>
```

```
  </query-method>
  <jboss-ql>
    ...
  </jboss-ql>
  <read-ahead>
    <strategy>on-find</strategy>
    <page-size>4</page-size>
  </read-ahead>
</query>
```

The page-size element defines the number of records to be loaded at a time. One of the disadvantages of this approach is that the CMP engine loads all the CMP fields and foreign key fields for CMR regardless of whether or not they are used in the transaction. JBoss solves this problem by using named load groups. Load groups are named groups of columns that should be loaded together. Suppose you want to display all the purchase orders as a list and want to display only the ID, user ID, and date. You can define a load group for these fields and associate that to the read-ahead strategy as shown below:

```
<entity>
  <ejb-name>PurchaseOrderEJB</ejb-name>
  <load-groups>
    <load-group>
      <load-group-name>list</load-group-name>
      <field-name>poId</field-name>
      <field-name>poUserId</field-name>
      <field-name>poDate</field-name>
    </load-group>
  </load-groups>
  <query>
    <query-method>
      <method-name>findAll</method-name>
      <method-params/>
    </query-method>
    <jboss-ql>
      ...
    </jboss-ql>
    <read-ahead>
      <strategy>on-find</strategy>
      <page-size>4</page-size>
      <eager-load-group>list</eager-load-group>
    </read-ahead>
  </query>
</entity>
```

In the example above, a named load group called list, which contains purchase order ID, user ID, and date, is defined. This load group is then linked to the finder query using the eager-load-group element. This means that when this finder is executed, JBoss will only select the three columns mapped to the aforementioned fields.

19.11.1.2 The On-load Strategy

JBoss provides an alternative strategy called on-load that will load data for the next few entities that follow the current entity, when the current entity is loaded (similar to a database cursor). This is under the assumption that the users access data sequentially. Again, similar to the on-find strategy, the data is kept in a cache and not immediately associated with entity bean instances. The snippet below shows how the on-load strategy can be implemented:

313

```
<entity>
  <ejb-name>PurchaseOrderEJB</ejb-name>
  <load-groups>
    <load-group>
      <load-group-name>list</load-group-name>
      <field-name>poId</field-name>
      <field-name>poUserId</field-name>
      <field-name>poDate</field-name>
    </load-group>
  </load-groups>
  <query>
    <query-method>
      <method-name>findAll</method-name>
      <method-params/>
    </query-method>
    <jboss-ql>
      ...
    </jboss-ql>
    <read-ahead>
      <strategy>on-load</strategy>
      <page-size>4</page-size>
      <eager-load-group>list</eager-load-group>
    </read-ahead>
  </query>
</entity>
```

If you want the CMP engine not to use any read-ahead strategy, you can specify it as follows:

```
<read-ahead>
  <strategy>none</strategy>
  ...
<read-ahead>
```

With the above option, the CMP engine falls back to the process of lazy loading.

19.11.2 Optimized Loading

When the CMP engine loads an entity bean instance, it normally loads all the CMP fields even if all the fields are not accessed in a transaction. JBoss allows you to specify groups of fields that should be eagerly or lazily loaded. This means the fields in the eager load group are loaded during the entity bean load, and those in the lazy load group are loaded as and when they are accessed. You can specify eager and lazy load groups at entity bean level as shown below:

```
<entity>
  <ejb-name>PurchaseOrderEJB</ejb-name>
  <load-groups>
    <load-group>
      <load-group-name>eager</load-group-name>
      <field-name>poId</field-name>
      <field-name>poUserId</field-name>
      <field-name>poDate</field-name>
    </load-group>
    <load-group>
```

```
            <load-group-name>lazy</load-group-name>
            <field-name>poEmailId</field-name>
            <field-name>poLocale</field-name>
            <field-name>poValue</field-name>
        </load-group>
    </load-groups>
    <eager-load-group>eager</eager-load-group>
    <lazy-load-group>lazy</lazy-load-group>
</entity>
```

In the above example, the purchase order ID, user ID, and date are eagerly loaded, and e-mail ID, locale, and value are lazily loaded.

19.11.3 Read-Ahead for Relationships

Same as in finders and selects, you can eagerly load CMR fields when the source entity is either found or loaded. You specify the read-ahead strategy for relationships within the ejb-relationship-role element as shown below:

```
<jbosscmp-jdbc>
    <enterprise-beans>
        <entity>
            <ejb-name>O_LineItemEJB</ejb-name>
            <load-groups>
                <field-name>id</field-name>
                <field-name>itemId</field-name>
                <field-name>categoryId</field-name>
            </load-groups>
            ...
        </entity>
        <entity>
            <ejb-name>PurchaseOrderEJB</ejb-name>
            ...
        </entity>
    <enterprise-beans>
    <relationships>
        <ejb-relation>
            <ejb-relation-name>PurchaseOrder-LineItem</ejb-relation-name>
            <foreign-key-mapping/>

            <ejb-relationship-role>
                <ejb-relationship-role-name>
                    PurchaseOrderEJB
                </ejb-relationship-role-name>
                <key-fields>
                    <key-field>
                        <field-name>poId</field-name>
                        <column-name>po_id</column-name>
                    </key-field>
                </key-fields>
                <read-ahead>
                    <strategy>on-load</strategy>
                    <page-size>4</page-size>
                    <eager-load-group>4</eager-load-group>
                </read-ahead>
            </ejb-relationship-role>
```

```
        <ejb-relationship-role>
          <ejb-relationship-role-name>
            O_LineItemEJB
          </ejb-relationship-role-name>
          <key-fields/>
       </ejb-relationship-role>
     </ejb-relation>

  </relationships>
</jbosscmp-jdbc>
```

This means that when the CMP engine loads a purchase order entity instance, it loads the first four line items with line item ID, item ID, and category ID.

JBoss 3.0

Administration and Deployment

Handbook

20

20.1 The EAR Deployer

20.2 The JBoss EAR Deployment
Descriptor

20

EAR Configuration

In this chapter, we look at the features available with JBoss for deploying EAR files. JBoss allows the deployment of standard J2EE EAR files by simply copying them to the directories monitored by the deployment scanner, as discussed in *Section 15.3: The Deployment Process.*

20.1 The EAR Deployer

JBoss provides a deployer that is capable of deploying EAR files. This is the `org.jboss.deployment.EARDeployer` class, which implements the `org.jboss.deployment.SubDeployer` interface by extending the class `org.jboss.deployment.SubDeployerSupport`. This EAR subdeployer accepts all files and directories that end with the string `ear`. This means that the EAR deployer can deploy EAR files in both exploded and unexploded format, stored in the directories monitored by the deployment scanner.

The EAR deployer is an MBean configured in the root configuration file `jboss-service.xml` in the `\conf` directory of the configuration set you use as shown below:

```
<mbean
   code="org.jboss.deployment.EARDeployer"
   name="jboss.j2ee:service=EARDeployer">
```

When this MBean starts, it registers itself with the main deployer as a subdeployer. This enables the main deployer to delegate the deployment of EAR components to the main deployer.

20.2 The JBoss EAR Deployment Descriptor

In addition to the standard EAR deployment descriptor (application.xml), JBoss allows a JBoss-specific deployment descriptor for EAR files. This file should be present in the \META-INF directory of the EAR file and should be called jboss-app.xml. The structure of this file is:

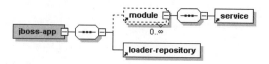

The jboss-app.xml file is mainly used for:

❑   Deploying SAR components as part of the EAR

❑   Defining a named classloader repository for the EAR

20.2.1 SAR Components

In *Section 4.2.1.2: JBoss SAR Components*, we saw the use of SAR components for deploying MBean services within JBoss. You can deploy SAR components as part of a standard J2EE EAR application. To package a SAR component, you need to create a standard Java archive with the extension sar that contains all the MBean and supporting classes for the MBean. In the \META-INF directory, you need to have a file called jboss-service.xml containing the MBean definition.

You can also deploy MBeans in exploded format. In this case you need to make the MBean deployment descriptor visible to the SAR deployer. The easiest way to achieve this is to name the file in the format *-service.xml and copy it to the \deploy directory of the configuration set you use. In this case you need to make sure that all the supporting classes (including the MBean class) are made available to the classloader. To do this, you can create a standard Java archive containing the class files and store it in the \lib directory of your configuration set.

For example, you can package all the datasource and JMS destination services required for the Petstore application as SAR components within the Petstore EAR file, instead of configuring them separately. One advantage of doing this is that you have a self-contained application without any external dependency and it is the only deployment unit you need for deploying it on remote servers. This means you can just drop the EAR file to somewhere visible to the EAR deployer, without worrying about any external configuration. This involves three main steps:

1. Package SAR files
2. Create the JBoss EAR deployment descriptor
3. Package the EAR

20.2.1.1 Package SAR files

Package the MBean services you want to deploy as a SAR file. SAR files are similar to vanilla JAR files, with the \META-INF directory containing a file called jboss-service.xml. This file should contain all the MBean definitions you require. Additionally, you may include all the dependent classes in the SAR file.

For example, if you are packaging the datasource definition for Petstore as a SAR component, you can create a jboss-service.xml file with the contents shown below (refer to *Section 8.2.1: Configuring Datasources* for a description of this file's contents):

```xml
<?xml version="1.0" encoding="UTF-8"?>

<!-- Datasources used for Petstore -->

<server>

  <mbean
    code="org.jboss.resource.connectionmanager.LocalTxConnectionManager"
    name="jboss.jca:service=LocalTxCM,name=jdbc/petstore/PetStoreDB">

    <depends optional-attribute-name="ManagedConnectionFactoryName">

      <mbean
        code="org.jboss.resource.connectionmanager.RARDeployment"
        name="jboss.jca:service=LocalTxDS,name=jdbc/petstore/PetStoreDB">
        <attribute name="JndiName">jdbc/petstore/PetStoreDB</attribute>
        <attribute name="ManagedConnectionFactoryProperties">
         <properties>
          <config-property name="ConnectionURL" type="java.lang.String">
            jdbc:oracle:thin:@youroraclehost:1521:yoursid
          </config-property>
          <config-property name="DriverClass" type="java.lang.String">
            oracel.jdbc.driver.OracleDriver
          </config-property>
          <config-property name="UserName" type="java.lang.String">
            megadeath
          </config-property>
          <config-property name="Password" type="java.lang.String">
            euthanasia
          </config-property>
         </properties>
        </attribute>
        <depends optional-attribute-name="OldRarDeployment">
         jboss.jca:service=RARDeployment,
         name=JBoss LocalTransaction JDBC Wrapper
        </depends>
      </mbean>
    </depends>

    <depends optional-attribute-name="ManagedConnectionPool">

      <mbean
        code=
        "org.jboss.resource.connectionmanager.JBossManagedConnectionPool"
        name=
```

```
 "jboss.jca:service=LocalTxPool,name=jdbc/petstore/PetStoreDB">
 <attribute name="MinSize">1</attribute>
 <attribute name="MaxSize">50</attribute>
 <attribute name="BlockingTimeoutMillis">5000</attribute>
 <attribute name="IdleTimeoutMinutes">15</attribute>
 <attribute name="Criteria">ByContainer</attribute>
 </mbean>

</depends>

<depends optional-attribute-name="CachedConnectionManager">
   jboss.jca:service=CachedConnectionManager
</depends>

<depends optional-attribute-name="JaasSecurityManagerService">
   jboss.security:service=JaasSecurityManager
</depends>

<attribute name="TransactionManager">
 java:/TransactionManager
</attribute>

<depends>jboss.jca:service=RARDeployer</depends>

 </mbean>

</server>
```

You then need to create a standard Java archive with the extension .sar with the jboss-service.xml file in the \META-INF directory. Call this file db.sar.

20.2.1.2 Create the JBoss EAR Deployment Descriptor

Now we need to create a JBoss-specific EAR deployment descriptor. This file should be called jboss-app.xml and should contain the following content:

```
<jboss-app>
  <module>
    <service>db.sar</service>
  </module>
</jboss-app>
```

You can have any number of module elements under the jboss-app element if you want to deploy more than one SAR component as part of the EAR.

20.2.1.3 Package the EAR

Now you need to package the EAR file. Here, you will need to include the db.sar file at the root level of the JAR, and the jboss-app.xml file along with the standard application.xml in the \META-INF directory of the JAR file.

> *The application.xml file should include the definitions for all the standard J2EE components such as WAR, RAR, and EJB.*

The listing below shows the structure of the EAR file for the Petstore customer application:

```
META-INF/
          application.xml
          jboss-app.xml
asyncsender-ejb.jar
...
cart-ejb.jar
...
db.sar
...
petstore.war
petstore-ejb.jar
...
xmldocuments.jar
```

20.2.2 Loader Repository

One major disadvantage of the JBoss unified classloader repository scheme is that it is impossible to have multiple versions of the same class across different EAR files, as JBoss will always use the first version that is loaded. This is because the unified classloaders will use the class already present in the repository.

However, you can circumvent this problem using scoped classloading in EAR files. This is achieved using the `loader-repository` entry in the JBoss-specific application deployment descriptor, `jboss-app.xml`:

```
<jboss-app>
  <loader-repository>
    petstore:service=LoaderRepository
  </loader-repository>
</jboss-app>
```

This EAR will use its own loader repository and will look into this repository before falling back to the default repository. The content of the `loader-repository` element should be a valid JMX object name. You can use any name for the loader repository, as long as it is a valid JMX object name.

You can also specify the class for the object that acts as the load repository using the `loader-repository-class` element. This class should implement the `org.jboss.mx.loading.LoaderRepository` interface. The default value for this class, if not specified, is `org.jboss.mx.loading.HierarchicalLoaderRepository2`.

> **In version 3.0.2 and earlier versions, because of a bug in the code, JBoss always tries to read the loader repository class from application.xml and not jboss-app.xml file. However, in most cases, you won't need to change the default value.**

JBoss 3.0

Administration and Deployment

Handbook

21

21.1 Scheduling Tasks

21.2 System Properties

21

Additional JBoss Configuration

In this chapter we will have a look at some of the custom features available with JBoss that are not part of the standard J2EE specification.

21.1 Scheduling Tasks

Many enterprise applications use some sort of scheduling to run specific tasks at regular intervals. One way of achieving this is to rely on operating system services such as cron on Unix and scheduled tasks on Windows. However, J2EE 1.3 doesn't specify any standard way of scheduling tasks as part of the specifications.

> *EJB 2.1 in J2EE 1.4 specifies a container-managed timer service that can be used for scheduling tasks.*

JBoss provides an MBean that can be used for scheduling tasks that need to be run at regular intervals. The MBean definition is:

```
<mbean
    code="org.jboss.varia.scheduler.Scheduler"
    name="petstore:service=DataPopulationScheduler">
```

Obviously you can configure the object name to something appropriate for the service you want to create.

This MBean supports the following attributes:

Attribute	Function
InitialStartDate	Used to specify the instance at which the task is run, for the first time. It supports the following values: ❏ NOW: This will run the task for the first time a second after the service is started. ❏ Number of milliseconds after 1st of January 1970. ❏ A date string that can be parsed by java.util.SimpleDateFormat.
InitialRepetitions	Used to specify the number of times the schedule task should be repeated. If you want to repeat the task forever, you can specify the value as -1.
StartAtStartup	If set to true, the scheduler will start immediately after the MBean is started. If this is set to false, you need to explicitly invoke the MBean operation startSchedule() to start scheduling.
SchedulablePeriod	The interval in milliseconds between each call to the perform() method to run the task. This value must be bigger than 0.
SchedulableClass	This is one option for defining the task that is scheduled. In this case you need to provide a class that implements the interface org.jboss.varia.scheduler.Schedulable. This interface defines a single method called perform() that provides two arguments specifying the time on which the scheduled task was called and the number of remaining repetitions. The scheduler will call this method at configured intervals.
SchedulableArguments	Used to specify the arguments passed to the constructor of the class that implements the Schedulable interface.
SchedulableArgumentTypes	Used to specify the argument types passed to the constructor of the class that implements the Schedulable interface.

Attribute	Function
SchedulableMBean	Instead of specifying a class that implements the Schedulable interface, you can specify the object name of an MBean whose method is run at regular intervals by the scheduler, using this attribute.
SchedulableMBeanMethod	Used to specify the MBean operation that is scheduled.

21.1.1 Scheduling Petstore Data Population

In this section we will write a small example to run Petstore data population at start-up and then every twenty-four hours thereafter. To do this we need to perform the following steps.

21.1.1.1 Write a Schedulable Implementation

Our Schedulable implementation will take the URL to the Petstore populate servlet as an argument to the constructor. Them every time the perform() method is called it will make a URL connection to the servlet to repopulate the Petstore database:

```
package com.wrox.jboss.chapter21;

import org.jboss.varia.scheduler.Schedulable;

import java.net.URL;
import java.net.URLConnection;
import java.io.IOException;
import java.io.InputStream;

public class PetstoreScheduler implements Schedulable {

   private String populateServletURL;

   public PetstoreScheduler(String arg0) {
     populateServletURL = arg0;
   }

   public void perform(java.util.Date date, long param) {

     try {
        System.out.println("Repopulating Database:" + date);
        URLConnection con =
           new URL(populateServletURL).openConnection();
        con.setDoInput(true);
        con.setDoOutput(true);

        InputStream in = con.getInputStream();
        while(in.read() != -1) {
        }
        in.close();
```

```
            System.out.println("Repopulated Database:" + date);
        } catch(IOException ex) {
            ex.printStackTrace();
        }
    }
}
```

To compile the class above you need to have the `scheduler-plugin.jar` file available in the `\lib` directory of the `default` configuration set in the classpath.

21.1.1.2 Write the MBean Service Descriptor

This will define the scheduler for running the task for repopulating the Petstore database:

```xml
<?xml version="1.0" encoding="UTF-8"?>

<server>

    <classpath codebase="lib" archives="scheduler-plugin.jar"/>

    <mbean code="org.jboss.varia.scheduler.Scheduler"
      name="petstore:service=DataPopulationScheduler">
        <attribute name="StartAtStartup">true</attribute>
```

Define the name of the schedulable class:

```xml
        <attribute name="SchedulableClass">
            com.wrox.jboss.chapter21.PetstoreScheduler
        </attribute>
```

Define the arguments and argument types:

```xml
        <attribute name="SchedulableArguments">
          http://localhost:8080/petstore/Populate
        </attribute>
        <attribute name="SchedulableArgumentTypes">
          java.lang.String
        </attribute>
```

Define the initial start date as now, number of repetitions as until server shutdown, and repetition period as 24 hours:

```xml
        <attribute name="InitialStartDate">NOW</attribute>
        <attribute name="InitialRepetitions">-1</attribute>
        <attribute name="SchedulePeriod">86400000</attribute>
    </mbean>

</server>
```

The above contents should be stored in a file called `jboss-service.xml`.

21.1.1.3 Package the SAR component

Now we will package the SAR component. For this, create a JAR file by the name `schedule.sar` with the contents shown below:

```
META-INF/
            jboss-service.xml
com/
    wrox/
        jboss/
            chapter21/
                    PetstoreScheduler.class
```

21.1.1.4 Include the SAR in the EAR

To do this first we need to add a `service` element in the `jboss-app.xml` file with the contents shown below as explained in *Section 20.2.1.2: Create the JBoss EAR Deployment Descriptor.*

```
<jboss-app>
    ...
    <module>
        <service>schedule.sar</service>
    </module>
</jboss-app>
```

The structure of the Petstore EAR file should be as shown below:

```
META-INF/
            application.xml
            jboss-app.xml
asyncsender-ejb.jar
...
cart-ejb.jar
...
petstore.war
petstore-ejb.jar
...
schedule.sar
...
xmldocuments.jar
```

Once you deploy the EAR file, you will be able to configure the scheduler through the JMX console as shown below. You can access the MBean by clicking on the JMX object link service=DataPopulationScheduler under the `petstore` domain from the JMX console home page:

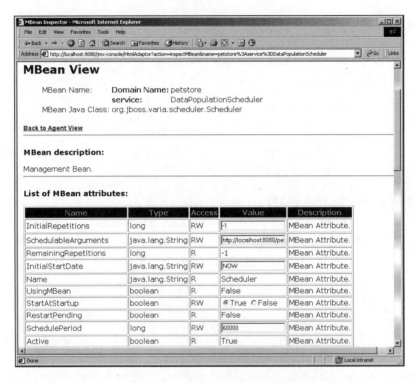

Upon first deploying the service you might find that it doesn't work immediately upon deployment. This is because we configured the scheduler to start NOW, but the SAR subdeployer runs before the AbstractWebContainer deployer such that the WAR has not been deployed yet and thus the URL our data scheduler needs is not available. However, upon subsequent invocations of the scheduler it will function fine.

21.2 System Properties

JBoss provides an MBean for populating system properties, which are useful for defining global settings. You can access system properties using the following code:

```
Object myProperty = System.getProperty("propertyName");
```

The MBean is normally defined in the file properties-service.xml available in the \deploy directory of the configuration set in use, and its definition is:

```
<mbean
  code="org.jboss.varia.property.SystemPropertiesService"
  name="jboss.util:type=Service,name=SystemProperties"/>
```

This MBean supports the following attributes:

Attribute	Function
Properties	This is used to specify a set of name/value pairs of system properties. Each property should start on a new line.
URLList	This is used to specify a comma-separated list of URLs pointing to files in the standard Java properties file format.

The listing below shows an example of using this MBean:

```
<server>
  <mbean
    code="org.jboss.varia.property.SystemPropertiesService"
    name="jboss.util:type=Service,name=SystemProperties"/>
    <attribute name="Properties">
      myProperty=123
      yourProperty=xyz
    </attribute>
    <attribute name="URLList">
      ./conf/test.properties,http://fred.com/test.properties
    </attribute>
  </mbean>
</server>
```

The example above sets two system properties: myProperty to 123 and yourProperty to xyz. It also reads the files test.properties stored in standard Java properties file format, in the \conf directory of the configuration in use and on the HTTP URL http://fred.com/, and sets the properties stored in those files as system properties.

JBoss 3.0

Administration and Deployment

Handbook

Index

Index

A Guide to the Index

The index is arranged hierarchically, in alphabetical order, with symbols preceding the letter A. Most second-level entries and many third-level entries also occur as first-level entries. This is to ensure that users will find the information they require however they choose to search for it.

E

WROX PRESS INC.

Wrox writes books for you. Any suggestions, or ideas
about how you want information given in your
ideal book will be studied by our team.
Your comments are always valued at Wrox.

Free phone in USA 800-USE-WROX
Fax (312) 893 8001

UK Tel. (0121) 687 4100 Fax (0121) 687 4101

NB. If you post the bounce back card below in the UK, please send it to:
Wrox Press Ltd., Arden House, 1102 Warwick Road, Acocks Green, Birmingham. B27 9BH. UK.

Registration Code : 81208I7I2K6N2TN01

JBoss 3.0 Deployment and Administration Handbook - Registration Card

8120

Name

Address

City _____ State/Region

Country _____ Postcode/Zip

E-mail

Occupation

How did you hear about this book?

☐ Book review (name)
☐ Advertisement (name)
☐ Recommendation
☐ Catalog
☐ Other

Where did you buy this book?

☐ Bookstore (name) _____ City
☐ Computer Store (name)
☐ Mail Order
☐ Other

What influenced you in the
purchase of this book?

☐ Cover Design
☐ Contents
☐ Other (please specify)

What did you find most useful about this book?

What did you find least useful about this book?

Please add any additional comments.

What other subjects will you buy a computer
book on soon?

What is the best computer book you have used this year?

How did you rate the overall
contents of this book?

☐ Excellent ☐ Good
☐ Average   ☐ Poor

Note: This information will only be used to keep you updated
about new Wrox Press titles and will not be used for any other
purpose or passed to any other third party.

Check here if you DO NOT want to receive further support for this book. ■

8120

wrox

PROGRAMMER TO PROGRAMMER™

POSTAGE WILL BE PAID BY ADDRESSEE

BUSINESS REPLY MAIL

FIRST CLASS MAIL   PERMIT#64   CHICAGO, IL

WROX PRESS INC.
29 S. LA SALLE ST.,
SUITE 520
CHICAGO IL 60603-USA

NO POSTAGE
NECESSARY
IF MAILED
IN THE
UNITED STATES